Marijuana and the Workplace

MARIJUANA AND THE WORKPLACE

Interpreting Research on Complex Social Issues

Edited by
CHARLES R. SCHWENK
and
SUSAN L. RHODES

QUORUM BOOKS
Westport, Connecticut • London

Library of Congress Cataloging–in–Publication Data

Marijuana and the workplace : interpreting research on complex social
   issues / edited by Charles R. Schwenk and Susan L. Rhodes.
      p.   cm.
   Includes bibliographical references and index.
   ISBN 1–56720–291–8 (alk. paper)
   1. Drugs and employment—United States.   2. Drugs and employment—
Research—United States.   3. Employees—Drug testing—United
States.   4. Marijuana—United States.   5. Drug abuse—United States.
I. Schwenk, Charles R.   II. Rhodes, Susan L.
HF5549.5.D7M37   1999
331.25—dc21   99–27819

British Library Cataloguing in Publication Data is available.

Library of Congress Catalog Card Number: 99–27819
ISBN: 1–56720–291–8

First published in 1999

Quorum Books, 88 Post Road West, Westport, CT 06881
An imprint of Greenwood Publishing Group, Inc.
www.quorumbooks.com

Printed in the United States of America

∞

The paper used in this book complies with the
Permanent Paper Standard issued by the National
Information Standards Organization (Z39.48–1984).

10 9 8 7 6 5 4 3 2 1

Contents

Contents

Chapter 1

Introduction

SCOPE AND SUBJECT OF THE BOOK

This book is about the effects of marijuana on users' performance at their work. Many people have opinions on this topic and these opinions vary widely. Some have estimated that in the mid to late 1980s, the use of marijuana and other illegal drugs cost approximately $100 billion per year in lost productivity to American companies (Bompey, 1988; Segal, 1990). More recent estimates put the cost in 1995 at $69.4 billion (Institute for a Drug-Free Workplace, 1998). A widely publicized 1998 report published by the National Institute on Drug Abuse (NIDA) and the National Institute on Alcohol and Alcohol Abuse (NIAAA), *Economic Costs of Drug and Alcohol Abuse, 1992* (Harwood, Fountain & Livermore, 1998), used sophisticated modeling techniques to estimate a total cost of drug and alcohol abuse that year at $246 billion, including $82 billion associated with lost productivity. The report did not address the effects of marijuana apart from those of other illicit drugs, and its details actually showed no impact for current or recent drug abuse on workplace productivity as indicated by individuals' earnings or hours worked. Nevertheless, advocates of increased mandatory employee drug testing cited the study as proof of the need for stronger measures to eliminate use of illicit substances by workers.

The harmful effect of marijuana on job performance has become widely accepted as a "fact" hardly needing further empirical testing. A survey conducted in October of 1995 by the Institute for a Drug-Free Workplace and the Gallup Organization showed that 71% of American employees either agreed or strongly agreed with the statement: "Periodic drug testing in the workplace reduces accidents and product defects." Further, 43% agreed or strongly agreed that, "Drug use by employees in your organization seriously affects your ability to get the job done." Thirty-eight percent felt employee drug use on or off the job greatly affected their companies' productivity; 41% felt it affected quality of products or services; 42% felt it affected workplace safety; and 42% felt it affected employee attendance (Institute for a Drug-Free Workplace, 1998).

In 1988, the loss of productivity caused by employees' consumption of marijuana and other drugs was considered serious enough, and well enough documented, to cause the U.S. Congress to pass the Drug-Free Workplace Act, which required all firms receiving federal government contracts to take steps to eliminate employee drug use. Anti-drug programs are now in place in 90% of Fortune 200 companies (*Wall Street Journal*, May 19, 1998, p. 1). Although currently only 22.5% of workers in small businesses are subject to drug testing, 52.2% of workers employed at medium-sized businesses and 68% at large businesses are subject to such testing (Substance Abuse and Mental Health Services Administration, Research and Study Update, December 17, 1997). The publication of the NIDA/NIAAA *Economic Costs of Drug and Alcohol Abuse, 1992* report spurred the House of Representatives to hold hearings in May, 1998 on the status of drug testing among small employers and led to passage in October of the Drug Free Workplace Act of 1998, Title 9 of the Omnibus Appropriations Bill of that year. This legislation allocates $10 million for voluntary programs aimed at increased implementation of drug-free workplace programs by small businesses (Institute for a Drug-Free Workplace, 1999).

Marijuana is by far the most frequently used illicit substance. Drug-free workplace policies have not explicitly targeted marijuana as the primary cause of lost productivity, but since the number of individuals using any other illegal drug is very small, the justification for anti-drug initiatives based on lost productivity must come primarily from the impact of cannabis on worker behavior.

Though national policy-makers appear to believe that the evidence that marijuana impairs job performance is clearly available and conclusive, some observers argue that marijuana's effects are currently unknown and that its use may have no negative effect at all on job performance. Crow and Hartman (1992: 923–925) critically evaluate the claim that drug use costs $100 billion annually and discuss ways such claims become "common knowledge" through the interaction of the media and politically motivated "experts." Some have expressed the concern that the sensitive political nature of this question has inhibited research on this topic and that there may be too little research to provide the basis for an objective discussion to replace the current "public debate" on this issue (Kleiman, 1989: 6–7).

Singer (1971) analyzed widely cited figures on the prevalence of heroin addicts in New York City and argued that, like the $100 billion statistic critiqued by Crow and Hartman, much of the published information on this topic came from highly questionable sources and had little or no actual documentation. The term "mythical numbers" was coined by Singer to describe the sort of generally accepted but empirically unfounded figures he observed. He found that mythical numbers had great "vitality," as journalists, politicians, and activists all referred to each other's speeches and writings without examining where the data originally came from. More recently, Reuter (1984) pointed out that such numbers have "continuing vitality." He argues that mythical numbers tend to gain widespread currency when those producing the numbers have an interest in minimizing or maximizing them, and when no substantive public resource allocations actually depend upon them.

Insight into the construction and use of mythical numbers comes from an examination of the 1998 report *Economic Costs of Drug and Alcohol Abuse, 1992* published by the NIDA and the NIAAA (Harwood, Fountain & Livermore, 1998). This report estimated the cost of alcohol and drug abuse in 1992, the most recent year for which sufficient data were available for analysis, and the numbers it contains were widely publicized, especially the $246 billion grand total. While this report appears to justify congressional action to enforce a drug-free workplace, closer scrutiny suggests that the figures it presents exemplify mythical numbers, even though the study uses rigorous methods and provides valid estimates of the costs it identifies. Its authors advise caution in the use of their findings, but such disclaimers appear to have failed to impress advocates committed to the anti-drug cause. Press releases accompanying the report's publication emphasized the alarming size of the total cost of drug and alcohol abuse it estimates (Institute for a Drug-Free Workplace, 1998, 1999); however, only a fraction of the $246 billion total was attributed to sources related to worker productivity.

Lost productivity was responsible for a large part of the economic costs described in the NIDA/NIAAA report, over 70% of the total, but less than half (46%) of this productivity reduction is associated with work performance, the $82 billion estimated impact of drug and alcohol induced morbidity on earnings and employment status. This portion of the cost of drug and alcohol dependence and abuse is clearly relevant to workplace drug policy, but even these costs have to be dissected before they cease to be mythical numbers. Of the $82 billion that the NIDA/NIAAA report estimates as the cost of lost wages and unemployment due to substance misuse in 1992, no losses were actually associated with *abuse* of any type of drug or alcohol. Alcohol *dependence* at some point in the respondent's lifetime was found to have a statistically significant negative association with male workplace outcomes, and current drug dependence was negatively correlated with hours worked for females. Current abuse of or dependence on alcohol had no significant relationship to productivity for men or women, nor did the appearance of these problems during the past year. Women's lifetime history of drug or alcohol misuse was similarly ineffective (Harwood et al., 1998: §5.3).

Economic Costs certainly documents negative economic effects related to drug use, but its findings do not provide evidence that workplace testing for illicit substances is cost effective for employers. In fact, the results reported in its "Lost Productivity" section are consistent with those of the studies relevant to marijuana and job performance included in this volume, failing to show a consistent causal relationship between use of this substance and work behavior.

The vitality of mythical numbers is one of the factors leading many Americans to become pessimistic about the chances that marijuana policy can be made rationally. Discussion of the issue is highly polarized. Advocates often only acknowledge evidence that supports their position. They vilify their opponents and may argue that objective inquiry is impossible or even inappropriate in relation to marijuana and other drugs. The purpose of this volume is to challenge this contention. Methodologically sound studies have been conducted on the effects of marijuana from a variety of research perspective and disciplines including cognitive and social psychology, economics, and anthropology. These studies examine marijuana use in a diverse range of cultural contexts. We review this body of work and reprint examples of high quality research using several different methods. Sampling the existing evidence about the effect of marijuana use on job performance, we evaluate its quantity and quality and attempt to clarify the decision problems faced by public and private policy-makers in relation to workplace drug use.

The following sections of this introductory chapter discuss the history of marijuana use and regulation, provide descriptions of marijuana's subjective effects, and examine the nature of the current U.S. public debate on marijuana policy. The introduction goes on to present an overview of the existing research on marijuana's effects and to outline the methods used in selecting the studies included in this book. Subsequent chapters cover the major streams of research identified by the first author, with examples of especially instructive work in each of the fields. A concluding chapter deals with the nature of the decision problem presented by regulation of workplace drug use and suggests ways in which policy-making in this area could be improved.

BACKGROUND INFORMATION ON MARIJUANA

History of Marijuana Use

Before examining the available research on marijuana and job performance, we wish to present basic information about the character of the substance and its cultural and political history. As we analyze the theoretical and practical implications of our current knowledge dealing with the effect of cannabis on work, we will see that different societies and different subcultures have used this plant in very different ways. Also, there is little agreement among users or observers as to the actual effect of acute intoxication or long-term use. Perhaps this diversity results in part from the lengthy history of humanity's relationship with marijuana and the many ways it has been employed.

There are at least three species of the marijuana plant. Cannabis sativa and cannabis indica are the most commonly cultivated. A third species, cannabis ruderalis, is native to Siberia and does not have a history of cultivation. Cannabis sativa is the most common of these species and has been cultivated for approximately 10,000 years (Stafford, 1992: 157). The cannabis sativa plant often reaches a height of 14–16 feet and produces strong fiber with a variety of uses, including the manufacture of clothing, paper, and rope. The seeds are rich in oil and have historically been used for food and in the manufacture of oil-based products such as soap. The leaves and flowering tops of the plant are the parts with the greatest concentration of resin, the substance containing the plant's psychoactive elements. Cannabis indica is less widely cultivated for fiber because it seldom reaches the height of cannabis sativa; however, its leaves and flowering tops generally contain more resin than do those of cannabis sativa, making it more useful as an intoxicant. The principal mind-altering compound found in marijuana is tetrahydrocannabinol (THC). Though THC is often referred to as the single active ingredient in marijuana, there are actually a large number of tetrahydracannabinols found in the plant. Delta-6 and delta-9 tetrahydrocannabinol are the psychoactive ingredients and delta-9 tetrahydrocannabinol is sometimes used in experiments in place of marijuana.

Cannabis sativa was probably the first species to be domesticated and widely spread around the globe. Scythians and other tribes introduced the plant into northern Europe. Cannabis seeds and leaves have been found in Germany in a site dated at 500 B.C. and archeological records show that the plant was growing in England by 400 A.D. Hemp fibers were used for rope and cloth and the seeds were used for food and oil.

Cannabis indica probably originated in India but has also spread worldwide. It was probably known to the Egyptians and was brought by Arab traders to the Mozambique coast of Africa in the thirteenth century. From there, it spread to the interior of the country. It spread to Europe as a result of Napoleon's military expedition into Egypt as well as the British colonization of India. In the 1790s, physicians attached to Napoleon's army brought samples of hashish back to France and W. B. O'Shaugnessy, a doctor with the British East India Company and a professor of chemistry at the University of Calcutta introduced marijuana into Western medicine when he published a monograph describing the history of the use of marijuana in the East and his own use of the drug as an analgesic and as a treatment for rheumatism and convulsions. Marijuana was recommended as a treatment for psychiatric disorders by Jean Joseph Moreau de Tours, who suggested that it might be used by doctors as a way of helping them to empathize with the psychotic states experienced by asylum inmates.

Moreau gave a sample of marijuana to Theophile Gautier, a leading French literary figure, which eventually led to a wider awareness of marijuana in European culture. Moreau administered marijuana to Gautier and others including Charles Baudelaire in a group called "Le Club des Haschischins." Baudelaire described his experiences in the following way, "If you are smoking, by some sort of transposition or intellectual quid pro quo, you will feel yourself evaporating and will attribute to your pipe, in which you feel yourself crouching and packed together like tobacco, the strange power of smoking yourself."

Hemp has been grown for its fiber in the United States since the early 1600s. It was cultivated by the settlers at Jamestown in 1611 and hemp seeds were brought to New England by the Puritans in the 1630s. Hemp was widely culti-vated in the colonies from that time and was often subsidized. In the 1760s, there were legal penalties in the state of Virginia for farmers who did not grow hemp. Both George Washington and Thomas Jefferson cultivated hemp for its fiber though there is no evidence they used it for medicinal, much less for recreational, purposes. At the time of the American Revolution, hemp was probably the single most widely used fiber for clothing and was widely used in the production of paper. The invention of the cotton gin lead to the decline of hemp by improving the efficiency with which cotton could be processed and reducing the cost of cotton cloth relative to hemp cloth. Further, developments in the technology for processing wood fiber into pulp reduced the cost of wood-based as compared to hemp-based paper products (Stafford, 1992).

Interest in the ingestion of marijuana and derivative products for medicinal and recreational purposes began in the mid 1800s with the appearance of can-nabis preparations such as "Tilden's Extract." In 1857 an American writer named Fitz Hugh Ludlow published a book entitled of *The Hasheesh Eater* describing his experiences with Tilden's Extract and other cannabis preparations, which, he claimed, allowed the user to make mental journeys to faraway lands and to un-earthly realms. This work may have been influenced by the writings of Baudelaire and the French hashish users as well as some of the opium-inspired poetry of Samuel Taylor Coleridge (e.g., "The Pains of Sleep," [1803]) and *Confessions of an English Opium Eater* (1822) by Thomas De Quincey, but it also shows that marijuana was used in America to assist flights of fantasy at an early date.

The smoking of marijuana for recreational purposes began to increase in the early 1900s particularly in southern states bordering Mexico where it was brought across the border by Mexican laborers (it has been suggested that the prohibitions against recreational use of marijuana have been partly driven by Nativist fears of the introduction of a "foreign" drug). In these areas, marijuana was considered a cheap substitute for liquor though many users preferred liquor when they could get it. Marijuana became more attractive as a substitute for alcohol after the passage of the Eighteenth Amendment to the Constitution prohibiting the man-ufacture and sale of liquor in 1920. Its use became less popular after the repeal of the Eighteenth Amendment in the late 1930s, only to regain popularity in the 1960s as a "counterculture" drug, the intoxicant of choice among non-conformist youth.

Effects of Marijuana

Regarding the subjective experience of marijuana intoxication, the range of reported experiences is extremely wide. Tart (1971) designed a questionnaire dealing with more than two hundred possible subjective experiences and received responses from 150 individuals who had smoked marijuana more than a dozen times. The experiences reported by these individuals included the following:

hallucinations	blurring of vision
increased vividness of colors	decreasing vividness of colors
increased peripheral vision	decreased peripheral vision
increased auditory acuity	synesthesia
increased hunger	diminished hunger
increased vividness of smells	time flowing more slowly
time flowing more rapidly	time appears to stop
objects seeming more massive	decreased anxiety
increased anxiety	increased relaxation
increased paranoia	"freaking out"
telepathy	precognition
out-of-body experiences	increased energy
decreased energy	pain diminishes
pain increases	body feels heavier
body feels lighter	body feels larger
increased awareness of the body	loss of awareness of the body
greater interest in sex	diminished interest in sex
greater sexual pleasure	diminished sexual pleasure
memory loss	improved cognitive function
diminished cognitive function	more sociable
more withdrawn	diminished self control
diminished anger	enhanced sleep
disturbed sleep	more vivid dreams
increased propensity to laughter	

This short list of effects will serve to demonstrate a fact often observed by users of this drug: its effects vary widely. Tart found that age, education level, previous experience with the drug, gender, and mood state strongly affected the subjective experience of marijuana. It seems likely that users' expectations, shaped by their cultural and social backgrounds and the environmental context of their use of the substance, also have significant effects on their experiences.

William Burroughs in an article published in the *British Journal of Addiction*, made the following observation based on his own experiences and those of his friends with cannabis indica.

Marijuana is a sensitizer, and the results are not always pleasant. It makes a bad situation worse. Depression becomes despair, anxiety, panic. I have already mentioned my horrible experience with marijuana during acute morphine withdrawal. I once gave marijuana to a guest who was mildly anxious about something ("On bum kicks" as he put it). After smoking half a cigarette he suddenly leapt to his feet screaming, "I got the fear!" and rushed out of the house. (Burroughs, 1957: 127)

History of Marijuana Prohibition in the United States

The earliest prohibitions against recreational use of marijuana were enacted in states bordering Mexico. In 1915, California made the nonmedical use of marijuana illegal, and in 1919 Texas did so. This fact is, of course, consistent with the theory that prohibitions against marijuana were part of a Nativist backlash against a "foreign" drug. Marijuana was later prohibited in Louisiana (1924) and New York (1927).

Efforts at marijuana prohibition at the federal level began in 1930 when H. J. Anslinger was appointed commissioner of the newly created U.S. Narcotics Bureau. In the mid 1930s he produced a series of articles as part of a publicity campaign against marijuana aimed at encouraging other states to pass laws against its use and to set the stage for federal legislation dealing with the drug. By 1937, all but two of the forty-eight states had passed laws prohibiting the use of marijuana.

Anslinger's publicity campaign strikes the modern reader as extreme. Perhaps his most famous slogan was "Marijuana, the Assassin of Youth." He claimed that marijuana could produce insanity in users, which could lead them to murderous rage. He also claimed that marijuana harmed users' health in a variety of ways and could even lead to death. During congressional hearings he reportedly told legislators, "You smoke a joint and you're likely to kill your brother." Anslinger was not the only American to hold these opinions at the time. These and other claims can be found in films of the period such as *Reefer Madness* (1936). However, Anslinger's position as one of the top government law enforcement officials seems to have given his claims added weight in the minds of legislators and citizens.

Hearings were held by the U.S. House of Representatives to determine whether there should be a federal law prohibiting the use of marijuana. In the 1930s there was concern about the constitutionality of a such a federal law since such prohibitions were seen as a matter for the states. Therefore, with the support of the U.S. Narcotics Bureau, the House decided to impose a transfer tax on marijuana to be collected by the federal government. This was the origin of the Marijuana Tax Act passed by both the House and Senate and signed into law by President Franklin D. Roosevelt in August of 1937.

The act did not prohibit the use of marijuana for medical purposes, and under its provisions there could still be legitimate use of the drug. For legitimate users, the act imposed a tax of $1 per ounce while for "illegitimate users" the tax was $100 per ounce. Failure to pay the tax was a felony. Further, the act classified marijuana as a narcotic and imposed penalties for its sale and use of five to ten years imprisonment for a first offense and ten to twenty years for a second offense.

This law effectively put an end to the manufacture of medicinal products prepared from marijuana by companies such as Lilly Pharmaceuticals and Squibb. It also banned the importation of hemp seeds used in the manufacture of such products as soap and paint unless the seeds had been sterilized and could not be used to grow hemp plants (Stafford, 1992).

THE CURRENT PUBLIC DEBATE ON MARIJUANA

Democracy and Personal Identity

The term "public debate" is, perhaps, an inaccurate description of the discussion of marijuana use as it is currently conducted in political campaigns and media news reports. Like many public policy questions, those related to cannabis have become highly polarized. Most of those speaking publicly on issues such as pre-employment testing for marijuana and the marijuana-free workplace advocate one of two diametrically opposed positions on the harm caused by the substance and the appropriate governmental action with regard to it.

This pattern of polarized, antagonistic public dialog has been identified by political theorist Benjamin Barber as symptomatic of what he calls "thin democracy" (Barber, 1984: 3–24). Barber points out a number of features of American political institutions and culture that encourage this type of highly contentious interaction among policy advocates. Framers of the U.S. Constitution were, for the most part, strong believers in the aphorism "That government is best which governs least." In one of the most famous documents written in support of the Constitution's ratification, *Federalist Paper No. 51*, James Madison argued in favor of keeping political advocates and the state itself in check by pitting "faction against faction" (Barber, 1984: 87–98).

Barber argues that the American model of limited government and competitive public discourse has been very successful in discouraging tyranny and promoting individual freedom from state-imposed burdens. He is critical, however, of its ability to develop strong community ties among citizens and to resolve long-term political conflicts. From his perspective, we have entered a period in which the political traditions and values of the U.S. put the country at great risk for hypercompetitive, extremely fragmented group conflict. The author contends that American democracy is "thin" because of these tendencies, which make the system vulnerable to demagoguery, inaction, and policy gridlock. By defining political participation almost exclusively in terms of voting, thin democracy fails to empower individual citizens and gives them few opportunities to learn much about policy choices beyond what they read in headlines or see in television newscasts.

Along with the features of the American political system, which Barber argues lead us toward polarized conflict and thin democracy, there appear to be deeply rooted patterns in human thought and behavior that may also propel us in the direction of joining cohesive, exclusive groups. Social psychologists, organization theorists, and analysts from a variety of other perspectives have observed that individuals construct their own social identities. Through interpreting and re-interpreting our memories of ourselves and our past experiences, sometimes se-lectively including and excluding unpleasant or unflattering events, we develop a view of the world and our place in it. Construction of an identity involves putting together an internally consistent and self-contained world view that sup-ports our concept of who we are. Part of this process may involve the identifi-cation of those who do not share one's world-view or who represent a threat to it (Aho, 1994: 26–33). One's own world-view is more clearly defined through a process of identifying opponents. Selecting and labeling enemies facilitates strong commitment to one's own role and identity.

If human psychology and the whole history of the U.S. polity lead our society toward deep, intractable political divisions, is there any way to alter this pattern? Barber outlines the components of what he views as "strong democracy." He feels that greater grass roots citizen participation in government and community affairs is needed, and that the quality and quantity of political discussion must be in-creased. These goals can be furthered by providing forums for dialog between members of competing groups and between policy-makers and the public, such as local and national town meetings, policy debates and media call-in programs. Citizen information and education should be maximized, along with equal access to these goods. Everyone should be encouraged to become involved with com-munity issues and institutions. Barber emphasizes the need for more participatory policy-making, in contrast to some observers, who see highly contentious politics as the result of an already-too-high level of mass mobilization (Barber, 1984: 117–162).

In the controversy surrounding marijuana use and regulation, it appears that the public policy discussion is dominated by two, polarized factions. By identi-fying the assumptions of the adherents of these two positions, it may be possible to better understand the main points of disagreement and even to promote rec-onciliation between the partisans on each side. It is important to remember that supporters of both positions believe they are promoting positive values. For com-mitted advocates in both camps, the issues in the marijuana debate are moral issues and they view their perspective as occupying the moral high ground. Since followers of each school of thought have their own rhetoric, and often use lan-guage that conveys different meanings to opponents than they intend, we will attempt to use neutral language in describing the assumptions of each side. We will call the two positions the "Responsible Living" position and the "Individual Liberty" position.

Social Identities of Marijuana Partisans

Those who are in favor of less regulation of marijuana see themselves as making a reasonable effort to balance the needs of society with the need for individual freedom. Those in favor of more regulation see themselves as passionate defenders of the interests of those who are harmed by the drug. These are essential parts of the identity of the members of both sides in the debate. We can learn a great deal about the self-image of these individuals by observing how they describe their opponents. Those who favor further efforts to reduce the use of marijuana tend to describe their adversaries as irresponsible and licentious while those who favor fewer efforts in this direction describe their opponents as puritanical and fascistic.

Supporters of the Responsible Living position maintain that American culture puts great emphasis on satisfying personal needs and wants. This can lead to a kind of excessive hedonism and the single-minded pursuit of instant gratification. They feel that recreational use of drugs, including marijuana, is a manifestation of this excess, so drug use should be discouraged. If it were possible to eliminate drug use by persuasion and rational argument, they would prefer to handle the drug problem this way. However, since people are constantly bombarded by messages promoting instant wish gratification, reasoned argument is often not sufficient to deter them from engaging in behaviors even though they generally regret them later. Thus, legal prohibitions may be necessary to help people behave the way they themselves would want to behave after sober reflection.

Respect for the law is an important part of this world view. While proponents of this view admit that some laws may be immoral and such laws should be opposed and perhaps even broken, they do not see the use of marijuana as an act of conscience but rather one of hedonism. They feel that if marijuana users wish to be free to smoke, they should work to change the law but obey it until it is changed.

Further, they argue, if employers are lax about drug use, it creates a climate in which those who are ambivalent about marijuana use are more likely to succumb to the temptation, much like permitting smoking on the job makes it more difficult for employees to quit. Marijuana use may mask other problems on the job. If, for example, employees feel they need to reduce stress, the stress itself may be an indication that certain aspects of the job need to be changed.

For members of this faction, marijuana use on the job is a serious enough problem to justify attempts to create a drug-free workplace. The lack of clear and consistent support from research for the claim that marijuana reduces performance does not dissuade them. The fact that researchers have not yet demonstrated the harmful effects of marijuana on performance does not provide a strong enough argument to counteract the argument that marijuana use is excessively hedonistic and illegal. They feel that the burden of proof should be on the opponents of pre-employment testing to provide a stronger case. Unless it can be proven that marijuana does not increase on-the-job accidents, employers are responsible for discouraging its use in the interests of their employees and customers.

On the other hand, those who support the Individual Liberty position feel that it is unnecessary to create a marijuana-free workplace and that pre-employment testing creates problems of its own. They argue that since research has not proven that marijuana has negative effects, there are no compelling reasons to outlaw it and to eliminate it from the workplace. Further, they do not see marijuana use as a part of the commercial culture that inundates us, but rather as something that helps reduce the power of self-indulgent commercialism.

Regarding the importance of obeying the law, members of this faction point to the amount of harm this law has done and say that this law is disobeyed *because* it is unjust. This points out that both sides hold different causal models. This side assigns more causal significance to the law itself than does the Responsible Living side, and feels that the law itself has caused much of the harm attributed to marijuana use.

Since pre-employment marijuana testing is part of the legalistic or prohibitionistic method of dealing with marijuana use, partisans on this side see it as a waste of money and an unnecessary threat to personal liberty. Typically, partisans on each side state their views and pay little attention to the views of the other side. When partisans on each side share the same public platform, they tend to talk past one another and attempt to distort opposing views in order to make them appear ridiculous. It is clear from such exchanges that each side is ego-involved in a perspective that serves to define their identity. Partisans' self-concepts and identities are threatened by the opposing side.

Within such partisan contexts, it is easy to see how mythical numbers become common currency. Those on each side judge data on the basis of its usefulness to their cause. Both unconscious psychological biases and more calculating political motives will tend to encourage committed activists to view the policy implications of any empirical findings as much more important than the way in which they were obtained.

How do we address complex policy issues like the control of marijuana use when there are such divergent views on the nature of the problem? The first step is to recognize that partisan public debate is not a productive way to address this issue. The second step is for those interested in the issue to take a close look at the research to see what it does and does not say about marijuana and job performance. To do this, it is necessary to be familiar with the methodological limitations of each of the approaches in research. This will allow us to determine how each type of research addresses the issue and what it adds to our understanding.

In this book we have identified four major approaches to research on the effects of marijuana on performance and have discussed their strengths, weaknesses, and limitations. Because we feel that it is important for readers to critically evaluate this research, we have included articles with examples of each type of research in order to help them form their own views of the value of the alternative approaches. A careful examination of the material in each reading dealing with the ways data were collected will expose the limitations of each approach to research. The research reviews in each chapter will help readers make sense of the individual studies.

RESEARCH SUMMARIZED IN THIS BOOK

A search of the *Medline* biomedical database revealed a great deal of research that, if interpreted with appropriate caution, provides information relevant to the role of marijuana in the workplace. Much of this work was done by medical researchers and addresses the effects of marijuana on mental and physical health, so its relevance to job performance may not be immediately apparent. Many of the tasks subjects performed in these studies, however, seem to have direct relevance to skills required for effective performance at many jobs.

Over two hundred research studies were initially screened to select the set of slightly over one hundred studies to be reviewed. The first author made the judgments about which studies should be included in this review. He developed the overall framework for discussing and integrating the contributions of different research methodologies. This framework is presented in Tables 1.1 and 1.2.

The principal criterion for screening studies was whether the dependent variables were clearly related to job performance. This lead to the exclusion of studies dealing only with marijuana's possible effects on physical or mental health and on violent or criminal behavior. Literature reviews on the health consequences of marijuana (e.g., Doblin & Kleiman, 1995; Grinspoon & Bakalar, 1993, 1995; Husain & Khan, 1985) do not provide consistent evidence that recreational use of marijuana produces any long-term health consequences that might have negative effects on job performance. Further, it is possible to draw meaningful conclusions from the literature on the effects of marijuana on job performance without discussing the literature on the health effects of marijuana.

Studies of the effects of marijuana on violent behavior, socially deviant behaviors, and criminal conduct have also been excluded though these topics have been addressed in earlier research (e.g., Halikas, Weller, Morse, & Hoffman, 1983). Since deviant behavior would not always reduce job productivity, and since problem behaviors that lead to termination, disciplinary actions by supervisors, or absenteeism are already examined in research on pre-employment drug testing, it is possible to discuss marijuana's effects on job performance without including these studies.

Since marijuana has long been the subject of intense public debate, a researcher's private opinions about the morality of marijuana use may affect his or her selection of studies and discussion of the results. Therefore, special care had to be exercised in selecting the final set of studies. First, the review was restricted almost entirely to articles published in refereed journals and research monographs. While peer review is certainly not a guarantee of high-quality research, it provides a useful initial screen. Second, the decision about whether or not to include a study was made after having identified the independent and dependent variables but before examining the study's findings in order to minimize the chance that knowledge of the findings would influence the decision on inclusion. Table 1.1 deals with the research methodologies used to examine marijuana use and performance.

Table 1.1
Categories of Research Related to the Effect of Marijuana on Job Performance

Methodology	Definition of Use	Definition of Performance	Findings (Methodological Concerns)
Controlled Experiments	Acute intoxication	Performance at job-related tasks	Intoxication reduces quality of performance at tasks requiring ability to learn and remember information. Effect sizes are small. Not shown to reduce motivation. (External Validity)
Surveys	Self-reports of frequency of use	Wages, Hours worked	Reported use negatively related to learning, memory, and hours worked but positively related to wages and other measures of achievement in young men. Pattern of relationships different for young women. (Causality)
Pre-employment Drug Testing	Testing "Dirty" or Self-reports	Absences, Accidents, Discipline, Turnover	Those who test positive for marijuana use prior to employment have significantly higher rates of performance problems. Effect sizes are small. (Sample Selection Bias)
Anthropological Field Studies	Self-reports confirmed by observation	Pay, Work output	Level of use is positively related to some measures of job performance but overall, no significant differences between users and non-users. (Control for Observer Biases)

Four major streams of research related to the question of the effects of marijuana use on job performance were identified: controlled experiments, survey research, pre-employment drug testing, and ethnographic field research. Each stream represents a distinct approach to inquiry with its own strengths and weaknesses. As Table 1.1 shows, each stream has a different way of defining marijuana use, uses a different definition of performance, and embodies a different set of assumptions about research. As would be expected, the results of each stream are not always supportive of each other.

Table 1.2 deals with four broad categories of dependent variables related to job performance. In defining these categories and assigning studies to each, the authors attempted to adopt a conservative approach and select from a very broad range of dependent variables only those most clearly job-related and likely to directly affect job performance. The resulting categories are commonly discussed in personnel and human resource texts and included in aptitude tests such as the General Aptitude Test Battery (GATB).

The first category of job-related dependent variables is ATTENTION, LEARNING, and MEMORY, which deals with the relationship between marijuana and performance at tasks requiring people to learn, remember, and use information. These are skills that seem relevant to all jobs, though they are much more im-

Table 1.2
Volume of Research Summarized by Research Streams and Topics Covered

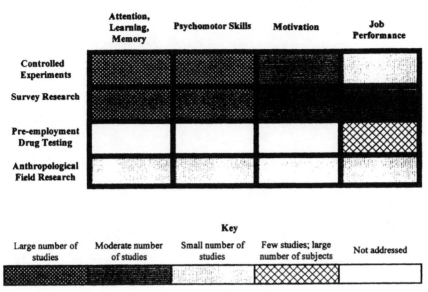

<table>
<tr><td></td><td>Attention, Learning, Memory</td><td>Psychomotor Skills</td><td>Motivation</td><td>Job Performance</td></tr>
<tr><td>Controlled Experiments</td><td></td><td></td><td></td><td></td></tr>
<tr><td>Survey Research</td><td></td><td></td><td></td><td></td></tr>
<tr><td>Pre-employment Drug Testing</td><td></td><td></td><td></td><td></td></tr>
<tr><td>Anthropological Field Research</td><td></td><td></td><td></td><td></td></tr>
</table>

Key

Large number of studies	Moderate number of studies	Small number of studies	Few studies; large number of subjects	Not addressed

portant in some jobs than in others. The second is PSYCHOMOTOR SKILLS—such as reaction time and hand-eye coordination, skills which are not important in some kinds of work but very important in others. The third is MOTIVATION to achieve or to perform well. The fourth is actual JOB PERFORMANCE as measured in terms of pay, absences, or other measures of productivity on the job.

A BRIEF OUTLINE OF THE BOOK

In the next four chapters of this book we will discuss each of the four streams of research in turn. We will summarize the strengths and weaknesses of each methodology and include one or two representative studies in each chapter. At the conclusion of each chapter summary we have attempted to draw the reader's attention to some points of special interest in each of the studies we have chosen for inclusion. We hope that the reader will be impressed, as we were, with the variety of ways researchers have addressed the relationship between marijuana use and job performance. Once readers are familiar with the details of these studies, they will be able to critique our own conclusions about the four streams of research. In the final chapter we will describe the implications of the research for future inquiry on this topic as well as public and business policy.

Chapter 2

Controlled Experiments

Nearly all of the relevant controlled experiments follow the same basic procedure. Subjects are given marijuana (orally or in smoked form) or THC (the active ingredient in marijuana), and its effects on their performance in a variety of tasks is assessed. In this review the results of all studies are combined regardless of the means by which marijuana or THC are administered. Though Casswell and Marks (1973a) have argued that marijuana's effects differ by means of administration, the author's own reading of the literature suggests that the differences in effects are not sufficient to warrant separate treatment. The period of administration varies from a single administration to controlled administration over ninety-eight days (see Murray, 1986 and Pope, Gruber, & Yurgelun-Todd, 1995 for further discussions of these studies).

These experiments allow us to assess the effects of *acute intoxication* on performance at tasks constructed to test basic skills or abilities. Several of these basic skills and abilities are relevant to the performance at a wide variety of jobs, so it seems that this research should be relevant in estimating the effects of marijuana intoxication on performance at specific jobs requiring these skills.

ATTENTION, LEARNING, AND MEMORY

Because marijuana intoxication is commonly believed to make people inattentive, slow, and forgetful, a number of experiments have addressed this question (Abel, 1970, 1971; Block, Farinpour, & Braverman, 1992; Casswell & Marks, 1973a,b; Chait, 1990; Chait, Fishman, & Schuster, 1985; Darley & Tinklenberg, 1974; Dittrich, Battig, & von Zepplin, 1973; Dornbush, Clare, Zaks, Crown, Volavka, & Fink, 1972; Evans, Martz, Brown, Rodda, Kiplinger, Lemberger, & Forney, 1973; Heisman, Stitzer, & Yingling, 1989; Jones & Benowitz, 1976;

Klonoff & Low, 1974; Melges, Tinklenberg, Hollister, & Gillespie, 1970a, b; Meyer, Pillard, Shapiro, & Mirin, 1971; Miller, Drew, & Kiplinger, 1972; Pickworth, Rohrer, & Fant, 1997).

The tasks used to assess attentiveness, learning, and memory in these experiments are typically laboratory tasks that have little apparent similarity to job-related tasks but that do test certain basic cognitive skills. For example, some experiments have used the Goal-Directed Serial Alternation (GDSA) task (Melges et al., 1970a, b; Meyer et al., 1971) in which subjects are assigned a number between 106 and 114 and required to mentally perform sequential additions and subtractions while holding the results of the previous operation in mind. Thus, this task tests attention, memory, and ability to perform complex cognitive tasks. The tasks used in these experiments vary widely, but all are designed to test basic cognitive skills and few bear any surface similarity to job-related tasks. Other more innovative measures have also been used including some involving EEG readings, but these are even less similar to job-related tasks and so will not be discussed in detail here.

Most experiments have shown that marijuana intoxication reduces subjects' attention or concentration on tasks, their speed at learning new material and their short-term memory. Abel (1970) showed that smoking marijuana reduced subjects' ability to recall written material from a book they read twice at their own speed after smoking and, in a later experiment (Abel, 1971), that smoking marijuana reduced subjects' ability to recall words from lists they previously read. Dornbush et al., (1972) results using a similar research design replicated those of Abel. Miller et al. (1972) found that marijuana affected memory for narrative material but not performance on another memory task (the Stroop Color-Word Test). Several of these studies showed that subjects who had smoked marijuana tended to produce more irrelevant material to "fill in" gaps in their recollections. Casswell and Marks (1973a) and Melges et al. (1970a, b) found that smoking marijuana reduced subjects' performance at the GDSA task discussed above, though Evans et al. (1973) found that *low* doses of marijuana did not influence performance at a task similar to the GDSA. Dittrich et al. (1973) found that subjects showed less ability to recall lists of two-syllable nouns after using marijuana than after using a placebo. Chait (1990) and Chait et al. (1985) have shown that some negative effects persist, but with diminished intensity, over periods of twenty-four hours. Block et al. (1992) found that smoking marijuana impaired learning but that prolonged breath holding also impaired performance, suggesting that some of the performance effects of marijuana may be due to the manner in which it is smoked.

Experiments on the effects of marijuana on the ability to recall material already in long-term memory have shown no overall differences attributable to marijuana intoxication (Darley, Tinklenberg, Roth, Vernon, & Koppel, 1977; Parker, Birnbaum, Weingartner, Hartley, Stillman, & Wyatt, 1980). One study that explored both short-term and long-term memory showed that intoxicated subjects required more trials to learn word lists but that they recalled more of the material they had learned when tested three days later than subjects who were not intoxicated while learning the lists (Rickles, Cohen, Whitaker, & McIntyre, 1973).

PSYCHOMOTOR SKILLS

Since psychomotor skills are important in a large number of jobs, and since driving performance is central to the performance at a variety of jobs, research results on the effects of marijuana on driving performance are relevant to the discussion of its effects on job performance. Some of the experiments previously cited in connection with the effects of marijuana on attention, learning, and memory also included tests of psychomotor and driving performance. A few additional studies have also been identified (Azorlosa, Heishman, Stitzer, & Mahaffey, 1992; Braff, Silverton, Saccuzzo, & Janowsky, 1981; Bech, Rafaelsen, & Rafaelsen, 1973; Chait & Perry, 1994; Clark, Hughes, & Nakashima, 1970; Hansteen, Miller, Lonero, Reid, & Jones, 1976; Jones & Stone, 1970; Kelly, Fotlin, Emurian, & Fischman, 1990; Klonoff, 1974; Kvalseth, 1977; Manno, Kiplinger, Haine, Bennett, & Forney, 1970; Manno, Kiplinger, Scholz, Forney, & Haine, 1971; MacAvoy & Marks, 1975; Mathew, Wilson, Humphreys, Lowe, & Weith, 1993; Melges, 1976; Moskowitz, Shea, & Burns, 1974; Moskowitz, Zeidman, & Sharma, 1976; Rafaelsen, Beech, Christiansen, Christrup, Nyobe, & Rafaelsen, 1973; Robbe, & O'Hanlon, 1993; Roth, Tinklenberg, Whitaker, Darley, Kopell, & Hollister, 1973; Vachon, Sulkowski, & Rich, 1974; Wilson, Ellinwood, Mathew, & Johnson, 1994).

Research dealing with psychomotor performance covers a wide range of tasks testing hand-eye coordination, reaction time, spatial and temporal judgments, etc. Marijuana intoxication has been shown to cause a greater rate of errors in estimates of distance (Bech et al., 1973) and in estimates of time, which could affect judgments in driving and operating machinery (Hollister & Gillespie, 1970; Jones & Stone, 1970; Melges et al., 1971; Vachon et al., 1974). It also affects visual tracking (MacAvoy & Marks, 1975; Melges, 1976; Roth et al., 1973) and visual information processing (Braff et al., 1981; Casswell & Marks, 1973b) as well as reducing reaction time and coordination of movements important for operating industrial machinery as well as driving (Kvalseth, 1977; Manno et al., 1970; Manno et al., 1971; Moskowitz et al., 1974). In general, these experiments suggest that acute marijuana intoxication impairs performance, particularly at more complex tasks.

The effects of marijuana intoxication on performance in driving simulators and controlled driving tests are somewhat more ambiguous, suggesting that in situations more similar to actual driving situations (or to actual work situations) users may be able to "suppress the marijuana high" (Murray, 1986: 34). Crancer, Dille, Deloy, Wallace, and Haykin (1969) found that marijuana intoxication reduced the accuracy of speedometer readings but did not affect use of the brakes, accelerator, or steering. Though Hansteen et al. (1976) showed decrements in driving skills for high doses of marijuana, and Klonoff (1974) found that intoxicated drivers performed less well on city streets from which other traffic had been excluded, Robbe and Hanlon (1993) found that in a controlled driving protocol, including driving in high-density urban traffic, higher doses impaired performance slightly but that the only significant effect of lower doses was that they caused drivers to drive more slowly, a trait that would not necessarily produce less safe driving. Further, the effects of marijuana varied from individual to individual in the Klonoff (1974) study, with 32% of subjects given a low dose and 16% given a high dose improving their driving performance.

MOTIVATION

Experiments on the motivational effects of marijuana intoxication bear on the claim that marijuana leads to an *amotivational syndrome* (McGlothlin & West, 1968). Some have claimed that this syndrome reduces effort and leads to poorer performance at jobs and school work (Hendin, Pollinger, & Ulman, 1981; Margolis & Popkin, 1980; Miranne, 1979).

Research has dealt with the effects of intoxication on the psychological phenomenon of "depersonalization." Mathew et al. (1993) define depersonalization as "an alteration in the perception or experience of the self in which the usual sense of one's own reality is temporarily lost or changed" and discuss the fact that this psychological state is associated with fatigue, depression, schizophrenia, and other conditions that could negatively affect worker motivation (Mathew et al., 1993: 431). Both Melges et al. (1970b) and Mathew et al. (1993) used scales developed by Dixon (1963) and found that marijuana intoxication caused increased levels of depersonalization. Mathew et al. (1993: 433–435) found that depersonalization increases to a maximum approximately thirty minutes after smoking marijuana and returns to baseline within two hours.

These experiments show that ingestion of marijuana produces measurable psychological effects sometimes associated with mental illness but not that the depersonalization measured in these studies was associated with lower productivity, since neither of the studies included measures of the behavioral consequences of the depersonalization. Castillo (1990) has shown that depersonalization can be produced by meditation in otherwise healthy and productive individuals, and this suggests that depersonalization by itself is not evidence of reduced motivation to work or productivity.

JOB PERFORMANCE

The experiments that deal most directly with work performance involve administration of marijuana to subjects and the measurement of performance in controlled settings over periods as long as ninety-four days (Cohen, 1976) and ninety-eight days (Kagel et al., 1976). Cohen (1976), Mendelson, Babour, Kuehnle, Rossi, Bernstein, Mello, and Greenberg (1976a) and Foltin, Fischman, Brady, Bernstein, Capriotti, Nellis, and Kelly (1990) found no significant differences between the performance of subjects given marijuana and those who were not. Foltin et al. (1990) found that subjects given marijuana increased their work activity more when rewarded for work than did those in the placebo condition.

The Kagel et al. (1980) piece deserves special mention because it represents the contribution of experimental economics and specifically the "micoeconomy" to the study of this topic. In this experiment, subjects spent ninety-eight days in a controlled environment in which they could do work in exchange for symbolic currency that could be exchanged for items of value. Subjects used marijuana within this controlled environment, and this allowed researchers to assess the relationship between use and productivity measured in terms of output per hour worked. They found no significant relationship between hours worked and marijuana use. However, marijuana use was associated with a statistically significant increase in subjects' output per hour (1980: 386–387). Overall, this experiment does not support the claim that marijuana reduces work productivity. Further, it raises the interesting possibility that marijuana use may, in some circumstances, be associated with higher productivity.

In summary, the controlled experimental research supports the conclusion that marijuana intoxication does have negative effects on attention, short-term memory, learning, and some psychomotor skills in controlled settings and that the effects appear to be dose related. The evidence from controlled experiments does not support the conclusion that marijuana use reduces motivation. However, the results of these experiments do not tell us about the magnitude of marijuana's effects in the field because the artificial conditions of the laboratory will influence the magnitude of the effects observed in the experiments. It is difficult to be sure how these results relate to actual job settings in which those who use marijuana are probably not continuously in a state of acute intoxication.

METHODOLOGICAL ISSUES

The great strength of laboratory research is that it allows the experimenter to manipulate the independent variables of interest (in this case, ingestion of marijuana) and to determine the effects of these manipulations on dependent variables of interest (in this case, task performance) because the use of experimental control allows the researcher to rule out third-variable causes. The experimenter designs the experiment and thereby exercises control over the setting. Further, the random assignment of subjects to experimental conditions ensures that systematic differences between subjects will not be confounded with experimental treatments in producing differences observed between experimental conditions. The experimenter also can achieve a high degree of specificity in the operationalization of the variables used in the experiment. The process of thinking through the exact operational definition of a variable to be used in an experiment is a valuable way of refining a researcher's understanding of the variable and improving on the rather vague definition of variables found in many field studies.

Precise definitions of variables and control over experimental procedures makes it possible for other researchers to replicate an experiment to make sure the results are consistent. Also, the ability to manipulate the variable of interest while controlling other variables allows laboratory researchers to make statements about causality that are not possible in field settings in which experimental control is absent. In a field study, any relationship between the variables of interest may be due to the presence of confounding variables. Thus, field researchers do not know with certainty that one variable such as marijuana use really causes changes in another variable, such as performance on particular tasks. However, if a controlled experiment has been properly designed, the experimenter can show that marijuana use causes differences in task performance, at least within the conditions of the experiment.

The great weakness of this method is that the results are always open to questions of *external validity* because the variables may not be operationalized in the laboratory in the same way that they occur in the field (in this case, acute intoxication as it is produced in the lab may not have the same effects as occasional recreational use of marijuana). More importantly, subjects' motivation to perform well at a laboratory task may be less than their motivation level in their jobs or careers. This may be especially true if there were no incentives or rewards for good performance. Since many of the effects of acute intoxication on performance may derive from marijuana's specific effects on attention span, subjects with greater motivation to pay attention and perform well at a task may be less affected by marijuana. This speculation is supported by the research suggesting that, at lower doses, users may be able to suppress the effects of marijuana intoxication on their behavior (Murray, 1986: 34) and that their behavior in actual driving conditions may be less affected by marijuana than their performance on driving simulators.

In general, the artificiality of the conditions in a controlled experiment is not necessarily a weakness. It merely makes it necessary that caution be exercised in interpreting the results. In attempting to apply the laboratory results to the field, it is important to develop a definition of acute intoxication that would allow us to determine whether an employee was intoxicated to a level that matches the level achieved in the controlled experiments. The existing literature provides no generally accepted definition of acute marijuana intoxication. The problem of developing a definition for marijuana is much greater than for alcohol. The effects of acute alcohol intoxication (slurred speech, poor coordination, etc.) are similar in most users, and the severity of these effects is highly correlated with blood alcohol level. These statements do not appear to be true of marijuana. The effects appear to vary widely from user to user and there is no agreement on the blood level of THC which constitutes intoxication. If, however, we assume that all employees who smoke marijuana do so to the point of intoxication, it appears that the intoxication lasts approximately two hours. Thus, if a person smokes at work or performs work within two hours of smoking, the research on ACUTE intoxication should be relevant in predicting the effects of marijuana on their job performance.

COMMENTS ON THE KAGEL ET AL. EXPERIMENT

The experiment we have chosen to include is one dealing directly with work performance rather than with factors that might contribute to work performance (attention, learning, memory, motivation, or psychomotor performance). It is also one of the experiments requiring subjects to spend a relatively long time in residence at the experimental facility. In many of the experiments on the effects of marijuana, subjects spend only a few hours in controlled settings where a specific amount of the drug is administered in a controlled way and subjects are then required to complete the experimental tasks. Such experiments maximize the level of experimental control, but they do not show us how subjects perform in actual work settings when using an amount of the drug with which they feel comfortable. In attempting to design an experiment that will provide a more realistic setting, the experimenters have had to give up some experimental control. Subjects were occasionally permitted outside the experimental area, and they were able to purchase and use varying amounts of marijuana though the experimenters recorded each subject's level of use.

There are a few points of contact between this article and the others included in this book. First, this experiment makes use of relatively young subjects (ages eighteen through twenty-seven). Thus, it focuses on the population sampled in the National Longitudinal Survey of Youth, which is analyzed in the articles by Kaestner in the chapter on survey research. A good deal of research focuses on younger workers because they are the most likely to use marijuana. Second, since this experiment examines marijuana use in a more realistic setting than most laboratory experiments, it parallels the field work of Dreher reproduced in the chapter on Ethnographic research.

APPENDIX A

Marihuana and Work Performance:
Results from an Experiment

John H. Kagel, Raymond C. Battalio, and C. G. Miles

ABSTRACT

Determining the relationship between marihuana and economic activity is an important factor in establishing social policy in this area. The effects of marihuana availability and consumption on production, hours worked, and output per hour are reported from an experimental microeconomy involving resident volunteer human subjects. The statistical analysis shows no effect of marihuana on total output or total hours worked for experimental as compared to control conditions, although marihuana use was generally associated with a simultaneous decision to engage in passive leisure activities in the period immediately following smoking. These results suggest a hypothesis about the general relationship between marihuana and economic activity that is used to integrate the results of several other studies with those reported here.

I. INTRODUCTION

In order to establish a meaningful framework for social policy-making with respect to marihuana, both the United States and Canadian commissions on marihuana and drug abuse have cited the need to establish a description and evaluation of the relationship of marihuana and economic activity. The United States Commission has been particularly concerned with identifying the social losses in terms of reduced productivity, unemployment, and absenteeism arising from marihuana use (21, pp. 3, 35). Likewise, the Canadian Commission has been concerned with potential adverse effects associated with regular marihuana

This article originally appeared in the *Journal of Human Resources*, Volume 15, pp. 373–395, 1980.

use on the capacity to carry out vocational responsibilities and on the qualities that have played an important part in the development of our present society, such as acquisitiveness, the willingness to defer present pleasure for future rewards, and the capacity to tolerate the tedium of routine tasks (6, pp. 266, 273). More recently, the director of the National (U.S.) Institute on Drug Abuse cited a continuing need to understand the relationship between marihuana and work performance. Further, while he had earlier thought that the marihuana issue was a "joke" relative to other problems of drug abuse, the increasing levels of exposure to marihuana in the population "merits the very greatest concern" (Robert L. DuPont as interviewed in *Science* [15]).

Most of the research on marihuana has been conducted by physicians and has been directed at determining the health effects of the drug. These researchers have, in general, not examined the problems of marihuana intoxication as related to work performance, and economists have generally shied away from the problem. The little evidence there is on the relationship between regular marihuana use (and use of other forms of the cannabis plant) and economic activities appears to be inconsistent. From clinical reports of physicians and psychologists in North America, researchers have hypothesized an "amotivational syndrome" associated with heavy, continuous cannabis consumption, an important characteristic of which involves decreased motivation to work (12). However, in Jamaica, where cannabis is an integral part of the lifestyle of members of the lower socioeconomic strata, users, almost without exception, maintain that cannabis enhances their ability to work and permits them to face, start, and carry through the most difficult and distasteful manual labor (Rubin and Cornitas [22]).

In this paper we present data from a series of three experiments designed to investigate the relationship between marihuana and socioeconomic behavior conducted at the Addiction Research Foundation of Ontario, Canada. The experiments were conducted in a planned economic environment in which volunteer subjects from the national economy, who were regular marihuana users, agreed to reside continuously for 98 days. The planned environment was designed as a microeconomy in which the volunteers earned their income by performing manual job tasks that were paid for on a piecework basis. Access to virtually all consumption goods during the experiment, including meals, was through income earnings. In addition, subjects could save for future consumption since unspent income was convertible to Canadian currency after completion of the study.[1] The length of the study makes it one of the longest periods of controlled investigation of marihuana use, uncomplicated by other drugs, ever conducted and provides significant information on the effects of repeated cannabis administration on regular users, which is not available from earlier studies.

In the next section we describe the structure of the economy and the design of the experiments. Then, following a statistical analysis of the effects of marihuana on total output, hours worked, and output per hour, is an analysis of behavior during the periods immediately following smoking. We conclude with a discussion of the distinguishing characteristics of the experimental economy compared to conditions typically faced by potential labor force participants in the United States and Canada, and indicate the extent to which the experimental results might he generalized, assuming legalization of marihuana within these national economies.

Due to the relative novelty of laboratory experimentation in economics, it is important in evaluating the results of the experiment that readers have a clear concept of what one can hope to learn from studies such as the one reported here. As the director of the National Institute of Drug Abuse (NIDA) notes, small-scale experiments using volunteers have important limitations in terms of obvious subject preselection biases, artificialities arising from bringing natural behavior into the laboratory, limited sample sizes, etc. Consequently, the main contribution of such studies, and the reason why NIDA and other government agencies continue to fund such studies, is that ". . . they narrow the parameters for discussion. It's no longer credible to say that *all* marihuana smokers have an x or y negative health outcome. That's a limited but valuable finding" (Robert L. DuPont as interviewed in *Science* [15]). This role of laboratory experiments in providing rigorous pretests of concepts prior to the collection of extensive field data is widely recognized in the biological and a number of the behavioral sciences.[2] It is a contribution that is receiving increased recognition within the economics profession also (Smith [23]).

II. EXPERIMENTAL DESIGN

The Economy

For each experiment, two groups of volunteer subjects, an experimental group and a control group, lived and worked in separate planned economic environments. These microeconomies occupied adjacent wings of the fourth floor of the hospital facilities of the Addiction Research Foundation (ARF). Subjects agreed to live in the economy continuously for the length of the experiment.

Income was earned by weaving sash belts on primitive, portable handlooms. Standards for acceptable belts were established by the experimenters, and subjects received $2.50 (Canadian currency) in the form of cash-value tokens for each acceptable belt turned in. Volunteers quickly learned how to weave belts, so that within a week virtually all belts produced met the specifications. Material required for weaving belts was provided free of charge and was always available. Subjects could work anywhere on the ward, at any hour of the day or night, and for any length of time. This flexibility in work schedules, while optimal for studying the alleged amotivational syndrome resulting from marihuana use, makes it impossible to observe directly the effects of the drug on such work related variables as absenteeism and tardiness.

The living area for each experimental and control group was approximately 56 feet by 123 feet. It included five bedrooms, four workrooms, four lounges (one with a TV and record player), and a dining room in addition to five rooms for staff. Ten subjects, sleeping two each in the five double bedrooms, were confined to this area, originally designed to service 16 patients under normal hospital conditions. Sleeping privileges, heat, lights, and room-cleaning services were provided free of charge. All other items of consumption had to be purchased using the cash value of tokens earned from weaving belts.

The store on the floor sold consumables subject to frequent repurchase, such as tobacco cigarettes, soft drinks, candy, alcoholic beverages, toiletries, etc., and was open virtually 24 hours a day. Meals were purchased from the hospital cafeteria and snack bar or from food-to-go outlets outside the hospital. Other retail items could be purchased from outside the hospital through a purchasing agent. Prices of these goods and services were set to match, as closely as possible, actual prices prevailing in Toronto where the experiment was conducted. Individual or collective use of the entertainment facilities (television, stereo, etc.) was obtained through a single rental fee of 10–15 cents per hour. Earnings could also be used to make payments on prior debts or for outside apartment rent. A bank existed in which subjects could deposit unspent earnings, but no interest was paid.

Individuals remaining in the economy for the entire experiment received a $200 bonus and were allowed to convert their cash balances into Canadian currency. Subjects leaving the economy forfeited three-quarters of their cash balances in addition to losing the bonus.

Volunteers spent most of their time confined to the premises of the microeconomy. However, they were able to leave the ward (under escort) at regularly scheduled times (several times a week) to use the gymnasium and sauna facilities at the ARF (at off-peak hours) and to exercise (weather permitting) in the outdoor courtyard of the Foundation. Swimming facilities outside the Foundation were also available at regularly scheduled intervals, and subjects could go on escorted night walks in the area. In addition, an occasional (two–three times a study) day outing was permitted, provided there would be minimal contact with the general population. When subjects were off the ward, they were accompanied by one nurse and one attendant at all times, and experimental and control groups were not permitted to use a facility at the same time. Nominal fees were charged for most of these events. Notwithstanding these efforts, living in the microeconomy involved considerable restrictions on subjects' activities and invasion of personal privacy, as subjects had to be located each half-hour to make regularly scheduled activity checks.

Except for the restrictions on subjects' movements inherent in the observation procedures employed, the experimental economy corresponded to a fully operationalized, albeit relatively simple, economic system. The average effective hourly wage rate equaled or exceeded existing wage rates for manual labor in Toronto at the time. Subjects worked an average of well over 40 hours per week and earnings were substantial, with more than half the subjects leaving the experiment with $2000 accumulated savings and six subjects having more than $4000 saved. Analysis of income, consumption, and saving behavior in the economy showed it to be consistent with Goldsmith's [12] analysis of saving behavior within the U.S. economy (Kagel et al. [13]). Further, measures of the dispersion of wage earnings were remarkably similar to the comparable measures reported for narrowly defined occupational categories in the United States and other market economies (Battalio et al. [3]).

Subjects

Subjects were recruited for the experiments through placing advertisements in underground newspapers, posting notices at the nearby University of Toronto campus, and advertising in other media likely to attract suitable subjects—that is, unattached individuals with a prior history of marihuana use who could readily drop out of the national economy for a three-month period. Local newspaper stories covering a pilot study (Miles et al. [17, 18]) and the first experiment, plus word-of-mouth communication about the nature of the studies, provided a considerable amount of free advertising. A series of pre-enrollment interviews were designed to provide potential volunteers with information concerning the studies and to screen out undesirables such as narcotics users and individuals with drinking and assorted psychiatric problems. Recruitment for each of the experiments was done separately preceding each study.

Subjects in the first two experiments, which were restricted to males, were between 21 and 27 years of age. In the third experiment, restricted to women, volunteers were between 18 and 25 years of age. Subjects' education ranged from grade 9 to university level, with over half of the subjects having studied at the college or university level. In addition, half the subjects were either employed or students prior to the time they enrolled in the study.[3] The other half had a wide variety of work experience prior to enrollment, but were currently unemployed. The length of unemployment ranged from one or two days to one year or more. The two most frequent explanations subjects gave for joining the experiment were the desire to earn money and general interest in the question under investigation, with a number of them citing both motives as the basis for volunteering.

Volunteers had typically been using marihuana for about two years prior to enrollment. Table 2.1 shows marihuana use during the 5–6 month period following termination of the study, systematic use records prior to entry into the experiment being unavailable.[4] These data must be interpreted cautiously as they are based on subject's self-reports.

Of the 60 subjects recruited, four dropped out during the studies; the two women who left Experiment III dropped out when the study was more than two-thirds completed.[5] Dropouts were evenly divided between the experimental and control groups. Reasons for quitting varied. Three of the four subjects who quit were low income earners; the fourth forfeited a considerable sum of money, about $1500, as a result of leaving early.

The recruitment procedures employed were not intended to, nor did they, result in a sample of subjects representative of the North American population as a whole. The sample is not even likely to be fully representative of the pop-

Table 2.1
Marihuana Use of Subjects Outside the Experimental Economy

	Use			
	None	Low	Medium	High
Number of subjects	3	14	9	21

Notes: Low use: Less than twice a month. Covers the range from "I have had about 12 tokes—it gets passed around at parties—it's almost a question of manners" to "I may get high about every third week. Once in a while, when there is some good stuff around, it's nice on a weekend." None of the subjects reported owning their own supply as a matter of course.

Medium use: More than twice and less than 10 times a month. Many subjects reported regular weekend use in a social context; others reported a period of daily use followed by total abstinence.

High use: More than 10 times per month, with most subjects reporting daily use.

$N = 47$, as all subjects did not report for postexperiment interviews.

ulation of casual or regular users of marihuana in North America, although it is undoubtedly representative of a large percentage of the population between the ages of 18 and 27. The unrepresentative nature of the sample naturally precludes any direct extrapolation of the results of the experiment to the population as a whole. However, it does not mitigate using the results to shed light on the behavioral processes underlying the relationship between cannabis use and work performance (Campbell and Stanley [8], especially pp. 23–24), which is what the experiments were designed to do.

Experimental Treatments[6]

In Experiments I and II, subjects were randomly assigned to one of the two wards upon entering the economy and remained there throughout the experiment. In Experiment III, this initial random assignment of subjects was adjusted during the predrug (baseline) period in an effort to equate mean output levels between groups. This involved switching half the subjects between wards. Efforts at group matching generally make it more difficult to achieve significant differences between groups, if they exist, unless appropriate corrections are taken (Boneau and Pennypacker [5]). However, in the present study, introducing these corrections resulted in no change in the test outcomes reported in the text.

During the first 17 days of each experiment, referred to as the predrug period, no marihuana was available. The purpose of the predrug period was to provide time for subjects to learn the job task. This period also provides measures of production and hours worked unaffected by marihuana, which can be used to control statistically for intersubject variability in economic activity (Winer [26]). During the predrug period, neither the subjects nor the staff knew when the experimental treatments would begin or to what experimental condition a group would be assigned.

In Experiments II and III, the experimental treatment consisted of required smoking of two (1 gram) cigarettes, each containing 8 mg. of Δ^9 THC (hereafter referred to simply as THC), the major active compound in hashish and marihuana. A single cigarette of this dose level contains enough active material to produce a reliable "high" in an experienced user, with two cigarettes insuring intoxication. Cigarettes were smoked consecutively at 8:15 p.m. each evening. In addition to the required smoking, members of the experimental group could purchase unlimited numbers of cigarettes containing 2 mg. of THC at 50 cents each.[7] In Experiment I, in the week immediately following the predrug period, subjects could purchase unlimited numbers of marihuana cigarettes containing 8 mg. of THC at 50 cents each with no required smoking. This was followed by a 27-day period of mandatory smoking of two 8 mg. THC cigarettes as in Experiments II and III, with unlimited members of 8 mg. THC cigarettes available for purchase at 50 cents each. This, in turn, was followed by a 15-day period in which the THC content of the mandatory and purchased cigarettes changed abruptly to 12 mg. per cigarette.

The control conditions also differed between Experiment I and Experiments II and III. In Experiment I, the control group was required to smoke two 1-gram placebo cigarettes at 8:15 p.m. each night under essentially the same conditions as the experimental group and could purchase unlimited numbers of these placebo cigarettes at 50 cents each. Control problems encountered in administering the placebo treatment—subjects readily detected that they were smoking inactive cigarettes and objected, quite strongly at times, to having to do so—led to the elimination of placebos in Experiments II and III, although subjects still had to gather as a group at 8:15 p.m. and remain together for approximately the same amount of time as did the experimental subjects. Television, records, and other entertainment facilities were available for all groups during the mandatory smoking period, and subjects could, and frequently did, bring their work to these sessions. Control subjects in II and III could purchase unlimited numbers of marihuana cigarettes containing 2 mg. of THC at 50 cents each. The low THC content of these cigarettes precluded subjects from attaining a "high" anywhere approaching that of the experimental group, while eliminating the control problems encountered in Experiment I as a consequence of the complete absence of marihuana.[8]

The experimental treatments described above were altered near the end of each experiment. These alterations consisted of two parts: (1) short cross-over periods during which treatment conditions were changed for one or both groups—for example, the placebo group in Experiment I was allowed to purchase 15 mg. THC cigarettes for a 13-day period in order to study the acute effects of such large intakes, and (2) a final period ranging from 7 to 10 days, depending upon the experiment, during which all marihuana was removed and subjects were allowed to move freely between wards preparatory to leaving the study. The re-socialization period is omitted from the analysis as the data show uniform drop-offs in output and hours worked independent of treatment conditions or the experiment and seem to have more to tell us about end-of-experiment effects of studies such as this than anything about marihuana. We do not report any formal analysis of the changeovers in experimental conditions, as this would extend the length of this report considerably while adding little to the conclusions reached from the analysis of the main experimental effects. We conclude by noting that subjects had no prior notice of when crossovers would begin or what they would consist of, nor any information about when the final socialization period would begin, although all subjects knew when the experiment would end.

Variables Measured

Records of output, earnings, and consumption were made as a routine part of running the economy.[9] In addition, a record was made each half-hour of the dominant activity of each subject. Raters were instructed to check one activity only, with the activities listed in order of priority; that is, if a subject was engaged in two activities simultaneously, the one higher on the list was checked. The activities, in order of their ranking, were: working, eating, toilet, passive leisure activities, sleeping, conversation, consultations (with staff), table tennis, making music (playing an instrument), game, art work, writing, reading, off ward, and miscellaneous.

Working included all activities associated with the productive task, including having the product checked by an attendant and collecting payment. Working was also checked when a subject was apparently engaged in production but had temporarily stopped, for example, to light a cigarette or blow his nose. Activity checks for working serve as a proxy measure in the analysis for time spent working.[10]

Passive leisure activities consisted of subjects being in or on their beds (or another horizontal surface) and being awake, or passively using one of the entertainment facilities (TV, radio, or record player). This activity was not checked when a subject was working, eating or recreating (playing ping-pong, cards, or some impromptu game, writing, doing art work, or making music) while listening to entertainment facilities. However, this activity would be checked when subjects were talking while using the entertainment facilities, as conversation was checked only when a subject was in interaction with another to the exclusion of other higher priority activities. Measures of passive leisure activities are particularly relevant in our analysis of the postsmoking effects of marihuana.

Table 2.2

Changes in Production, Hours Worked, and Output per Hour[a]

	Experiment I		Experiment II		Experiment III	
	Experimental	Control	Experimental	Control	Experimental	Control
Number of subjects	10	9	9	10	10	10
Number of days of treatment[b]	49	49	53	53	56	56
Milligrams of THC/person/						
day (S_m)	18.67	None	16.74	1.54	16.32	1.52
	(1.47)		(.33)	(.43)	(.09)	(.35)
Daily production						
Belts/person	4.38	5.51	7.49	11.06	5.47	5.32
predrug period (S_m)	(.34)	(.92)	(.99)	(1.54)	(1.22)	(1.22)
Mean change relative to	91%	60%	64%	36%	43%	71%
predrug period						
t-statistic	1.55		.81		-1.38	
(probability $t \neq 0$)[d]	(.14)		(.43)		(.19)	
Daily working time						
Hours/person	8.20	8.85	8.20	9.37	8.17	7.34
predrug period (S_m)	(.47)	(.77)	(.88)	(.69)	(.66)	(.99)
Mean change relative to						
predrug period						
t-statistic	1.17		-.69		-2.43*	
(probability $t \neq 0$)[d]	(.26)		(.50)		(.03)	
Output per hour						
Predrug period[c]	.53	.61	.92	1.13	.61	.65
(S_m)	(.02)	(.07)	(.08)	(.10)	(.09)	(.08)
Mean change relative to	95%	75%	86%	47%	93%	77%
predrug period						
t-statistic	1.36		2.62*		.90	
(probability $t \neq 0$)[d]	(.19)		(.02)		(.38)	

[a]All experiments had a 17-day predrug period.

[b]In both Experiments I and II, one subject left during this period. Data for these subjects have been excluded from the analysis.

[c]Predrug production levels computed over the last 9 days of the predrug period. For the first week of the predrug period, production was close to zero as subjects learned the job task.

[d]Probability levels computed on the basis of a two-tailed alternative to the null hypothesis that change in Experimental less change in Control was equal to zero.

(S_m) = standard error of the mean. Reported in parentheses below mean values.

*Significant at the 5 percent level.

III. EXPERIMENTAL RESULTS

Overall Effects of Marihuana

Since the subjects in the experiment were paid on a piecework basis, the number of belts produced provides the primary measure of economic productivity in the economy. Table 2.2 reports the results of tests for the effects of marihuana on average daily belts produced during the main experimental period relative to production during the predrug period. Production was adjusted relative to predrug production levels (1) to reduce the variance resulting from the substantial intersubject variation in production levels observed during the predrug period, and (2) to correct the group means for differences in predrug production levels. The t-tests were conducted under the assumption that the production ratios were lognormally distributed within each group. Sensitivity tests conducted under the assumption that these ratios were normally distributed, or using the change in the number of belts produced relative to predrug production levels (a gains analysis), yield essentially the same results as those reported.[11]

The data in Table 2.2 support the null hypothesis that there were no significant differences in production between the experimental and control groups in any of the experiments. In fact, in two of the three studies, the experimental group showed greater increases in production than the control group. Further, in Experiments II and III, the absence of any differences in production between the experimental and control groups cannot be attributed to the control groups' smoking sufficiently large numbers of 2 mg. THC cigarettes to equal the experimental groups' intake. As shown in Table 2.2, the average daily THC intake in the control group was about 1.5 mg. per person (less than one cigarette a day), compared to about 16.5 mg. in the experimental group (counting purchased cigarettes as well as mandatory smokes).

An overall assessment of the outcome of the experiments can be conducted using Fisher's Z-statistic for combining t-tests (Winer [26]). This statistic is designed to combine evidence from a series of experiments conducted at different times or places and using independent random samples, as is the case here. Employment of the combined test does nothing to alter our acceptance of the null hypothesis of no difference between groups ($Z = .53$, probability $Z \neq 0 = .59$). Further, examination of the production data for the control groups in all three experiments shows changes in production levels for the placebo group in Experiment I falling between the values reported for the control group in the other two experiments, suggesting that while the use of placebos may have led to control problems in terms of running the experiment, these problems did not have especially adverse effects on production.

The data in Table 2.2 show considerable increases in the level of production, relative to the predrug period, in all the experiments. This growth in production under essentially constant experimental conditions reflects the effect of learning by doing, a phenomenon quite commonplace within the national economy (see Ferguson [10] for a summary of this research). This immediately raises the question of whether there were any systematic differences in learning curves between the experimental and control groups. To test for this, we fit a 2-component error components model to the pooled cross-section and over-time data from each experiment (Madalla [14], Avery and Watts [2]) and tested for interaction effects between time periods and experimental treatments.[12]

Statistically significant interaction effects (at the 5 percent level) were found only in the case of Experiment II. Plotting these data, we found that during the first two weeks of mandatory smoking, output for the experimental group fell below that of the control group, only to catch up and surpass it thereafter. While the initial drop-off and later recovery of production is consistent with notions of subjects' developing tolerance to marihuana, we note that (1) both statistical tests and plots of data reveal no similar effects in the other experiments, and (2) tolerance effects alone do not explain why the production levels of the experimental subjects should consistently surpass those of the controls beginning with the third week of mandatory smoking. Thus, the over-time analysis shows no systematic differences between patterns of learning-by-doing uniquely attributable to the effects of marihuana.[13]

Having found no systematic effects of marihuana on production, we now are interested in determining its effects on the component parts of the production: hours worked and output per hour (efficiency). Table 2.2 shows the results of t-tests for these effects. As with production, the tests are conducted on changes in hours worked and output per hour relative to predrug values, assuming a lognormal distribution of the ratios across individuals.

The data show a statistically significant reduction in hours worked associated with marihuana in Experiment III, an insignificant effect of the same sign in Experiment II, and just the opposite result in Experiment I. Combined evaluation of these results using Fisher's Z-statistic shows no significant effect ($Z = -1.06$, probability $\neq 0 = .28$). The absence of any decrease in hours worked associated with marihuana in Experiment I cannot be attributed to the control problems associated with the use of placebos in that study. When we look at the data on mean changes in hours worked, we find that the control group in I looks more like the control groups in II and III than the experimental group in I looks like experimental groups in II and III, indicating a relatively varied response to marihuana in terms of hours worked under conditions of the experiment.

Table 2.2 also shows that marihuana was associated with increased output per hour or efficiency in the experiments. This effect is statistically significant in Experiment II by itself and in combined evaluations across all three studies ($Z = 2.65$, probability $Z \neq 0 < .01$). It was the improvements in output per hour associated with marihuana that prevented the significant reductions in hours worked in Experiment III from turning into significant reductions in output, and that turned the smaller reductions in hours worked in Experiment II into increases in total output for the experimental group in that study. While diminishing marginal productivity as a result of increased hours worked would, other things equal, result in differences in hours worked and output per hour being opposite in sign, it by no means dictates that they would be self-canceling with respect to their effects on production—as they were.

Pooled cross-section and over-time analysis of the data on hours worked and output per hour shows statistically significant interaction effects between experimental treatments and time periods only in the case of hours worked in Experiment II. Plots of the data from this study show hours worked falling initially for the experimental group, with no corresponding drop-off for the controls, only to have this difference disappear with the passage of time. The pattern of interaction effects here match, and largely explain, the interaction effects reported earlier for Experiment II with respect to number of belts produced.

Postsmoking Effect of Marihuana

Other experimental studies have shown clear dose and time-response effects associated with marihuana. While the effects differ among individuals, the subjective measures of the effects correlate significantly with a number of objective behavioral and psychological variables. The onset of these effects is almost immediate with smoking the more potent forms of marihuana and, depending on dose, they usually last several hours, while milder effects may endure for longer periods [6, 20, 21]. This research suggests that we look at activities in the periods immediately following cannabis consumption, when subjects were sure to be "stoned," to understand more completely the relationship between marihuana and production in the experimental economy.

To characterize the postsmoking effects of marihuana, we examine behavior for the two-and-one-half-hour period immediately following smoking. The THC level of cigarettes smoked may well have been such that major effects lasted longer than this period. However, previous research (Miles et al. [18], Canadian Commission Annex A [6]) indicates that intoxicating effects were at their maximum and were present throughout the two and one-half hours following smoking.

Table 2.3 compares work time and time spent in passive leisure activities for the experimental and control groups between 8:30 and 11 p.m. Comparison are again based on ratios of experimental period values relative to predrug observations.[14] In Experiments II and III, there were statistically significant reductions in hours worked following mandatory smoking in the experimental group as compared to behavior of the control group over the same time period. In both experiments, the differential reduction in work time in the postsmoking period was proportionately greater than the differential reductions in total hours worked reported earlier in Table 2.2. In Experiment II, the postsmoking differential accounted for about 85 percent of the differential in total hours worked, whereas in Experiment III it accounted for about 30 percent of the differential. In other words, the tendency reported in Table 2.2 for marihuana to reduce hours worked in Experiments II and III was disproportionately concentrated in the period immediately following smoking when intoxication effects were at their maximum. Interestingly, we found no postsmoking effects of marihuana on work time in Experiment I. Once again, the behavior of the control group is quite similar across experiments, with the behavior of the experimental group in I being responsible for the different outcome in that study.

A combined evaluation of the postsmoking effects of marihuana on work activities across all three experiments shows a statistically significant drop-off in hours worked in the period immediately following smoking ($Z = -2.56$, probability $Z \neq 0 = .01$). However, as the data from study I indicate (as well as

Table 2.3
Postsmoking Effects of Marihuana on Time Spent Working and on Passive Leisure Activities between 8:30 and 11:00 P.M.[a]

	Experiment I[b]		Experiment II[c]		Experiment III[c]	
	Experimental	Control	Experimental	Control	Experimental	Control
Work time						
Percentage of time/person	46	51	52	35	42	37
predrug period (S_m)	(7)	(6)	(7)	(5)	(4)	(5)
Mean change relative to						
predrug period	-47%	-55%	-72%	-33%	-89%	-57%
t-statistic		.44		-2.67*		-2.48*
(probability $t \neq 0$)[d]		(.67)		(.02)		(.02)
Passive leisure activities						
Percentage of time/person	9	14	15	18	12	14
predrug period (S_m)	(2)	(3)	(3)	(4)	(1)	(2)
Mean change relative to	627%	206%	371%	211%	424%	333%
predrug period						
t-statistic		2.12*		2.68%		1.27
(probability $t \neq 0$)[d]		(.04)		(.02)		(.22)

[a]Number of subjects and number of days in predrug period same as in Table 2.
[b]Number of days = 42, as 7 days of self-regulated consumption following the predrug period have been excluded.
[c]Number of days same as in Table 2.
[d]Probability levels computed on the basis of a two-tailed alternative to the null hypothesis that change in Experimental less change in Control was equal to zero.
(S_m) = standard error of the mean.
*Significant at the 5 percent level.

inspection of individual subject data from studies II and III), this response was not universal across all subjects, but appeared to vary as a function of individual subject and/or situational characteristics.[15] Nevertheless, the average response for the population in question was one of scheduling work activities away from the period when marihuana intoxication was at its maximum.

Consistent with folklore and clinical reports [6], the data on passive leisure activities reported in Table 2.3 show increases in this activity category for experimental subjects in all three studies, being statistically significant in studies I and II. A combined evaluation across studies also proves significant at the 1 percent level ($Z = 6.80$, probability $Z \neq 0 < .01$).

The data in this section provide some of the first direct evidence to corroborate survey research results which indicate that regular cannabis users (1) frequently define the use of marihuana as incompatible with certain aspects of their regular daily behavior, and (2) devote the period immediately following consumption primarily to a passive form of activity ([6] and Ames [1]). A direct analysis of postsmoking effects of marihuana on production and output per hour is not possible, as production data were maintained on a daily rather than an hourly basis, and output per hour is defined as total daily production divided by daily hours worked.

IV. EVALUATION OF EXPERIMENTAL RESULTS

In evaluating the results of the experiments, we must, as the director of the National Institute of Drug Abuse notes, clearly distinguish between using the results to draw implications beyond the conditions of the experiments vs. using the results to answer questions of interest within the experimental setting. To draw implications beyond the conditions of the experiment is to generalize the results. As with any kind of empirical research, the question of generalizability is an empirical issue that must ultimately be answered through further empirical research or by using existing results (Campbell [7]).

We start with the easy task first—using the results to answer questions of interest within the institutional context of the experiments. Quite clearly, the results reported here disprove any contention that the heavy use of marihuana is *inherently* incompatible with maintaining productivity levels [21] and the capacity to carry out vocational responsibilities [6]. In an institutional setting with a relatively high piecework wage rate, unlimited access to the factors of production, and a completely flexible work schedule, we found that large scheduled doses of marihuana had no adverse effects on production. This was so, even though the job task involved fairly demanding manual labor and subjects worked an average of well over 40 hours a week. While there was some tendency for marihuana to be associated with less time spent working, particularly in the periods immediately following smoking, these effects were sufficiently well contained, and offset by increased productivity during other times, that they did not significantly affect production; that is, subjects altered their labor-leisure mix on the job to compensate for the effects of increased off-the-job leisure resulting from mandatory smoking. Further, with unlimited availability of high quality and inexpensive "legalized" marihuana in Experiment I, there was negligible smoking in addition to required amounts, with subjects in all of the experiments complaining at times that required smoking levels were "too great." Thus the results also disprove any contentions that legalization will *necessarily* result in unusually high levels of marihuana use.

The question of generalizability concerns the implications of the experimental results for the potential effects of marihuana under working conditions faced by labor force participants in the United States and Canada. Direct extrapolation of the results of the present studies to argue that heavy, regular marihuana use *does not*, in general, interfere with labor productivity and ability to work would be *unwarranted* on a number of grounds. These would include obvious problems of sample representativeness relative to the general population and important differences between the experimental and national economies; for example, perhaps marihuana had less negative effects on output and productivity in the microeconomy than in a national economy because of boredom from the restricted environment that marihuana helped relieve. Finally, the results tell us nothing about the very long-term effects of marihuana use, as the experiments covered a three-month period with even less time than that under mandatory-smoking conditions. Nevertheless, the results of the present studies and others reported in the literature suggest certain regularities in the relationship between marihuana and work performance that have important implications for behavior in national economies. These are discussed below.

Central to understanding the behavioral relationship between marihuana and work performance is the fact, documented here and elsewhere, that cannabis is a drug whose major effects occur almost immediately after smoking and last for several hours, but can only be maintained beyond that period with renewed consumption. Presumably the people who smoke marihuana do so because these after-effects are in some sense beneficial. Further, the reason they don't smoke marihuana all the time, such as in the experiments reported here, is that there are some costs associated with use. Included in these costs are the purchase price of the marihuana itself. However, equally as important are costs in the form of diminished work productivity in the period following smoking. The fact that subjects in the present experiment tended to schedule work away from periods immediately following smoking, in conjunction with comments recorded in the nurses' log notes, suggest this hypothesis. Other studies, aimed at directly investigating this proposition uniformly support it. These studies range from investigation of agricultural productivity in Jamaica (Rubin and Comitas [22]), to studies of psychomotor tracking performance and visual signal detection acuity [6, Annex A], to investigations of the problem-solving abilities of laboratory animals (Tehr et al. [24]).[16] Further, the decrement in productivity or performance levels is a direct function of the quantity of marihuana consumed and the degree of complexity of the job task [6, pp. 52–66]. This suggests that the behavior one can expect to observe with respect to marihuana use and work will be quite varied, depending upon differences in relative costs and benefits of use in different situations. For example, Biernachi and Davis, in a survey report on moderate to regular marihuana users (special-occasion users to those who smoke several times a week) in North America, noted:

> The most distinguishing characteristic of this mode is that use is regulated or scheduled so that the perceived effects or aftereffects of the drug do not interfere with other activities in which the user is engaged. That is, the [moderate-regular] user finds the use of marihuana pleasurable, but also defines it as incompatible with other investments and commitments emanating from his total life situation. . . . [Consequently] his use of the drug is typically restricted to leisure settings and hours. (Quoted in [6], p. 195.)

In marked contrast, Rubin and Comitas [22] found that lower income farmers in Jamaica commonly used ganja (marihuana) while working, citing its use as an important motivating factor enabling them to start and carry through the most difficult and distasteful tasks.[17] Although independent tests showed that smoking reduced efficiency in terms of objective measures of energy expenditure and time required to perform common agricultural tasks, Rubin and Comitas do not associate its use with an amotivational syndrome. Rather, they suggest that the marginal value of time for these workers was low, independent of marihuana, reducing the cost of use considerably, particularly when compared to costs to North American workers:

> In a village where the ethical code includes hard work and long hours in the field, such farmers (those for which there is insufficient agricultural land to maintain full employment) face a dilemma. They can leave the area and search for work elsewhere, and some do. They can complete their own cultivation quickly and obtain other work in their spare time; some also do this, but such work is generally difficult to obtain. Or, they can work longer hours in the field and expend more kilo-calories than would be necessary to exploit the available land. In this way, they maintain a subjective impression of enhanced physical efforts and capacity for work. The heavy use of ganja during agricultural pursuits may be related to this alternative. (Rubin and Comitas [22], p. 79)

Finally, the results of an experiment by Mendelson and Meyer [16] would seem to rule out cultural and/or genetic differences between Jamaicans and North Americans as the basis for the differences in smoking patterns reported above. In their experiment, Mendelson and Mayer found subjects, under conditions of self-regulated use, smoking marihuana at levels previously thought atypical for North American culture, well above any of the self-administered or mandatory use levels found in the experiments reported here. Mendelson and Meyer provide no explanations for these high use levels. In terms of the present framework, however, this heavy use would be explained by the fact that the primary job task (accumulating points on a 4-digit hand counter) was one whose productivity had been shown to be unaffected by marihuana use even under maximal intoxication, while a ceiling was placed on maximum daily earnings, both factors reducing considerably the opportunity costs of smoking. Even more telling, Mendelson and Meyer note a marked tendency for subjects to schedule cannabis consumption away from those time periods during which experimental activities requiring cognitive and motor skills were scheduled and for which subjects were paid contingent on performance levels—a behavior for which they provide no explanation, but one which is readily accounted for in the present framework and which is consistent with the behavior pattern reported by Biernachi and Davis above.

The present analysis implies that part of the reason we found no difference between experimental and control groups in the studies reported here was that subjects effectively limited marihuana use to required smoking. This limitation was, in turn, related to the relatively high effective hourly wage rate (over $2.50/hour in 1972 Canadian dollars) and the fact that for most subjects earning money was a major factor motivating their volunteering for the experiments. An incident occurring in the pilot study conducted prior to the experiments reported here (Miles et al. [18]) supports this interpretation. Midway through this study, subjects were "on strike" for a week during which time they threatened to leave the experiment if wages were not raised. We can interpret the strike week as a period in which a prior decision had been made to reduce labor supply sharply as a bargaining tactic, or one in which the expected wage rate was sharply reduced as a consequence of the strong possibility that subjects would leave the economy and forfeit three-quarters of all accumulated savings. Irrespective of the preferred interpretation, the effect of the "strike" was to sharply reduce the costs of any decreases in labor productivity associated with smoking. As a consequence, smoking increased by about one-third on average and increased uniformly across all subjects. Further, with the successful completion of the strike, subjects returned to normal work patterns and the amount of cannabis consumed decreased for all subjects.

This analysis suggests that formal modeling of the effects of marihuana on work behavior be done within the context of a full cost pricing model (e.g., Becker [4]) accounting for the fact that while the direct time cost of smoking is small, its use serves as an input into both household and income earning production functions. Unfortunately, the development and testing of such a model lies beyond the scope of the present paper. Nevertheless, the formulation presented here focuses attention on the fact that, under conditions of self-regulated consumption, when and how much cannabis is consumed, and consequently its relationship to economic activities, is an endogenously determined variable. Thus, its effects cannot be understood independently of economic parameters in the environment—in particular, wage rates, the nature of the job task, and the relative valuation placed on goods with high market prices.

NOTES

1. The development and successful operation of a planned economic environment explicitly designed for the analysis of socioeconomic behavior, with the degree of economic complexity and thoroughness of data collection reported here, represents a significant methodological innovation in the experimental analysis of economic behavior. It is the closest thing to Morgenstern's [19] suggestion that large isolated communities be built explicitly for conducting economic studies. For a discussion of some of the practical problems involved in running a microeconomy with continuous recording of subject data, see Congreve and Miles [9].

2. The only conclusive way to determine whether deleterious effects are associated with long-term marihuana use for a completely representative sample of smokers would be a large-scale prospective study similar to those that identified the determinants of heart disease and the hazard of tobacco. Such a study would cost over $2 million, and would be two years in planning, and it would be at least four more years before any results would be obtained [15].

3. Experiment I ran from May to August outside university terms. Subjects listing occupations as students in other studies would have to have dropped out of school temporarily.

4. In no case did subjects report heavier use of marihuana following the experiment than before it.

5. We terminated our analysis of Experiment III at the time the first subject started seriously discussing the possibility of leaving the study, as the nurses' log notes and the production data suggest that her quitting had an adverse effect on the morale (output) of others in her group. Since this subject was in the control group, failure to terminate the analysis at this point would tend to bias the results toward showing an absence of treatment effect.

6. Details of experimental treatments and procedures may be found in [6], Annex B, and Miles et al. [17].

7. A complete drug assay of the cannabis material used is contained in Miles et al. [17]. Although smoking was to some extent self-paced, the subjects were urged to smoke as quickly as they could, to inhale and hold the smoke, and not to leave long ends. This was true for both mandatory and self-regulated consumption. Under these circumstances, during the mandatory smoking period, the delivered dose, probably about 50 percent of the THC in the cigarettes, would constitute a relatively large dose (see [6], pp. 39–41, and Truitt [25]).

8. These complaints also took the form of attempts to smuggle marihuana onto the ward, which were partially successful. The amount of marihuana smoked surreptitiously is considered to be too minor to affect the results.

9. A description of these measurement procedures and the results of independent checks for data accuracy are reported in Miles [17] and Kagel et al. [13].

10. Nurses' log notes indicate that it was uncommon for subjects to switch activities in efforts to bias these ratings.

11. The log normal assumption is preferred as it enables us to consider simultaneously the effects of marihuana on hours worked and output per hour using a simple t-test rather than Feiler's theorem (Finney [11], Ch. 2, especially pp. 41–43).

12. In this analysis, time periods were defined as consecutive 7-day periods starting at the end of the predrug period. Where a 7-day period would lead to overlapping experimental conditions, a 6- or 8-day period was used, and in Experiment II, the last time period was 4 days. All between-group comparisons have the same number of days in corresponding time periods. Complete specification of the model used in the analysis may be found in an earlier version of this paper available from the authors.

13. The absence of statistically significant interaction effects in Experiment I is of special interest as treatments varied from self-regulated to mandatory consumption, and between different levels of mandatory consumption. The absence of interaction effects under these circumstances ($F = 1.48$, degrees of freedom $= 6, 132$, probability $F \neq 1 = .19$) indicates an insensitivity of the results reported to these differences in treatment conditions.

14. Here we assumed the ratios to be normally distributed since they occasionally take on zero values for a given week. An analysis based on differences from predrug values (a gains analysis) shows essentially the same results as reported in the text.

15. There were statistically significant subject-by-treatment interaction effects at the 1 percent level with respect to postsmoking work activity in Experiment II using a pooled cross-section and over-time analysis. Plots of the data show that during the last two time periods differences between experimental and control subjects were virtually nonexistent in this study. Further, under self-regulated smoking conditions in Experiment I, subjects worked proportionately less time during the periods following marihuana consumption as compared to the rest of the day, with these differences being statistically significant at the

1 percent level using a paired t-test. This is what we mean by situational variability, although the basis for this behavior is unknown at present.

16. We should add that for rats, at least, later exposure to the same problem-solving tasks showed no difference between experimental and controls, indicating no residual learning deficits were associated with marihuana use (Tehr et al. [24]).

17. Smoking ganja while working is so widespread in Jamaica that it is not uncommon for an employer of a group of field hands to offer a ganja break, much as coffee breaks are offered in North America (Rubin and Comitas [22]).

REFERENCES

1. F. Ames. "A clinical and metabolic study of acute intoxication with cannabis sativa and its role in the model psychoses." *Journal of Mental Science* 104 (1958): 972–99.

2. Robert Avery and Harold W. Watts. "The application of an error components model to experimental panel data." In *The New Jersey Income-Maintenance Experiment*, Vol. II, ed. Harold W. Watts and Albert Rees. New York: Academic Press, 1977.

3. Raymond C. Battalio, John H. Kagel, and Morgan Reynolds. "Income distributions in two experimental economies." *Journal of Political Economy* 85 (December 1977): 1259–77.

4. Gary S. Becker. "A theory of the allocation of time." *Economic Journal* 75 (September 1965): 493–517.

5. C. A. Boneau and H. S. Pennypacker. "Group matching as research strategy: How not to get significant results." *Psychological Reports* 8 (1961): 143–47.

6. Canadian Commission of Inquiry into the Non-Medical Use of Drugs (Le Dain). *Cannabis: A Report of the Commission of Inquiry into the Non-Medical Use of Drugs.* Ottawa: 1972.

7. D. T. Campbell. "Prospective artifact and control." In *Artifact in Behavioral Research*, ed. R. Rosenthal. New York: Academic Press, 1969.

8. D. T. Campbell and J. C. Stanley. *Experimental and Quasi-Experimental Designs for Research.* Chicago: Rand-McNally, 1966.

9. G. Congreve and C. G. Miles. "Practical problems in running an experimental micro-economy." In *Experimentation in Controlled Environments*, ed. C. G. Miles. Toronto: Addiction Research Foundation, 1975.

10. C. E. Ferguson. *The Neoclassical Theory of Production and Distribution.* Cambridge, England: Cambridge University Press, 1969.

11. D. J. Finney. *Statistical Method in Biological Assay.* New York: Hafner Publishing Co., 1952.

12. R. W. Goldsmith. *A Study of Savings in the United States*, Vol. 1. Princeton, N.J.: Princeton University Press, 1955.

13. John H. Kagel, Raymond C. Battalio, R. C. Winkler et al. "Income, consumption and saving in controlled environments: Further economic analysis." In *Experimentation in Controlled Environments*, ed. C. G. Miles. Toronto: Addiction Research Foundation, 1975.

14. G. S. Maddala. *Econometrics.* New York: McGraw-Hill Book Co., 1977.

15. "Marihuana: A conversation with NIDA's Robert L. DuPont." *Science* 192 (May 1976): 647–49.

16. J. H. Mendelson and R. E. Meyer. "Behavioral and biological concomitants of chronic marihuana smoking by heavy and casual users." In Marihuana: A Signal of Mis-

understanding. *Technical Papers of the First Annual Report of the National Commission on Marihuana and Drug Abuse*, Vol. I. Washington: U.S. Government Printing Office, 1972.

17. C. G. Miles, G.R.S. Congreve, R. J. Gibbons, J. Marshman, R. Devenyi, and R. C. Hicks. "An experimental study of the effects of daily cannabis smoking on behavior patterns." *Acta Pharmacologica et Toxocologica* 34 (Supp. 1, 1974): 1–44.

18. C. G. Miles, Raymond Battallo, John H. Kagel, and G. F. Rhodes. "The effects of cannabis and negotiated wage rate changes on income and job performance in an experimental token economy." In *Experimentation in Controlled Environments*, ed. C. G. Miles. Toronto: Addiction Research Foundation, 1975.

19. Oskar Morgenstern. "Experiment and large scale computation in economies." In *Economic Activity Analysis*, ed. O. Morgenstern, New York: Wiley, 1954.

20. National Commission on Marihuana and Drug Abuse. *Marihuana: A Signal of Misunderstanding*, Appendix Vol. 1 and Vol. 2. Washington: U.S. Government Printing Office, 1972.

21. National Commission on Marijuana and Drug Abuse. *Drug Use in America: Problem in Perspective*. Washington: U.S. Government Printing Office, 1973.

22. Vera Rubin and Lambros Comitas. *Ganja in Jamaica*, London: Mouton & Co., 1975.

23. Vernon L. Smith. "Experimental economics: Induced value theory." *American Economic Review* 66 (May 1976): 274–79.

24. K. A. Tehr, H. Kalant, and A. E. LeBlanche. "Residual learning deficit after heavy exposure to cannabis and alcohol in rats." *Science* 192 (June 1976): 1239–51.

25. E. B. Truitt. "Biological disposition of tetrahydrocannabinols." *Pharmacological Review* 23 (1971): 273–78.

26. B. J. Winer. *Statistical Principles in Experimental Design*, 2nd. ed. New York: McGraw-Hill Book Co., 1971.

Chapter 3

Survey Research

Though the studies in the next section deal with a variety of topics, they share a common methodology. In these studies, people were asked, through the use of surveys, about their past marijuana use and the information they provided was used to assess the relationship between frequency of use (also called chronic use, recreational use, and long-term use) of marijuana and other variables related to job performance. The discussion of this research uses the same categories used for discussing controlled experiments.

ATTENTION, LEARNING, AND MEMORY

Partly because of the relative ease of using this research method as opposed to controlled experiments, a number of studies have assessed the relationship between self-reported marijuana use and performance at attention, learning, and memory tasks similar to those used in the controlled experiments previously discussed. In many studies, subjects provided information on past use at the same time they completed the performance tasks. While some have shown no significant differences attributable to long-term marijuana use (Bowman & Pihl, 1973; Culver & King, 1974; Mendelson et al., 1976; Satz et al., 1976; Weckowicz et al., 1977), the majority have shown significant negative relationships between history of use and performance on a variety of tasks (Agarwal, Sethi, & Gupta, 1975; Block & Ghoneim, 1993; Block, Farnham, & Braverman, 1990; Block, Farnham, Braverman, & Noyes, 1990; Carlin & Trepan, 1977; Entin & Goldzung, 1973; Gianutsos & Litwack, 1976; Millsaps, Azrin, & Mittenberg, 1994; Page, Fletcher, & True, 1988; Pope & Yurgelun-Todd, 1996; Rubin & Comitas, 1975; Schwartz, 1991; Schwartz, Gruenwald, Klitzner, & Fedio, 1989; Sethi,

Trivedi, & Singh, 1981; Varma, Malhotra, Dang, Das, & Nehra, 1988; Wig & Varma, 1977).

PSYCHOMOTOR PERFORMANCE

For the dependent variable of psychomotor performance, the results may be a bit different. The number of studies showing no differences (Bowman & Pihl, 1973; Culver & King; 1974; Grant et al., 1973; Mendelson et al., 1976b; Reed, 1974; Rochford et al., 1977; Satz et al., 1976; Weckowicz et al., 1977) is approximately the same as those showing negative relationships between marijuana use and performance (Block & Ghoneim, 1993; Block et al., 1990; Carlin & Trupin, 1977; Gianutsos & Litwack, 1976; Mendhiratta, Varma, Dang, Malhotra, Das, & Nehra, 1988; Page et al., 1988; Rubin & Comitas, 1975; Varma et al., 1988; Wig & Varma, 1977). These studies suggest that marijuana use may have a stronger relationship to attention, learning, and memory tasks than to psychomotor tasks.

Nonetheless, the foregoing studies demonstrate that those who report having used more marijuana in their lives perform less well at some tests of attention, learning, and memory. They may also perform worse at tests of psychomotor performance, though the relationship may be less clear-cut. A future meta-analysis of the existing studies would probably show that the average effect size across studies is small but statistically significant for attention, learning, and memory tasks and close to statistical significance for psychomotor tasks.

MOTIVATION

Several studies deal with the relationship between marijuana use and measures of achievement or achievement motivation (Brill & Christie, 1974; Kupfer, 1973; Mellinger, 1978; Mellinger, Somers, Davidson, & Manheimer, 1976; Miranne, 1979). Though Kupfer (1973) found that marijuana users had indications of lower motivation, including lower grades, the remainder of the studies cited above show no overall differences in indicators of motivation and Mellinger (1978) found that marijuana users had *higher* grades while Miranne (1979, 197) found that marijuana had no significant relationship to any of six measures of achievement or achievement orientation (including materialistic achievement orientation, educational aspirations, occupational aspirations, and grade point average) when other relevant variables were controlled.

JOB PERFORMANCE

One set of studies deals directly with the relationship between marijuana use and two measures of job performance, wages and labor force participation. These studies make use of the National Longitudinal Survey of Youth, a survey begun in 1979 with 12,500 respondents who were then between the ages of fourteen and twenty-one. The research on the relationship between marijuana and wages is based on the 1984 and 1988 waves of data from these subjects. Kaestner (1994a, b) provides a summary of prior studies of this database and gives the results of his own cross-sectional and longitudinal analyses of the 1984 and 1988 waves. In Kaestner (1994a) he examines the relationship between reported marijuana use and wages, which are one measure of performance. Categories of reported use were: lifetime use, use within the past thirty days, and a dichotomous variable indicating heavy use. His results show that in 1984, men (aged nineteen to twenty-six at that time) who had higher levels of lifetime marijuana use and higher levels of use within the last thirty days had significantly *higher* wages. These relationships were positive but not significant in 1988. In 1988, men (aged twenty-three to thirty at that time) who were classified as heavy users had higher wages than those who were not. For women, lifetime use was significantly related to wages in 1988. All relationships between measures of marijuana use and wages for men and women were positive in both 1984 and 1988, but none were statistically significant except those mentioned above (Kaestner, 1994a: 462).

Comparison of the 1984 and 1988 data reveals a negative, but not significant, relationship between marijuana use and wage *increases* for both men and women. The most conservative interpretation of these data seems to be that increases or decreases in marijuana use had no relationship to increases or decreases in wages between 1984 and 1988 (Kaestner, 1994a: 464).

Kaestner (1994b), using the same data set, examined the relationship between marijuana use and number of hours worked. Cross-sectional analyses for male respondents indicated significant negative relationships between lifetime use and current use of marijuana and hours worked in 1984 and in 1988. There was also a significant negative relationship between lifetime use of marijuana and hours worked in 1984 and in 1988. There was also a significant negative relationship between lifetime use of marijuana and hours worked in 1988 but not between current use and hours worked (Kaestner, 1994b: 148). For female respondents, the story is a bit different. Cross-sectional analyses showed that current use was not significantly related to hours worked in 1984 or 1988 and that no measures of lifetime use were related to hours worked in 1984, though lifetime use was negatively related to hours worked in 1988 (Kaestner, 1994b: 149). The longitudinal analysis using 1984 and 1988 data, however, was unable to detect any significant effects on changes in hours worked for either men or women, leading Kaestner to conclude there is no significant overall effect of marijuana use on labor force participation (Kaestner, 1994b: 141 & 145).

There are two points of interest in the results of Kaestner's studies. First, the variability of the parameter estimates was large in general, leading Kaestner to argue that "marijuana use is a highly idiosyncratic experience that has different effects on different people" (1994b: 145). Second, there is some suggestion from the results that marijuana may have a different relationship to job performance for women than men.

In summary, these results provide no support for the claim that the use of marijuana makes people less productive at their jobs. Further, the results of the cross sectional analyses may be contradictory. How is it possible that the use of marijuana could simultaneously cause a reduction in hours worked and an increase in wages? Unless marijuana actually *improves* people's efficiency at the job, it would appear that the relationship between marijuana use and job performance, if any, is the result of a third-variable cause.

METHODOLOGICAL ISSUES

There are at least two great strengths of this type of survey research. First, it enables researchers to collect data from large numbers of individuals; more than could be accommodated in controlled experiments because of limitations in time and resources. Second, it allows researchers to assess the effects of lifetime use, a variable that could not be manipulated in controlled experiments because it would be ethically wrong to conduct such experiments on human beings.

One important weakness of this type of research, however, has to do with the measurement of drug use. People do not always accurately report their drug use. More importantly, there is evidence that the inaccuracies in their reports are not simply random but are biased in systematic ways that might affect the observed relationships between marijuana and performance. Self-reports of drug use tend to understate use, and that degree of understatement is a function of the perceived desirability of drug use, among other factors (Harrison, 1995). Further, Schwenk (1985) has shown that cognitive processes may affect recollections of past behavior to make it more consistent with social norms. Thus, apparent relationships between lifetime drug use and performance may be partially due to biases in reporting of use.

There are at least three additional problems that must be taken into account in interpreting these results. First, few of the studies contained adequate controls for other drug use. Subjects who use marijuana may use other drugs and the effects of these other drugs may account for any apparent relationship between marijuana use and performance. Second, few studies adequately matched users with non-users on relevant variables that might affect their performance. If, for example, marijuana users were less intelligent than non-users, they should be matched with non-users on this variable. This problem is less common in the studies conducted since the mid 1980s. Third, survey research does not penetrate very deeply below the surface. The scope of information sought is usually emphasized at the expense of depth. Thus, survey research, as compared to ethnographic field research, is usually extensive rather than intensive (Kerlinger, 1973: 422).

Because of these weaknesses, these studies do *not* show that lifetime marijuana use makes people inattentive, slow, forgetful, clumsy, or unmotivated. They do, however, provide information that is a useful complement to the results of the controlled experiments.

COMMENTS ON THE KAESTNER ARTICLES

We have included two articles using survey research methodology in this book. They are both based on an excellent database, the National Longitudinal Survey of Youth. The survey includes questions on the use of specific drugs and the papers we have included deal with both marijuana and cocaine, though our comments will focus only on marijuana.

The first paper deals with the relationship between self-reported marijuana use and wages. Table 3.2 in the paper reveals that the correlations between all measures of marijuana use and wages are positive in both 1984 and 1988 for both men and women, and, in a few cases, these correlations are significant. This struck us as odd. Even more odd is the fact that the relationships between nearly all measures of cocaine use and wages are positive for both men and women. Few would seriously suggest that these positive relationships prove that marijuana and cocaine use makes people better workers. Yet people sometimes seriously suggest that *negative* correlations between marijuana use and other measures of psychological and physical well-being prove that marijuana leads to physical and psychological damage. The tendency to overinterpret such correlations can be counteracted by reminding ourselves that correlation does not imply causality.

Nonetheless, researchers sometimes seem more interested in addressing the negative relationships between marijuana use and performance than the positive ones. It is as important to understand why marijuana is positively associated with performance as it is to understand why it is negatively related to performance in particular contexts, and we invite the reader to speculate on possible reasons for the positive relationships. Table 3.3 deals with the relationship between marijuana use and changes in wages. None of the relationships are significant.

The second study examines the relationship between marijuana use and hours worked. Table 3.3 of this paper shows some positive and some negative relationships between these two variables but, overall, no consistent significant relationship.

It is interesting to consider the results of these studies in connection with the studies of pre-employment drug testing included in the next chapter. The Kaestner studies show no consistent negative relationships between marijuana use employment outcomes like wages and hours worked, but the pre-employment drug testing studies seem to suggest that those who test positive for marijuana may be more prone to accidents, involuntary turnover, and other negative job outcomes. In the concluding chapter of this book, we offer a possible explanation for this discrepancy, but readers are invited to develop their own speculations prior to reading ours.

The Effects of Illicit Drug Use on the Labor Supply of Young Adults

Robert Kaestner

ABSTRACT

This paper analyzes the effects of illicit drug use on the labor supply of a sample of young adults using data from the National Longitudinal Survey of Youth. The paper investigates whether the frequency and timing of marijuana and cocaine use are systematically related to labor supply, and presents both cross-sectional and panel data estimates. The cross sectional results are consistent with those of previous researchers, and suggest that illicit drug use has large, negative effects on labor supply. The longitudinal results, however, suggest that illicit drug use does not have a significant adverse impact on labor supply.

I. INTRODUCTION

There is widespread concern over the negative effects of illicit drug use on the workforce. Hundreds of companies in the United States have developed extensive alcohol and drug abuse programs alternatively aimed at prevention, detection and treatment of employees who use illicit drugs, and as detailed in Hayghe (1991) the numbers continue to grow. The federal government has also been quite active in its effort to control illicit drug use, particularly in the workplace. The Drug Free Workplace Act of 1988 requires federal government contractors to maintain drug free workplaces, and executive order 12,564 requires all federal agencies to establish drug free workplace policies. There is a general concern in

This article originally appeared in the *Journal of Human Resources*, Volume 24, pp. 126–155, 1994. The appendix accompanying the original article has been omitted due to space limitations. See the original publication for descriptive statistics included in its appendix.

the country that the ability of our workers is being seriously impaired by illicit drug use.

One of the most frequently cited consequences of illicit drug use is the consistency of labor force participation, including chronic absenteeism, although there have been relatively few systematic studies of the labor market effects of illicit drug use.[1] Johnson and Herring (1989) find that illicit drug use among young adults leads to delayed entry into the labor market. Kandel and Davies (1990) using data from the National Longitudinal Survey of Youth (NLSY), and Kandel and Yamaguchi (1987) using regional data, find that illicit drug use is positively correlated with weeks unemployed and increased job mobility (for example, quits) among young adults. Using a somewhat older and more limited sample, Alite et al. (1988) find no effect of illicit drug use on labor force participation. In one of the first studies found in the economics literature, Kagel et al. (1980) using a novel experimental design, report no significant effects of marijuana use on hours of work of young adults. More recently, Zarkin et al. (1992) find a slight negative impact of illicit drug use on weeks worked per year and skipped work days. The Zarkin et al. study uses a sample of individuals 18 and older drawn from the 1990 National Household Survey of Drug Use (NIDA 1991). Gill and Michaels (1992) and Register and Williams (1992) both use the NLSY data set and find significant effects of illicit drug use on labor force participation. Gill and Michaels (1992) report that a broad measure of past drug use is negatively correlated with the probability of being currently employed, but that a variable measuring use of hard drugs has no impact on the employment probability. The mixed nature of the Gill and Michaels (1992) findings also characterize the findings of Register and Williams (1992), who report that past marijuana use has a negative impact on the probability of being employed, but that a cocaine use has no effect. Most of these studies present some evidence suggesting that among young adults, drug users work less hours than nonusers over the course of the year. In addition, Gleason et al. (1991) report that 7 percent of respondents in the NLSY reported drug use on the job as of 1984. Thus, it is possible that drug users will be devoting less actual time to work, even if they are technically working the same amount of hours as comparable nonusers.

If illicit drug use is in fact responsible for a reduction in the labor supply of individuals, the economic implications of such an occurrence are significant. The reduced labor market experience of drug users will result in a decrease in the amount of worker on-the-job training, and other human capital investments associated with the employment relationship. The lower levels of human capital accumulation will decrease the productivity of the U.S. workforce, increase production costs, and lead to diminished living standards. These negative consequences of illicit drug use are what underlie the government's "war on drugs," and the explosion in private employer concern over illicit drug use.

This paper analyzes the effects of illicit drug use on the labor supply of a sample of young adults using data from the National Longitudinal Survey of Youth (NLSY). In particular, the paper investigates whether the frequency and timing of marijuana and cocaine use are systematically related to the quantity of labor supplied. As was noted above, there have been very few systematic studies of the effects of illicit drug use in the labor market, and even fewer based on economic theory. Thus, this paper makes a contribution in two ways. First, it outlines the relevant economic theory, and applies it to the problem of illicit drug use and labor supply. Second, it uses micro-data to obtain both cross-sectional and panel data estimates of the effects of illicit drug use on labor supply, and addresses several previously ignored empirical problems. The cross-sectional results of this paper are consistent with the findings found in most of the previous research, and suggest that illicit drug use has large negative effects on labor supply. The longitudinal results, however, suggest that illicit drug use does not appear to have a significant adverse impact on the hours of work supplied to the market. In particular, it is found that the effect of illicit drug use on labor supply is quite variable, and that there does not appear to be a common experience with regard to the relationship between illicit drugs and labor supply.

The balance of the paper will be divided into the following parts. The next section presents a simple theoretical model of drug use and labor supply. This section sets forth a framework of analysis, and specifies the ways in which drug use can be incorporated into the more general theory of consumer behavior. Section III describes the empirical model used to estimate the effects of illicit drug use on labor supply. This section is followed by a description of the data, including sample design and important variable definitions. A presentation of the results will follow the data section, and the paper will end with a summary of the main findings.

II. ANALYTICAL MODEL OF DRUG USE AND LABOR SUPPLY

The most straightforward way in which to incorporate illicit drug use into a labor supply model is to treat illicit drugs as a consumption good. Following Becker and Murphy (1988), an age specific utility function of the following general form can be specified;

$$(1) \quad U_t = u\,(L_t\,,\,D_t\,,\,S_t\,,\,X_t\,)$$

where L is the amount of leisure, D is the quantity of illicit drugs, S is the stock of drug consumption capital, X is a composite good representing other consumption, and $t = I$ to T indexes age. The inclusion of the stock of drug consumption capital in the utility function is a distinguishing feature of the current problem. Presently, it is assumed that drugs are potentially an addictive good as defined in Becker and Murphy (1988). Given the above preferences, a cost function can be defined that indicates the minimum cost of obtaining a certain level of utility. The cost function can be written as,

Appendix A

$$(2) \quad C_t = c\,(W_t\,,\,V_t\,,\,P_{xt}\,,:\,U_t = u\,(L_t\,,\,D_t\,,\,S_t\,,\,X_t\,)\,)$$

In Equation (2), W is the wage, V is the price of current drug consumption, which consists of two parts, the market price of illicit drugs and the user cost associated with the drug consumption capital, and P, is the price of other consumption.[2] The compensated demand functions for leisure (L), and illicit drugs (D), can be obtained by differentiating Equation (2) with respect to wages and the price of drugs. These demand functions will in general depend on all prices and the level of utility. For example, the demand for leisure can be represented as follows;

$$(3) \quad L_t = f\,(W_t\,,\,V_t\,,\,P_t\,,\,U_t\,)$$

From an empirical point of view, Equation (3) is limited, due to the fact that V, the price of current drug consumption, including the user cost associated with the drug consumption capital, is never observed, nor is the level of utility. A partial solution to this problem is to use the conditional cost function to represent preferences, as developed by Pollak (1969), Browning (1983), Browning and Meghir (1991). In the conditional cost framework, illicit drugs are treated as a conditioning variable that affect preferences, but are not of primary interest (Browning and Meghir 1991). The consumer minimizes the cost of achieving a certain level of utility, given that the quantity of some goods (for example, illicit drugs) are predetermined.[3] Thus, Equation (2) can be rewritten as follows;

$$(4) \quad C_t = c\,(W_t\,,\,D_t\,,\,P_t\,,:\,U_t = u\,(L_t\,,\,D_t\,,\,S_t\,,\,X_t\,)\,)$$

where the quantity of the conditional variable is substituted for its respective price. The model can be put into an intertemporal framework by assuming that the lifecycle conditional cost function is additive, which implies that preferences are implicitly separable.[4] This specification is completely consistent with the idea that illicit drugs are an addictive good, since each age specific conditional cost function includes the current quantity of illicit drugs which is determined by past and future consumption. The age specific, compensated conditional demand functions can be derived from the lifecycle counterpart to Equation (4), and for leisure this derivation results in the following;

$$(5) \quad L_t = g\,(W_t\,,\,D_t\,,\,P_{xt}\,,\,U_t\,)$$

where demand for leisure will be a function of prices, quantities of the conditioning variables, and the unobserved level of utility (Browning 1983). The model assumes perfect foresight and complete certainty, which implies that the consumer knows all future prices, and takes account of the effect of current drug use on future utility and wages. The model outlined above can be easily extended to the family. The utility function would then include all family members' (for example, husband and wife) leisure and the quantity of drugs would refer to total household consumption of drugs.[5]

As noted by Browning and Meghir (1991), the use of conditional cost functions, and the resulting conditional demands, has several advantages. First, the conditional approach eliminates the need to specify the underlying model of the conditioning goods, which in this case is the current consumption of illicit drugs.[6] Second, the conditional approach is empirically valid even when individuals are at a corner solution, which is a common occurrence with regard to drug use. Third, the conditional approach eliminates the need to use measures of the "full" price of illicit drugs, which are not observable. Finally, since the primary purpose of this paper is to identify the effect of illicit drug use on labor supply, the conditional approach facilitates the direct estimation of such an effect, as opposed to simply the sign and magnitude of the cross price effect.

III. EFFECT OF ILLICIT DRUG USE ON LABOR SUPPLY

In terms of the conditional demand approach outlined above, an increase in illicit drug use will result in an increase or decrease in leisure, depending on whether leisure and drugs are not complements or substitutes. Since it is a model of compensated demand, there is no income effect. It seems reasonable to expect drug use and leisure to be complements, thus, the expectation is that drug use will decrease labor supply, and increase leisure. This expectation is based on the assumption that the household production of the commodity that uses illicit drugs as an input is a relatively time intensive activity; given the physiological effects of most illicit drugs, individuals probably do not substitute greater quantities of drugs for time in the production of some good, say "euphoria" as in Stigler and Becker (1977). Thus, persons who consume drugs would be expected to have a preference for a more time intensive consumption bundle than comparable nonusers.

On the other hand, if drug use is a goods intensive activity, we would expect increased drug use to be positively related to labor supply. The production of "euphoria" might necessitate a much greater market input component (in other words, drugs) than time (leisure) input. In addition, Becker and Murphy (1988) suggest that drug users will have a higher rate of time preference than nonusers, and thus would prefer current consumption, including leisure, to future consumption.

IV. EMPIRICAL MODEL OF DRUG USE AND LABOR SUPPLY

The specific functional form of Equation (5) used in this paper is a modified version of that found in Browning, Deaton, and Irish (1985). In their paper, the authors (BDI) derive a theoretically consistent empirical demand function that is linear in parameters, and in which the unobserved component related to lifetime utility enters additively.[7] In addition, the demand function specified by BDI is consistent with the conditional cost framework used in this paper.[8] This particular form of the demand function is advantageous to work with since it can be estimated using OLS methods, and the unobserved variables can be eliminated using the fixed effect estimator. As in Browning and Meghir (1991), the introduction of the conditioning variable (in other words, illicit drugs) into the empirical model can be achieved by making the parameters associated with the price variables in the cost function, dependent on the quantity of illicit drugs. If it is also assumed that other consumption is separable from leisure and illicit drug use, the following model will result;

$$(5a) \quad H_t = a_0 + a_1 \ln OW_t + a_2 OW^5_t SW^{-5}_t + a_3 D_t + a_4 Z_t + a_5 \ln U + e_t$$

where everything is as defined previously, $H_t = T - L_t$ is the hours of work, OW_t indexes the own or respondent's wage, SW_t indexes the spouse's wage (in a family labor supply model), Z_t is a vector of exogenous variables, including among others the number of children of various ages, the respondent's age and education, the a's are parameters to be estimated, and e is a stochastic error term. Illicit drug use is expected to be an endogenously determined variable, and in light of this fact an appropriate estimation method needs to be implemented. In this paper, an instrumental variables (IV) approach will be used.

Before turning to the problems of measurement error and sample selection, one additional point relating to Equation (5a) needs to be addressed. The wage of the spouse (SW_t) is not observed in the data, but the spouse's age and education are included. In place of the ratio of wages found in Equation (5a), the spouse's age and education are included in the vector Z_t hr, thereby making the identification of the instrumental parameter a_2 impossible. The age and education of the spouse are the primary determinants of the spouse's wage. Since the main purpose of the paper is to identify the effects of drug use, and not to estimate the structural cross wage effect, Equation (5a) will be estimated as a semi-reduced form.[9]

Given the data that will be used in the analysis, both the wage and quantity (in other words, frequency) of drug use might be expected to be measured with error. The wage is treated as an exogenous variable, but is calculated using annual hours of work which results in the wage being endogenous in a statistical sense. In addition, drug use is expected to be endogenous. Thus, it is appropriate to use some type of instrumental variables in place of these two measures. The primary instruments that will be used to estimate the wage will be the individual's age, actual past labor market experience, education, and score on the armed forces qualification test.[10] The instruments that are used to estimate the drug use measures are several personal and family characteristics such as the respondent's age, education, household composition at age 14, frequency of religious attendance in 1979, and a measure of their perceived self-esteem.[11] As Kaestner (1991) demonstrates, the wage and drug use are also expected to be simultaneously determined, and thus, the regressions that estimate both of these measures will be reduced form estimates.

Equation (5a) still suffers from the empirical problem associated with the presence of nonworkers, and will have to be estimated using appropriate methods. An individual's hours of work and market wage are only observed for those who work, and thus, Equation (5a) will be estimated for a sample of employed individuals. As is well known, this type of "sample selection" criteria tends to result in biased estimates of the true parameters (Heckman 1976). In this paper, the two stage procedure due to Heckman (1976, 1979) will be implemented, although other methods were tried and yielded qualitatively the same results.[12]

The empirical analysis was carried out in the following order. First, a reduced form labor force participation model is estimated by standard probit methods, which yields estimates of the inverse mills ratio used to correct for sample selection bias. Second, a reduced form drug demand model is estimated using the entire sample. Next, a reduced form wage model is estimated using a sample of employed individuals, and correcting for sample selection. Finally, a semireduced form labor supply model is estimated using the predicted wage and predicted drug use, on a sample of employed individuals correcting for sample selection. The only equation that contains structural parameters is the labor supply model. This equation is identified since several of the exogenous variables that are used to predict both the wage and illicit drug use are excluded by assumption from the labor supply model. These variables include two indices measuring the respondent's psychological outlook, the respondent's adolescent family structure, mother's education, the respondent's religiosity and prior involvement in illegal activities.[13]

The empirical analysis will be implemented using two separate years of cross-sectional data, 1984 and 1988, and on a panel of data consisting of the two cross sections. Estimation using the limited panel will allow for the identification of the unobserved fixed effect in the model, which is potentially quite important. The cross-sectional estimates will suffer from the omitted variable bias associated with the unobserved characteristics of the individual, but remain informative since they will provide a set of estimates that are comparable with previous cross-sectional estimates. The empirical strategy is identical for the cross-sectional and longitudinal samples, although there are some significant differences. The differences will be easier to describe when the panel data estimates are presented, so the relevant discussion will be delayed until that point in the paper.

As the previous two sections have detailed, the empirical implementation of a labor supply model including a potentially addictive good like illicit drugs is quite complex. Several theoretical and statistical assumptions have been made that impose strong restrictions on the model. Previous research has shown that the parameter estimates of the labor supply model may be significantly changed by using an alternative set of assumptions (Mroz 1987; Browning, Deaton, and Irish 1985; Browning and Meghir 1991). Thus, the results of this analysis need to be interpreted in the context of these considerations.

V. DATA

The data used in the analysis come from the National Longitudinal Survey of Youth (NLSY) which is a longitudinal survey of the labor market experiences of young adults (Center for Human Resource Research 1990). The starting year of the survey was 1979 and included an initial sample of approximately 12,500 youths aged 14–21 at that time. The survey has been updated each year since 1979 with a broadening array of purposes and questions. The data contain detailed information on a respondent's labor market experience, family and personal background, and illicit drug use. Central to the purposes of this paper are the questions related to respondent's illicit drug use. In 1984, and again in 1988, the respondent was asked questions about their lifetime and current use of several illicit drugs, most notably marijuana and cocaine.[14]

The sample used in the analysis was selected based on the following criteria, which were established to eliminate several sources of heterogeneity. The respondent had to be at least 21 years old in 1984, be living independently or with their parents, but not in jail or other temporary quarters (for example, dormitory), and the respondent could not be enrolled in school, or have served in the military at any time between 1984 and 1988. In addition, those observations with missing data were deleted.[15] These restrictions resulted in a sample size of approximately 4,200 individuals in 1984, and 4,100 individuals in 1988. Descriptive statistics of the variables used in the analysis can be found in the appendix [omitted]. All analyses were done separately by marital status and gender. The analyses were done separately on the basis of marital status due to the expected impact of other family member characteristics (for example, wage) on the respondents' labor supply.[16] Separating the sample on the basis of gender is consistent with the many previous studies of labor supply (see Killingsworth 1983) that have demonstrated significant differences between male and female labor supply parameters.

The illicit drug use questions are limited in two major respects. First, as suggested by Mensch and Kandel (1988), there appears to be some underreporting in the NLSY 1984 wave, particularly with regard to cocaine use. The exact nature of the underreporting is not known, but Mensch and Kandel (1988) suggest that underreporting is more common among relatively light users, compared to more heavy users of illicit drugs, and more pronounced among females and minorities. Although the analysis accounts for a simple (in other words, random) type of measurement error, the underreporting issue remains a problem. The second problem related to the drug use questions, is the absence of a measurement of quantity of use; only the frequency of drug use is measured. Although frequency and quantity have been shown to be highly correlated, the two measures are clearly not equivalent (Stein et al. 1988). In fact, Stein et al. (1988) report that the quantity of drug use is a more powerful predictor of problems associated with illicit drug use. In addition the frequency of use was interval coded with relatively large groupings (see Table 3.1). This fact results in a more complex estimation

Table 3.1

Distribution of Total Sample by Frequency of Drug Use by Marital Status and Gender

	Married Males		Single Males		Married Females		Single Females	
	N	%	N	%	N	%	N	%
Lifetime Frequency of Cocaine Use								
1984								
0	555	84.3	995	78.3	965	91.1	1,002	84.5
1--9	55	8.4	118	9.3	52	4.9	87	7.3
10--39	19	2.9	72	5.7	21	2.0	47	4.0
40--99	13	2.0	41	3.2	7	.7	27	2.3
100+	16	2.4	44	3.5	14	1.3	23	1.9
1988								
0	706	73.4	588	61.9	1,011	83.1	716	74.0
1--9	161	16.7	188	19.8	127	10.4	145	15.0
10--39	44	4.6	81	8.5	51	4.2	57	5.9
40--99	24	2.5	44	4.6	17	1.4	28	2.9
100+	27	2.8	49	5.2	11	0.9	21	2.2
Cocaine Use Past Year								
1984								
(No) 0	618	93.9	1,060	83.5	1,018	96.1	1,065	89.8
(Yes) 1	40	6.1	210	16.5	41	3.9	121	10.2
1988								
(No) 0	892	92.7	783	82.4	1,169	96.1	869	89.9
(Yes) 1	70	7.3	167	17.6	48	3.9	98	10.1
Lifetime Frequency of Marijuana Use								
1984								
0	203	30.9	367	28.9	482	45.5	456	38.4
1--9	163	24.8	302	23.8	305	28.8	341	28.8
10--39	87	13.2	122	9.6	101	9.5	131	11.0
40--99	49	7.4	137	10.8	71	6.7	84	7.1
100+	156	23.7	342	26.9	100	9.4	174	14.7
1988								
0	299	31.1	262	27.6	524	43.1	346	35.8
1--9	253	26.3	254	26.7	367	30.2	299	30.9
10--39	121	12.6	124	13.1	142	11.7	137	14.2
40--99	84	8.7	80	8.4	178	6.4	58	6.0
100+	205	21.3	230	24.2	106	8.7	127	13.1
Marijuana Use Past Year								
1984								
(No) 0	455	69.1	687	54.1	870	82.2	823	69.4
(Yes) 1	203	30.9	583	45.9	189	17.8	363	30.6
1988								
(No) 0	758	78.8	633	66.6	1,088	89.4	755	78.1
(Yes) 1	204	21.2	317	33.4	129	10.6	212	21.9

strategy. As was noted above, instruments for the drug variables are obtained from auxiliary regressions, and given that the data on the frequency of drug use are discrete, simple OLS estimates will not be appropriate.

Table 3.1 is a frequency distribution of illicit drug use for the sample under examination, and presents the data by gender and marital status. One finding of note in Table 3.1 is the relatively large increase between 1984 and 1988 in the percentage of respondents reporting some lifetime use of cocaine. In 1984 about 15.7 percent of the married male sample and 8.9 percent of the married female sample report some prior cocaine use, and by 1988 these same figures are 26.6 percent and 16.9 percent. The same pattern can be observed for the sample of single individuals. The increase in the initiation into cocaine use over this age range is consistent with previous studies (Kandel and Logan 1984; Ravels and Kandel 1987). A surprising finding is that the percentage of respondents who report cocaine use in the last year is basically unchanged between 1984 and 1988, even though there was a substantial increase in the number of lifetime users.

Initiation into marijuana use has generally ceased over the age range observed for the current sample, as evidenced by the relatively unchanged prevalence of lifetime marijuana use, and the number of respondents who report using marijuana during the past year declines dramatically between 1984 and 1988. This pattern of marijuana use is evident for both married and single individuals. These figures imply a general decline in illicit drug use consistent with the data from the recent National Institute on Drug Abuse (NIDA) household surveys.

In general the prevalence of marijuana use is much higher than that of cocaine, as is the proportion of users who report relatively heavy marijuana use. It is also apparent that single individuals engage in more drug use than married people, and men have a greater frequency of use than women. Single men exhibit the greatest frequency of drug use; over 38 percent have tried cocaine by 1988, and over 72 percent have reported some marijuana use. Finally, the prevalence of illicit drug use among employed individuals (not shown), is very similar to that reported in Table 3.1. In fact, a comparison of means between the employed and not at work samples indicated that in most cases there were no significant differences in their patterns of illicit drug use. Indeed, when there were significant differences, the employed were observed to have higher levels of usage.

The levels of reported drug use in the 1988 NLSY survey compare favorably to those reported in the 1988 National Household Survey (NHS) on Drug Abuse (National Institute on Drug Abuse 1988). The sample of male respondents used in this paper have an age range of 25–32, and report lifetime prevalence of cocaine use of 32.3 percent, the exact same figure as that reported in the NHS survey for a similarly aged (26–34) group of males. For marijuana use, the current NLSY male sample report a lifetime prevalence of use of 70.7 percent, compared to 68.1 percent for the NHS. The same pattern is observed for the current NLSY sample of women, compared to those in the NHS. The women in the current sample report virtually the identical prevalence of cocaine use, 20.9 percent compared to 21.0 percent in the NHS, and a slightly greater prevalence of marijuana use, 60.2 percent compared to 56.2 percent in the NHS. This finding raises questions about the extent of underreporting in the NLSY, and particularly whether there was in fact substantial underreporting in 1984, as suggested by Mensch and Kandel (1988). Furthermore, Sickles and Taubman (1991) report on an unpublished NLS study that counters the Mensch and Kandel (1988) criticism, and suggests that the self-reports of illicit drug use in the NLS are reliable.

There is a certain degree of inconsistency in the self-reports of drug use in the NLSY that may have implications for the empirical results that follow. In an attempt to find out the potential magnitude of the measurement error in the data, the internal consistency of the respondents' reported drug use in 1984 was compared to their reported use in 1988. For marijuana, approximately 12 percent of those who reported some prior use as of 1984, report no prior use as of 1988, and for cocaine the same figure is 19 percent. In response to this finding, all models were estimated twice, once using the original drug variables, and another time using an internally consistent drug variable; that is, if the respondent reported prior drug use as of 1984, but no prior drug use as of 1988, the reported drug use as of 1988 was replaced with the 1984 value. The results of the two analyses were qualitatively the same, and the text reports those results that used an internally consistent measure.

The measure of labor supply used in this paper is the number of hours worked in the past 12 months on all jobs reported during this period. The hours of work measure refers to the usual number of hours worked per week times the number of weeks worked at the job(s) the respondent held during the past year. This measure of labor supply ignores the loss of work time due to absenteeism, a potentially important source of hours variation among drug users, and is a clear limitation of the current study. Labor force participation is defined as having worked for pay at some time during the past year.

A variety of measures of illicit drug use were used in the following regression analyses. Two linear measures of the lifetime frequency of illicit drug use were used; one measure took on values ranging from 0 to 4, corresponding to the coding scheme used in the survey, and which is listed in Table 3.1, and the other used the midpoints of the intervals used by the survey to code drug responses. A series of dummy variables were also created to represent the frequency of lifetime illicit drug use. For marijuana, the categories were the following: no use, 1–39 times, and 40 or more times of use. For cocaine, the categories were no use, 1–9 times, and 10 or more times. The differences in the way the data were collapsed reflect the differences in the distribution of users across the drug types. In addition, a dummy variable indicating membership in the relatively higher drug use categories was used separately. A measure of past year use of illicit drugs was also used in the analysis. The only information in the data was whether or not the person used marijuana or cocaine in the past year, and the variable was coded as a dummy variable with one indicating past year use.

The rest of the variables used in the analysis are somewhat standard, except for experience, and several of the variables used to predict drug use. Experience is the actual experience, and is the sum of actual weeks worked since 1975. As predictors of drug use, several personal and family background measures were included in the analysis, namely; a respondent's score on a series of questions relating to self-esteem (*ESTEEM*) as measured in 1980, the respondent's score on a series of questions measuring an individual's feeling of control over the world (*ROTTER*) as measured in 1980, the frequency of religious attendance (*RELIGION*) prior to 1979, and the number of illegal acts (*ILLACT*) committed prior to 1980. Details of the questions that constitute those variables can be found in the NLS handbook (Center for Human Resources 1990).

VI. CROSS-SECTIONAL ESTIMATES

As noted above, the cross-sectional estimates of a labor supply model are subject to a serious misspecification bias, since there are important unobserved variables that have been omitted from the model which are expected to be correlated with the other explanatory variables (for example, illicit drug use). The cross-sectional estimates, however, will provide a link to prior research and serve as a benchmark, and for these reasons a brief review of the findings are included. Although not specified in Equation (5a), a measure of nonearned income was included in the cross sectional model in keeping with the tradition found in the literature. To some extent, nonearned income is expected to be correlated with the omitted unobservable variables. This variable along with the wage and drug use measures are all treated as endogenous, and the actual values have been replaced with their respective predicted values. The predicted value of illicit drug use was obtained in a variety of ways, corresponding to the particular form of drug use involved. The predicted value for the linear measures of lifetime use was obtained by an OLS regression, the predicted value of the dummy variables representing lifetime use were obtained by an ordered probit procedure, and the predicted value of current use was obtained from a binary probit regression. In the dummy variables case, the predicted probability of being in a certain category of drug use was used in place of the actual value.[17]

Three separate samples were used in all of the analyses contained in this paper; a combined sample of married and single respondents, and separate samples chosen on the basis of marital status. When estimating the labor supply model using the combined sample, variables related to the respondent's spouse, and the variables measuring the number of children were interacted with a marriage dummy variable. For each sample, five separate models were estimated using one of the different measures of drug use; two linear measures of lifetime use; a set of dummy variables representing different levels of lifetime use, a dummy variable indicating relatively heavy use, and a dummy variable indicating current use. The measure of lifetime drug use, which may include current use, and current drug use were not entered together in the same model, due to severe problems of multicollinearity. The problem of multicollinearity also provides the explanation for why the models are estimated separately by type of illicit drug.

The cross-sectional results are listed in the appendix [omitted]. The results indicate that an increased frequency of marijuana use is associated with lower levels of labor supply for men, with somewhat larger and more significant effects for married as opposed to single men, and in 1988 as compared to 1984. For example, those married men who have used marijuana 40 or more times in their life, are expected to work between 503 (Model 3) and 587 (Model 4) hours less per year than comparable men using the 1984 estimate, or between 342 and 339 hours less per year using the 1988 estimate. In the case of cocaine, there does not appear to be any significant impact of cocaine use on the hours of work for males as of the 1984 interview. This conclusion is reversed, however, by 1988, and cocaine use is associated with less hours of work for both married and single men. For example, a married male who has used cocaine 20 times is expected to work 230 (Model 2) hours less than a similar male who is a nonuser. The same figure among single men would be 112 hours.

Among the female sample, it appears that increased marijuana use is only significantly related to hours of work for the sample of single women in 1988. Among this sample, those who used marijuana in the past year are expected to work 554 hours less than similar nonusers. A single women who has used marijuana 40 or more times in her life is expected to work between 518 (Model 4) and 587 (Model 3) hours less than a nonuser. In the case of cocaine, the only significant result is for current or past year cocaine use among single women in 1988, and this is only marginally significant at the .10 level.[18]

VII. PANEL DATA ESTIMATES

As suggested above, the presence of important unobserved individual characteristics, such as the level of lifetime utility, may cause the cross-sectional estimates to be biased. In order to account for these unobserved effects, the labor supply model represented was reestimated using a limited panel of data formed from the two cross-sections of 1984 and 1988. The empirical estimates were obtained from a model of first differences which will yield unbiased estimates if the unobserved characteristics, and their effects, are time invariant. For illustrative purposes, the empirical model can be written as follows:

$$(6) \quad H_{it} + b_0 + b_1 X_t + b_2 D_{it} + b_3 U + e_{it},$$

and

$$(7) \quad H_{it-1} = a_0 + a_1 X_i + a_2 D_{it-1} + b_3 U + e_{it-1},$$

where H represents hours, X are time invariant exogenous variables, D represents time varying drug use, U is the level of lifetime utility, $I = 1$ to N indexes

respondents, $t = 1$ to T indexes time, the b's and a's are parameters to be estimated, and the e's are error terms. The model was estimated in the following first
differenced form;

$$(8) \quad H_{it} - H_{it-1} = (b_0 - a_0) + (b_1 - a_1)X_i + b_2D_{it} - a_2D_{it-1} + e_{it} - e_{it-1}$$

The above formulation imposes no restrictions on the estimates across years,
except that the effect of the unobserved time invariant characteristic is constant.
This unrestricted form also facilitates estimation of the predicted values used as
instruments for the conditioning variables. For example, restricting the coefficients on current drug use to be equal in Equation (8), would necessitate that an
instrument for the first difference of drug use be obtained. Since in this case drug
use is a binary measure, this would necessitate estimating a nonlinear, panel data
(in other words, fixed or random effect) model which as illustrated by Chamberlin
(1982, 1984) is a nontrivial task. As currently formulated, instruments for drug
use and wages are obtained on the levels of these variables using both years (1984
and 1988) exogenous variables.[19] The use of levels for the right hand side variables, as compared to first differences, will also reduce the effect of measurement
error as a source of bias, particularly in the case of the binary variables. Jakubson
(1986) demonstrates that in the case of binary variables measurement error can
lead not only to a downward bias, but to the wrong sign.

The empirical estimates also account for sample selectivity due to nonparti-
cipation, although among the married male sample the problem is ignored since
over 95 percent of all married males in the matched sample work in both years.
The method is an extension of the Heckman (1976, 1979) procedure. First,
define $V = e_i - e_{it-1}$ from Equation (8). Next, note that only individuals who
are observed to work in both years are used in the analysis. Corresponding to the
two participation decisions, there will be two latent variables defined by two
auxiliary linear regression models with error terms U_1 and U_2. If it is assumed
that V, are U_1 and U_2 distributed as trivariate normal, then instead of the simple
binary probit selection model as is usually the case, a bivariate probit selection
model is appropriate.[20] The bivariate probit model corresponding to the participation decisions will include an unobserved person specific effect, and to obtain
consistent estimates of the selection terms (in other words, lambdas) it will be
necessary to account for this fact. This can be done by using the results found in
Chamberlain (1980), and the ideas behind his random effects probit model. The
unobserved person effect is assumed to be linearly related to the leads and lags
of the exogenous variables, and by including these variables in the selection
model for each year, and estimating this reduced form, consistent estimates of
the selection terms can be obtained. There is no inconsistency in treating the
unobserved person effect as a Chamberlain type of random effect in the selection
model, and a fixed effect in the hours model, since in the linear case (in other
words, hours), the two treatments are identical. The assumptions that underlie

this correction procedure are quite strong, but feasible alternative procedures are few.

Three samples of data were created from the original two cross sections. The first sample consists of individuals who were married in 1984, and who remained married to the same partner through 1988. The second sample consists of individuals who were single in 1984 and remained single through 1988. The last sample consists of all individuals present in both survey years with complete sets of data in each year. In this sample the spouse related variables are interacted with a marriage dummy variable corresponding to the formulations used in the cross-sectional analysis. The sample selection criteria related to age, school enrollment and the military also applies to these longitudinal samples. Finally, only the linear measures of lifetime drug use, and the binary measures of current drug use are used in the analysis. The omission of the categorial measures of lifetime drug use from the analysis was based on the instability of the cross-sectional results relating to this variable. In addition several other models which included the first differenced form of the drug use variables were estimated, two of which appear in Table 3.3 below.[21] These alternative specifications were used to test whether the results of Table 3.3 are sensitive to the expected multicollinearity between the current (1988) level of drug use and its lagged value (1984). In general, the results were not very sensitive to the choice of specification.

The essential relationship being identified in the longitudinal analysis is the relationship between changes in hours and changes in drug use, although the above formulation is not in the standard first difference form. In many studies this relationship is hard to identify due to little variation in hours, some or most of which is measurement error. In the current samples, there appears to be a relatively good deal of variation in hours between two time periods. The mean change in hours is 271 for males with a standard error of 826, and for females the same figures are 146 and 803. A related question is how much variation is there in drug use, and to what extent this variation is due to measurement error. In the case of cocaine, 15 percent of the male sample are observed changing their status with respect to past year use, and 21 percent increase their lifetime use. Among the female sample, 10 percent are observed changing their status with respect to past year cocaine use, and 16 percent increase their lifetime use of cocaine. For marijuana, 26 percent of the males change their status as past year users, and 18 percent increase their lifetime use. The same figures for the female sample are 20 percent and 18 percent respectively. Table 3.2 details the extent of the changes in drug use between 1984 and 1988 for past year marijuana and cocaine use for the total sample of matched respondents who were employed in both years.

Table 3.3 lists the parameter estimates associated with the drug use measures of equation (8). The signs on the 1984 values of drug use have been reversed for ease of exposition, since the regression package assumes an additive form of the model. Examining the results pertaining to males, the left half of Table 3.3, it can be seen that there does not appear to be a consistently significant relationship

Table 3.2
Changes in Drug Use Status—Past Year Marijuana and Cocaine Use

	1988 Drug Use							
	Marijuana				Cocaine			
	Nonusers		Users		Nonusers		Users	
1984 Drug Use	N	(%)	N	(%)	N	(%)	N	(%)
Males								
Marijuana								
Nonusers	795	(53)	95	(6)				
Users	297	(20)	303	(20)				
Cocaine								
Nonusers					1,197	(80)	108	(7)
Users					110	(7)	75	(5)
Females								
Marijuana								
Nonusers	874	(69)	64	(5)				
Users	193	(15)	145	(11)				
Cocaine								
Nonusers					1,104	(87)	61	(5)
Users					69	(5)	42	(3)

Notes: All percentages will not add to 100 percent due to rounding. The sample on which these numbers are based consists of all respondents present and employed in both survey years (1984 and 1988).

between marijuana use and hours of work. In contrast to the cross-sectional estimates, the point estimates of the effect of increased lifetime use are positive, although the standard errors are quite large. For current or past year marijuana use, the results are insignificant, but negative for the sample of single respondents and the total sample, which includes those respondents changing marital status between the four years. Again, the standard errors of the estimates are quite large. In the case of cocaine use, the results are similar to those for marijuana in that the signs of the effects change across samples, and the estimates have relatively large standard errors. A significant negative effect is observed, however, for the measure of lifetime cocaine use among the total sample of respondents.

The results of Table 3.3 are quite disconcerting, and raise several questions. Theoretically, the effect of one type of drug use, say cocaine, should be consistent across marital status, although the nature of the relationship between illicit drugs and leisure could differ by drug type. The illicit drug under examination and leisure should be complements or substitutes regardless of an individual's marital status. If, however, the imprecise measure of drug use used in this paper is related to the true measure differently according to marital status, then the variability of the results is expected.

Table 3.3

Parameter Estimates of the Effect of Illicit Drug Use on Hours Worked per Year, Longitudinal Estimates for Males and Females (Standard Errors in Parentheses)

Drug Type/Model	Males			Females		
	Total	Married	Single	Total	Married	Single
Marijuana Use						
1 Lifetime Use 1984	99.7	238.6	116.8	225.0	-297.6	185.9
(0,1,2,3,4)	(212.5)	(205.7)	(343.3)	(247.7)	(317.0)	(348.0)
Lifetime Use 1988	109.5	256.6	131.9	266.3	-370.1	194.4
(0,1,2,3,4)	(201.1)	(208.5)	(292.1)	(247.1)	(294.3)	(331.3)
2 Change in Use 88-84	116.5	245.1	153.0	247.4	-407.1	198.3
(0,1,2,3,4)	(197.4)	(204.1)	(261.9)	(245.6)	(291.1)	(328.8)
3 Current Use 1984	-302.6	472.9	-507.3	-503.3*	197.2	131.2
(0,1)	(325.8)	(317.4)	(339.4)	(313.5)	(355.1)	(353.7)
Current Use 1988	-512.2	486.8*	-420.9	-173.4	188.0	-17.6
(0,1)	(415.6)	(300.6)	(468.6)	(421.7)	(385.7)	(504.4)
4 Change in Use 88-84	-325.0	512.9*	-477.0	-368.4	937.0*	84.4
(-1,0,1)	(350.4)	(306.0)	(344.7)	(371.5)	(562.0)	(385.1)
Cocaine Use						
1 Lifetime Use 1984	-817.8***	-306.8	355.0	476.5	70.6	201.9
(0,1,2,3,4)	(280.0)	(263.1)	(333.8)	(507.8)	(613.8)	(351.4)
Lifetime Use in 1988	-531.5***	-98.6	161.1	413.5	-181.0	236.5
(0,1,2,3,4)	(194.8)	(214.9)	(211.5)	(412.8)	(468.9)	(251.4)
2 Change in Use 88-84	-252.8	-81.9	37.6	336.2	-403.1	245.1
(0,1,2,3,4)	(158.1)	(215.0)	(181.3)	(363.7)	(419.3)	(246.1)
3 Current Use 1984	-470.0	-125.3	655.3	-603.1*	-217.0	-131.2
(0,1)	(335.4)	(332.2)	(462.5)	(357.5)	(457.4)	(353.7)
Current Use 1988	-550.1*	371.9	245.8	129.1	-532.8	-17.6
(0,1)	(332.7)	(301.7)	(356.7)	(416.0)	(499.1)	(504.4)
4 Change in Use 88-84	-263.8	336.6	448.8	164.1	1011.3	-113.5
(-1,0,1)	(245.9)	(444.9)	(435.7)	(500.7)	(780.2)	(516.3)
Observations	1,490	380	501	1,276	423	371

Notes: In all models the actual value of drug use is replaced by its predicted value. In Models 1, 2, and 4, the prediction method was an OLS regression. In Model 3, a binary probit model was used to predict the probability of being a current user. All models included the following additional control variables: the predicted value of the natural logarithm of the wage, age, education, the number of children of various ages, race, the predicted value of nonearned income, spouse age, spouse education, and geographic indicators. For time varying variables (for example, children), both the 1984 and 1988 values were entered into the model. Also the signs on the 1984 variables have been switched, since the software package assumes an additive form.

*p < 10.

**p < .05.

***p < .01.

The right hand side of Table 3.3 presents the longitudinal results for the female sample. As was the case for males, there is a good deal of variability in the results across drug use types and marital groups, and the standard errors are relatively large. Large, negative effects of current marijuana and cocaine use are observed for the samples of single women and all women. Among the married women, however, current marijuana use is associated with large positive effects, that in one case approach commonly accepted levels of statistical significance.

The findings with regard to the other variables raises a question about the commonly found way longitudinal estimates of labor supply are obtained. It is almost universal to find that the empirical model restricts the coefficients on wages, and other important variables, to be time invariant. The results of this paper suggest otherwise. The parameter estimates associated with the wages and other variables from different years often differed dramatically from each other. The effect of time invariant variables also differed over time. The results associated with two representative models can be found in the appendix.

The impact of illicit drug use on labor supply may be most evident in regard to an individual's labor force participation, as opposed to their (conditional) hours of work. To test this hypothesis, an analysis of the effect of marijuana and cocaine use on labor force participation was implemented using the limited panel data. The analysis of labor force participation using panel data, however, presents several substantial empirical problems. As demonstrated by Chamberlain (1982), the nonlinear nature of these models prohibits the use of the simple fixed effect estimates. In addition, there is the endogeneity of illicit drug use that further complicates the analysis, as does the categorical nature of the drug use variables.

In light of these considerations, the empirical framework chosen for this analysis was based on the correlated random effects model of Chamberlain (1980, 1982). This model was chosen because it does not necessitate first differencing the drug use measures which is impractical given the categorical drug use data, and the endogenous nature of illicit drug use.[22] The results (not shown) of this analysis were consistent with those reported in Table 3.3. The parameter estimates of the effect of illicit drug use were imprecisely estimated, particularly with regard to past year use, and had different signs depending on the measure of drug use and the sample. The majority of the results indicated a positive effect of illicit drug use on labor force participation. The significant empirical problems associated with this analysis, however, demand that these results be interpreted with caution and represent an area of future research.

VIII. CONCLUSION

This paper has presented an empirical analysis of the effects of drug use on labor supply. Based on previous research, and the theoretical model currently presented, it was expected that drug use would most likely have a negative impact on the hours of work supplied to the market, though a positive result could not be ruled out. The findings of this paper do not appear to be totally consistent with such an expectation. In the cross-sectional results, the effect of illicit drug use on labor supply tended to be negative, and large in magnitude, particularly in 1988. The longitudinal estimates, however, were less supportive of the hypothesized relationship. The parameter estimates were not in general negative, as in the cross-section, and the variability of the estimates was also much greater. If, as is often argued in the literature, the longitudinal estimates are to be preferred, there appears to be no systematic effect of illicit drug use on labor supply. Furthermore, a preliminary analysis of the effect of illicit drug use on labor force participation yielded qualitatively similar results.

Taken at face value, these results would have important policy implications. They would suggest that drug use among young adults is a highly idiosyncratic experience that has different effects on different people. It should be pointed out that these results are not inconsistent with anecdotal evidence concerning the severe adverse impact on young adults' lives of heavy and continuous illicit drug use. The evidence contained in this paper pertains to a broad range of drug users, and the interest has been focused on estimating an average effect of drug use. It is this average effect that is not systematic. There does not appear to be a common experience with regard to drug use and labor supply, and public policies should reflect this fact if they are to be effective and cost efficient. The goal of policy would be to identify those individuals for which illicit drug use does become problematic, and further research is clearly needed in this area.

The results of this paper should be viewed as preliminary. The current analysis suffers from several problems, most notable of which is poor measures of drug use. Only very crude measures of illicit drug use were available, and the variability of the parameter estimates associated with drug use might very well be a function of this fact. The neoclassical model of labor supply, the starting point of this analysis, has also suffered from its share of empirical refutation. Several of the theoretical and statistical assumptions used throughout the paper are quite restrictive. These qualifications are important and necessitate more work in this area.

NOTES

1. In comparison to illicit drugs, there have been many more studies of the effects of alcohol use on labor market outcomes. Mullahy (1992) surveys the literature relating to alcohol use and the labor market.

2. Since changes in current consumption will alter the stock of drug consumption capital, the price of current consumption should include the effects of changes in the stock on utility. It is assumed that the changes in the stock of drug consumption capital are instantaneous.

3. The conditional framework has also been used to model goods that are rationed, as in Blundell and Walker (1982), but in the current case, illicit drugs are not rationed. The consumer is able to choose their optimal level, and at this point the conditional and unconditional cost functions will yield equal values.

4. For a discussion of implicit separability see Deaton and Muellbauer (1980) or Browning, Deaton, and Irish (1985).

5. An apparent drawback of the empirical model is that the measure of drug use actually used refers only to the respondent, and not the household. This implies that the drug use of one spouse is separate from the drug use of their partner.

6. This is a real advantage given the complexity of modeling the demand for addictive goods. See the papers by Chaloupka (1991) and Becker, Grossman, and Murphy (1991) for a discussion of the empirical analysis of the demand for addictive goods.

7. The demand function implies that preferences are "quasi-homothetic." See Browning, Deaton, and Irish (1985) for further discussion.

8. Equations 5.8 and 5.9 in Browning, Deaton, and Irish (1985, p. 521) illustrate that the empirical demand function specified in Equation (5a) in the text can be derived using the consumer's profit function or the cost function. The only difference between the two specifications is that instead of the unobserved price of utility, the lifetime level of utility enters into the model when the cost function is used.

9. In addition, the use for the semi-reduced form provides a way to sidestep the problem of the spouse not working. In essence the age and education of the spouse are capturing the effects of the actual wage for working spouses and the reservation wage for nonworking spouses. To the extent that the functional form of the empirical model becomes more adhoc, this procedure introduces the possibility of specification bias.

10. Several of the variables will be entered into the regression in a quadratic form (experience) or as a series of dummy variables (education). In addition, several geographic measures and demographic variables will be included in the model.

11. See the appendix for a complete list of the variables used to predict drug use, as well as the variables used to predict the wage [*Appendix omitted from this reprint. See appendix in original, Kaestner,* Journal of Human Resources, *24: 146–153.*]

12. The Heckman procedure was also estimated by FIML methods with virtually identical results although in a few cases the LIMDEP software did not converge. The alternative method for correcting selectivity bias due to Olsen (1981) was also implemented. The results were quite similar to those reported in the table. In addition, the issue of selectivity due to nonworkers was ignored, and the results were again similar to those reported.

13. The empirical model can be represented as follows:

Structural   **Reduced Form**

$H = f(D,W,X) + U_w$

$D = g(H,W,Y) + U_d$ $D = g^1(X,Y,Z) + V_w$

$W = h(D,Z) + U_w$ $W = h^1(X,Y,Z) + V_w$

$P = k(D,W,X) + U_p$ $P = k^1(X,Y,Z) + V_p$

where H = hours, D = drugs, W = wage, P = a latent variable which has a corresponding indicator equal to one of the individual works, X, Y, and Z are exogenous variables, and the U, and V, are error terms. All estimates were obtained from the reduced form except for the hours model.

14. The 1988 survey limited the illicit drug use questions to include only marijuana and cocaine.

15. The sample selection criteria used in the paper are intended to reduce unobserved

heterogeneity in the sample, but they also may have eliminated those individuals for whom drug use has the greatest adverse impact. For example, respondents who are in jail have been excluded from the analysis, although there are very few respondents in the data who are in fact in jail.

16. Empirically, tests of the validity of this strategy were carried out using the cross sectional samples and a reduced form model of hours of work, including a correction for sample selection. The results of these tests indicated that the parameter estimates differed by marital status, and that a simple dummy variable indicating married was not sufficient to account for the differences. The results were less strong for the male sample, but significant at the .05 level. Limiting the sample on the basis of marriage, however, gives rise to the possibility that the parameter estimates of the labor supply model will be biased if marriage and drug use are jointly determined.

17. The use of the predicted values on the right hand side has important implications for the standard errors derived from the OLS regression on hours. The estimated standard errors from the OLS regression are smaller than the true estimates (Murphy and Topel, 1985; Maddala, 1983). The derivation of the true standard errors would be quite complex given the nature of the auxiliary regressions, sample selection and instruments for quantitative variables, and beyond the scope of this paper.

18. The parameter estimates associated with the other variables in the model are similar to previous estimates found in the literature. The female uncompensated own wage elasticity evaluated at the mean number of hours was in the .4 to .5 range in 1984, and .1 to .3 range in 1988 for the different samples. The presence of young children resulted in a significantly lower level of labor supply for women. Among the male samples, the own wage uncompensated elasticity was between .35 and .45 in 1984, and approximately .3 in 1988. The presence of children had no significant impact on male labor supply.

19. For example, respondents' past experience in 1984 and 1988 are entered into the regression of the 1984 wage. Inclusion of exogenous variables from other years is consistent with Chamberlain's (1982, 1984) correlated random effects model for panel data. In the linear case (in other words, wage), this model is identical to a fixed effect model, but in the nonlinear case this model allows a relatively simple way to obtain panel data estimates for discrete variables.

20. A bivariate probit procedure is preferable, but due to problems of obtaining estimates that would converge using the LIMDEP software and this data set, separate probits were used instead. When bivariate probit estimates could be obtained, the results were virtually identical to those obtained when using the separate probits, even when the correlation of the underlying random variables was significant.

21. For example, a dummy variable was created that indicated whether the person was a current user in both 1984 and 1988, or had become a current user in 1988, versus never being a current user, or being a current user in 1984 and not being a current user in 1988. Another variable was a dummy variable that indicated a person became a heavy user in 1988 as compared to 1984. None of the results from these models differed significantly from those reported in the text.

22. The model can be written as follows:

(9) $LFP_1 = a_0 + a_1 D_1 + \phi + e_1$,

(10) $LFP_2 = a_0 + a_1 D_2 + \phi + e_2$,

(11) $\phi = b_0 + b_1 D_1 + b_2 D_2 + v$,

where *LFP* is a binary indicator of labor force participation, D represents drug use, ϕ is an unobserved person specific effect, a_i and b_i are parameters, and e_i and v are error terms that follow independent normal distributions. The model is a reduced form model. The structural parameters, a_t , are obtained by substituting Equation (11) into the other equations, and imposing cross-equation restrictions on the b_t , using a minimum distance estimator (Chamberlain, 1984). A problem is that illicit drug use D_i is endogenous and the predicted nature of illicit drug use needs to be incorporated into the derivation of the appropriate covariance matrix of the reduced forms (Maddala, 1983). In addition, the minimum distance estimator uses the matrix formed by the outer product of the first order conditions, which depend on the estimated parameters, and the derivation of this matrix may also be affected by the predicted nature of drug use. In this paper, the minimum distance estimates are obtained using a covariance matrix that ignores the predicted nature of the drug variables.

REFERENCES

Becker, Gary S. 1965. "A Theory of the Allocation of Time." *Economic Journal* 75 (299): 493–517.

Becker, Gary S., and Kevin M. Murphy. 1988. "A Theory of Rational Addiction." *Journal of Political Economy* 96 (4) 675–700.

Becker, Gary S., Michael Grossman, and Kevin M. Murphy. 1991. "An Empirical Analysis of Cigarette Addiction." National Bureau of Economic Research Working Paper 3322.

Blundell, Richard W., and Ian Walker. 1982. "Modeling the Joint Determination of Household Labor Supplies and Commodity Demands." *Economic Journal* 92 (366): 351–364.

Browning, Martin. 1983. "Necessary and Sufficient Conditions for Cost Functions." *Econometrica* 51 (3): 851–856.

Browning, Martin, and Costas Meghir. 1991. "The Effects of Male and Female Labor Supply on Commodity Demands." *Econometrica* 59 (4): 925–951.

Browning, Martin, Angus Deaton, and Margaret Irish. 1985. "A Profitable Approach to Labor Supply and Commodity Demands Over the Life-Cycle." *Econometrica* 53 (3): 503–543.

Center for Human Resource Research. 1990. *NLS Handbook 1990*. Columbus: Ohio State University.

Chaloupka, Frank. 1991. "Rational Addictive Behavior and Cigarette Smoking." *Journal of Political Economy* 99 (4): 722–742.

Chamberlain, Gary. 1984. "Panel Data." In *Handbook of Econometrics*, Vol. 2, ed. Zac Griliches and Michael Intrilligator, pp. 1247–1318. Amsterdam: North Holland.

Chamberlain, Gary. 1982. "Multivariate Regression Models for Panel Data." *Journal of Econometrics* 18 (1): 5–46.

Chamberlain, Gary. 1980. "Analysis of Covariance with Qualitative Data." *Review of Economic Studies* 47 (1): 225–238.

Deaton, Angus, and John Muellbauer. 1980. *Economics and Consumer Behavior*. Cambridge: Cambridge University Press.

Gill, Andrew M., and Robert J. Michaels. 1992. "Does Drug Use Lower Wages?" *Industrial and Labor Relations Review* 45 (3): 419–434.

Gleason, Philip M., Jonathan R. Veum, and Michael R. Pergamit. 1991. "Drug and Alcohol Use at Work: A Survey of Young Workers." *Monthly Labor Review* 114 (8): 3–7.

Hayghe, Howard V. 1991. "Survey of Employer Anti-Drug Programs." In *Drugs in the Workplace: Research and Evaluation Data, Volume II*, ed. Steven W. Gust, J. Michael Walsh, Linda B. Thomas, and Dennis J. Crouch, pp. 22–36. Washington, D.C.: U.S. Department of Health and Human Services.

Heckman, James J. 1976. "The Common Structure of Statistical Models of Truncation Sample Selection and Limited Dependent Variables." *Annals of Economic and Social Measurement* 5 (4): 475–492.

Heckman, James J. 1979. "Sample Selection Bias as a Specification Error." *Econometrica* 47 (1): 153–161.

Heckman, James J., and Mark Killingsworth. 1986. "Female Labor Supply: A Survey." In *Handbook of Labor Economics*, ed. Orley Ashenfelter and Richard Layard, pp. 41–83. Amsterdam: North Holland.

Jakubson, George. 1986. "Measurement Error in Binary Explanatory Variables in Path Data Models; Why Do Cross Section and Panel Data Estimates of the Union Wage Effect Differ?" Working Paper #209, Industrial Relations Section. Princeton, NJ: Princeton University.

Johnson, Robert J., and Cedric Herring. 1989. "Labor Market Participation Among Young Adults." *Youth and Society* 21 (1): 3–331.

Kaestner, Robert. 1991. "The Effect of Illicit Drug Use on the Wages of Young Adults." *Journal of Labor Economics* 9 (4): 381–412.

Kagel, John H., Raymond C. Battalio, and C. G. Miles. 1980. "Marijuana and Work Performance: Results from an Experiment." *Journal of Human Resources* 15 (3): 373–395.

Kandel, Denise B., and Mark Davies. 1990. "Labor Force Experiences of a National Sample of Young Adult Men." *Youth and Society* 21 (4): 411–445.

Kandel, Denise B., and John Logan. 1984. "Patterns of Drug Use from Adolescence to Early Adulthood." *American Journal of Public Health* 74 (7): 660–666.

Kandel, Denise B., and K. Yamaguchi. 1987. "Job Mobility and Drug Use: An Event History Analysis." *American Journal of Sociology* 92 (4): 836–878.

Killingsworth, Mark. 1983. *Labor Supply*. Cambridge: Cambridge University Press.

Maddala, G. S. 1983. *Limited Dependent and Qualitative Variables in Econometrics*. Cambridge, Mass.: Harvard University Press.

Mensch, Barbara S., and Denise B. Kandel. 1988. "Underreporting of Substance Use in a National Longitudinal Youth Cohort." *Public Opinion Quarterly* 52 (1): 100–124.

Mroz, Thomas. 1987. "The Sensitivity of an Empirical Model of Married Women's Hours of Work to Economic and Statistical Assumptions." *Econometrica* 55 (4): 765–799.

Mullahy, John. 1992. "Alcohol and the Labor Market." Unpublished. Department of Economics, Trinity College.

Murphy, Kevin M., and Robert H. Topel. 1985. "Estimation and Inference in Two-Step Econometric Models." *Journal of Business and Economic Statistics* 3 (4): 370–379.

National Institute on Drug Abuse. 1988. *National Household Survey on Drug Abuse*. Rockville, MD: U.S. Department of Health and Human Services.

Olsen, Randall J. 1988. "A Least Squares Correction for Selectivity Bias." *Econometrica* 48 (1): 1815–1820.

Pullak, R. A. 1969. "Conditional Demand Functions and Consumption Theory." *Quarterly Journal of Economics* 83 (1): 70–78.

Raveis, V. H., and Denise B. Kandel. 1987. "Changes in Drug Behavior from the Middle to Late Twenties: Initiation, Persistence, and the Cessation of Use." *American Journal of Public Health* 77 (5): 607–611.

Register, Charles, and Donald Williams. 1992. "Labor Market Effects of Marijuana and Cocaine Use Among Young Men." *Industrial and Labor Relations Review* 45 (3): 435–448.

Sickles, Robin, and Paul Taubman. 1991. "Who Uses Illegal Drugs?" *American Economic Review* 81 (2): 248–251.

Stein, Judith A., Michael D. Newcomb, and P. M. Bentler. 1988. "Structure of Drug Use Behaviors and Consequences Among Young Adults: Multitrait-Multimethod Assessment of Frequency, Quality, Work Site, and Problem Substance Use." *Journal of Applied Psychology* 73 (4): 595–605.

Stigler, George, and Gary Becker. 1977. "De Gustibus Non Est Eisputandum." *American Economic Review* 67 (2): 76–90.

White, Helene Raskin, Angela Aidala, and Benjamin Zablocki. 1988. "A Longitudinal Investigation of Drug Use and Work Patterns Among Middle-Class, White Adults." *Journal of Applied Behavioral Science* 24 (4): 455–469.

Zarkin, Gary, Michael French, and J. Valley Richal. 1992. "The Relationship Between Illicit Drug Use and Labor Supply." Working Paper, Research Triangle Institute.

APPENDIX B

New Estimates of the Effects of Marijuana and Cocaine Use on Wages

*Robert Kaestner**

ABSTRACT

Using the 1984 and 1988 waves of the National Longitudinal Survey of Youth, this study provides an update of several previous cross-sectional estimates of the effect of illicit drug use on wages, as well as the first longitudinal estimates of that effect. The cross-sectional results, which are generally consistent with the surprising findings of previous research, suggest that illicit drug use has a large, positive effect on wages. The longitudinal estimates, which control for unobserved heterogeneity in the sample, are mixed: among men, the estimated wage effects of both marijuana and cocaine use are negative, but among women, the effect of cocaine use remains positive and large. Because the longitudinal model is imprecisely estimated, however, those results are inconclusive.

INTRODUCTION

The adverse physical and psychological effects of illicit drug use have been well documented in the medical literature and widely publicized through an extensive public and private media campaign. Given the public's knowledge of the negative health consequences of illicit drug use, it is not surprising that illicit drug use is also commonly believed to adversely affect the social and economic aspects of users' lives. Despite these perceptions, a large segment of the U.S. population

*The author is Assistant Professor of Economics at Rider College and Faculty Research Fellow of the National Bureau of Economic Research. A data appendix with additional results, and copies of the computer programs used to generate the results presented in this paper, are available upon request to Robert Kaestner, Department of Economics, Rider College, Lawrenceville, NJ 08648. This article originally appeared in *Industrial and Labor Relations Review*, Volume 47, pp. 454–470, 1994.

engages in illicit drug use. In a 1991 survey of 18–34-year-olds, for example, approximately 60% of the respondents reported having used illicit drugs at some time in their lives, and approximately 23% reported using illicit drugs within the previous year (NIDA 1991).

One important focus of efforts to reduce illicit drug use has been the labor market. Concern that the ability of our workers is being seriously impaired by illicit drug use has spurred sizable expenditures to correct the problem. The fundamental goal of most drug prevention programs is to eliminate *all* illicit drug use, a goal that appears unrealistic in view of the fact that illicit drugs continue to be widely used despite extensive dissemination of information about their harmful effects. Thus, the merit of a "zero tolerance" drug policy depends critically on the effect of illicit drug use on the individual. If illicit drug use harms the user regardless of the particular drug used and even when the amount of the drug consumed is small, a zero tolerance policy is clearly defensible; otherwise, the wisdom of such a policy is questionable.

To date, little evidence of the type that would satisfy most economists has been produced to justify the extent and scope of the current drug prevention effort, particularly in the labor market. Since earnings are one of the best and most accessible measures of labor market success, several recent studies, using data from the National Longitudinal Survey of Youth (NLSY), have examined the impact of illicit drugs on the wages of young adults. In general, the evidence presented in these papers, directly contradicting the commonly held belief that drug use has an adverse impact on labor market outcomes, indicates that drug use has a *positive* effect on wages. The explanation most often suggested for this finding is the probable existence of unobserved heterogeneity in the sample; individuals who use drugs may also, for reasons unobserved by the researcher, be more productive than average.

The previous studies on this subject have all been cross-sectional in nature, and none of them, despite their careful execution, have been able to fully control for unobserved characteristics that could strongly affect the observed relationship between illicit drug use and wages. The purpose of this paper is to partially fill this gap in the literature by estimating, for the first time, a longitudinal or fixed effects model of drug use and wages. To the extent that some of the potentially important unobserved characteristics that have been omitted from previous studies are individual-specific and time-invariant, a fixed effects wage model will provide better estimates of the relationship between illicit drugs and wages. In addition, using the NLSY data of 1988, I provide the most up-to-date cross-sectional estimates of the effect of illicit drug use on the wages of young adults yet published.

ILLICIT DRUG USE AND WAGES

There have been several studies of the effects of illicit drug use on wages, and all of them have used the 1984 wave of the NLSY. Gill and Michaels (1992), using a switching regression framework, examined the effect of (1) use of any illicit drug and (2) use of hard drugs (cocaine and heroin) on the wages of a combined sample of men and women. They found a positive effect of drug use on wages, resulting primarily from differences in the return to unobserved characteristics. In a 1991 study (Kaestner 1991), I examined the wage effect of both lifetime and recent use of marijuana and cocaine, using a simultaneous equations model in which drug use and the wage were jointly determined. I found that both marijuana use and cocaine use positively affected wages of all four demographic groups chosen on the basis of gender and age. I also estimated a switching regression model, and found positive wage effects of cocaine and marijuana use consistent with Gill and Michaels's (1992) results. Using a model that was somewhat unconventional in terms of economic theory, Kandel and Davies (1990) estimated simple OLS wage regressions, and found no significant effect of marijuana or cocaine use on the wages of employed men.[1] Finally, Register and Williams (1992) examined the effect of marijuana and cocaine use on the wages of men, including the effect of on-the-job use and long-term use, using an instrumental variables approach. They found a positive wage effect of general marijuana use, but negative effects of on-the-job marijuana use and long-term marijuana use. They found no significant effect of cocaine use on the wage.

All of these previous studies started with the premise that illicit drug use results in deterioration of an individual's physical and psychological well-being, and consequently also decreases a person's productive capabilities. Drug use and wages were hypothesized to be negatively related.

The observed relationship between illicit drug use and wages could very well be positive, however, if illicit drugs are a normal good, since wages are an important determinant of income. Indeed, this hypothesis has received some empirical support. Sickles and Taubman (1991) reported findings suggesting that individuals with higher earnings capacity have a greater involvement in illicit drug use. Kaestner (1991) and Register and Williams (1992) explicitly recognized the potential income effect, and estimated a structural model of illicit drug use and wages. A second reason for estimating a structural model of drug use and wages is found in Gill and Michaels (1992) and Kaestner (1991). Those studies cast the basic consumer problem in a household production framework, in which the interdependence of drug use and wages resulted from the wage being the price of time used in producing goods.[2] Given these considerations, in this paper I use the following two-equation model to estimate the effect of illicit drug use on wages:

$$(1) \quad W_{it} = f\left(X_{it}, D_{it}, E_i, V_{it}\right)$$

and

$$(2) \quad D_{it} = g\left(Z_{it}, W_{it}, E_i, U_{it}\right).$$

In equation (1), W is the natural logarithm of the wage, X is a vector of exogenous variables affecting the wage, D is a measure of the quantity of illicit drug use, E is an unobserved person-specific effect, V is an error term, I indexes individuals, and t indexes time. Equation (2) has similarly defined variables, with Z being a vector of exogenous variables that affect drug use, and U the error term.

EMPIRICAL MODEL

Before empirical estimates of the model can be obtained, two issues need to be addressed. First, the functional form of equations (1) and (2) needs to be specified. For now, I assume these functions are linear. Second, the exogenous variables for each equation need to be chosen. For equation (1), these will include several human capital variables (for example, education, and experience), demographic variables (such as age, race, and marital status), geographic measures (such as region), and family/personal background variables (such as household composition at age 14 and self-esteem scale). The exogenous variables chosen for equation (2) will include all of those in equation (1), plus a measure of non-earned income, the frequency of religious attendance in 1979, the current number of dependent children of various ages, and the number of illegal acts committed in 1979. These last four variables will identify the parameter estimates of equation (1). I chose them based on the results of my 1991 study, which tested this set of variables for the over-identifying restrictions they impose. The parameters of equation (2) are under-identified, and therefore only the reduced form version of this equation will be estimated.

Both cross-sectional and panel data (fixed effect) estimates of the model will be obtained, and the implementation strategy will be the same in both cases. First, reduced form estimates of equation (2) will be obtained using the entire sample, and from these estimates a predicted drug use measure will be calculated. Next, estimates of the wage equation (1) will be obtained for a sample of employed individuals using the predicted drug use variable in place of its actual value, and correcting for the sample selectivity introduced by examining only employed individuals.[3] The Heckman (1976) two-step procedure will be used to correct for the potential sample selectivity bias.[4]

The choice of the fixed effects specification of the model is based on the expectation that the unobserved personal characteristics that influence the wage will also be correlated with the other variables in the model, particularly the drug use measures. Thus, this specification is preferred over the alternative random effect model, which assumes that the individual effect is uncorrelated with the other variables. The Chamberlain (1982) "correlated random effects" model, which allows for the correlation between the unobserved effect and the other explanatory variables, is identical to the fixed effects specification when the model is linear in the parameters, as is the current model. The specification of the fixed effects model used in this paper, however, is somewhat unconventional and a departure from what is usually found in the lite simplicity, assume that equation (1) can be written as follows for period t:

$$\text{(1a)} \quad W_{it} = b_0 + b_1 X_i + b_2 Z_{it} + b_3 E_i + V_{it}$$

and for period $t - 1$,

$$\text{(1b)} \quad W_{it-1} = a_o + a_1 X_1 + a_2 Z_{it-1} + b_3 E_i + V_{it-1}$$

The X are exogenous variables that are time-invariant (such as race), and the Z are exogenous variables that are time-varying (such as illicit drug use). The E in the above equations are the unobserved person-specific characteristics, which are assumed to be time-invariant. The standard way to obtain unbiased estimates of the parameters of the model is to take the difference of equations (1a) and (1b), and run an OLS regression. Furthermore, it is usually assumed that the a_i = b_i = b, which yields the following:

$$\text{(1c)} \quad W_{it} - W_{it-1} = b\,(Z_{it} - Z_{it-1}\,) + (V_{it} - V_{it-1}\,).$$

Note that the unobserved person effect has been eliminated by taking the difference. An alternative specification allows the a_i and b_i to differ and estimates the following:

$$\text{(1d)} \quad W_{it} - W_{it-1} = (b_o - a_o\,) + (b_1 - a_1\,)\,X_i + b_2 Z_{it} - a_2 Z_{it-1} + (V_{it} - V_{it-1}\,).$$

Although not common, specifying a model in which the parameter values change over time is a theoretically sound idea. For example, if the degree of racial discrimination changes over time, the impact of race on the wage will also change. Similar arguments can be made for the remaining variables, including the human capital variables such as education and experience.[5]

There are several benefits associated with specifying the model as in equation (1d). First, equation (1d) imposes the fewest restrictions on the model. The only restriction imposed in equation (1d) is that the effect of the unobserved person-specific characteristics (b_3) is the same in both time periods. Second, given the way the quantity of drug use is measured (described in detail below), the differencing of the drug use measure presents problems, and is not intuitively appealing.[6] Thus, including the level of drug use from each year of data in the model facilitates estimation, since standard methods can be used to obtain the predicted values of the level of drug use that are used in the second stage of estimation. The predicted values of drug use will be derived from the reduced form estimates obtained from a model that includes all exogenous variables from both time periods.[7] Third, taking differences of any qualitative variable (such as marital status) results in an arbitrary ordering being imposed on the data, and using the levels avoids this problem.

In addition, the panel data estimates will be obtained from a sample of individuals employed in both of the available time periods. The exclusion of those who were not employed in both of the periods introduces a potential sample selection bias that I address by including separate correction terms associated with the labor force participation decision in each year. Using an unrestricted model also facilitates the incorporation of the sample selection terms, since these variables enter the model in levels. The reduced form labor force participation equation will also be obtained using all the exogenous variables from both time periods.[8]

A potential drawback of this procedure is that the time-varying variables are often highly collinear, and this collinearity will affect the precision with which the parameters are estimated. Alternative models that use the differenced form of the drug use variables are estimated to test this hypothesis as it pertains to the drug use variables, which are the variables of interest in this paper. In addition, several of the variables that are technically time-varying will be treated as time-invariant, since there is very little variation over time in these measures. These variables include the respondent's age, since all respondents aged about four years between the two surveys, and the respondent's region of residence.

DATA

The data used in the analysis come from the National Longitudinal Survey of Youth (Center for Human Resource Research 1990). In its starting year, 1979, the survey sample consisted of approximately 12,000 youths aged 14–21. The survey has been updated each year since 1979, with a broadening array of purposes and questions. The questions elicit detailed information on respondents' labor market experience, family and personal background, and illicit drug use. Central to the purposes of this paper are the questions related to the respondent's illicit drug use. In 1984, and again in 1988, respondents were asked questions about their lifetime and recent use of several illicit drugs, most notably marijuana and cocaine.[9]

Several selection criteria were established to eliminate sources of heterogeneity: the sample included only those respondents who were at least 18 years old in 1984, were living independently or with their parents, but not in jail or other temporary quarters (such as a dormitory), and who were not enrolled in school, in the military, or self-employed. In addition, those observations with missing data were deleted. These restrictions resulted in samples of approximately 7,800 individuals in 1984 and 7,200 in 1988. A matched sample of individuals present in both years, who numbered approximately 5,700, was also created. Definitions and descriptive statistics of the variables used in the analysis can be found in the appendix.

The illicit drug use questions are limited in two major respects. First, as was suggested in Mensch and Kandel (1988), there may be some under-reporting in the NLSY 1984 data, particularly with regard to cocaine use. The exact nature of the under-reporting is not known, but Mensch and Kandel (1988) suggested that under-reporting is more common among relatively light users of illicit drugs than among heavier users, and more pronounced among women and minorities

Table 3.4
Distribution of the Total Sample by Gender and Frequency of Drug Use

Year	Lifetime Frequency of Cocaine Use	Men N	%	Women N	%	Lifetime Frequency of Marijuana Use	Men N	%	Women N	%
1984	0	2930	80.4	3655	87.3	0	1107	30.4	1804	43.1
	1–9	360	9.9	286	6.8	1–9	916	25.1	1161	27.7
	10–39	165	4.5	135	3.2	10–39	385	10.6	481	11.5
	40–99	93	2.6	60	1.4	40–99	356	9.8	274	6.5
	100–999	73	2.0	37	0.9	100–999	444	12.2	296	7.1
	1000+	23	0.6	15	0.4	1000+	436	12.0	172	4.1
1988	0	2204	67.4	3084	78.8	0	962	29.4	1608	41.1
	1–2	366	11.2	292	7.5	1–2	457	14.0	725	18.5
	3–9	249	7.6	222	5.7	3–9	433	13.2	451	11.5
	10–39	236	7.2	191	4.9	10–39	455	13.9	514	13.1
	40–99	106	3.2	72	1.8	40–99	271	8.3	227	5.8
	100+	109	3.3	51	1.3	100+	692	21.2	387	9.9

Year	Past 30 Day Frequency of Marijuana Use	Men N	%	Women N	%	Past 30 Day Frequency of Marijuana Use	Men N	%	Women N	%
1984	0	3458	94.9	4057	96.9	0	2622	72.0	3613	86.3
	1–2	89	2.4	71	1.7	1–2	243	6.7	200	4.8
	3–5	41	1.1	24	0.6	3–5	196	5.4	113	2.7
	6–9	30	0.8	17	0.4	6–9	158	4.3	78	1.9
	10–19	17	0.5	15	0.4	10–19	194	5.3	82	2.0
	20–39	7	0.2	2	0.0	20–39	130	3.6	61	1.5
	40+	2	0.1	2	0.0	40+	101	2.8	41	1.0
1988	0	3122	95.5	3818	97.6	0	2770	95.5	3590	91.8
	1–2	73	2.2	60	1.5	1–2	113	2.2	123	3.1
	3–5	33	1.0	22	0.6	3–5	104	1.0	64	1.6
	6–9	20	0.6	1	0.0	6–9	77	0.6	34	0.9
	10–19	12	0.4	7	0.2	10–19	102	0.4	41	1.0
	20–39	4	0.1	2	0.1	20–39	62	0.1	27	0.7
	40+	6	0.2	2	0.1	40+	42	0.2	33	0.8

Source: Figures are derived from the National Longitudinal Surveys of Labor Market Experiences—
Youth Cohort (Center for Human Resource Research 1990).

than among men and non-minorities. Although the present analysis accounts for a simple (that is, random) type of measurement error, under-reporting remains a potential problem.[10]

The second problem related to the drug use questions is the absence of a measure of quantity of use; only the frequency of drug use is measured. Although frequency and quantity have been shown to be highly correlated, the two measures are clearly not equivalent (Stein et al. 1988). In fact, Stein et al. (1988) reported finding that the quantity of drug use was a more powerful predictor of problems associated with illicit drug use than was frequency of use. In addition, the frequency of use was interval-coded with relatively large groupings (see Table 3.4).

Table 3.4 is a frequency distribution of illicit drug use for the sample under examination, and presents the unweighted data by gender. One finding of note in Table 3.4 is the relatively large increase between 1984 and 1988 in the percentage of respondents reporting some lifetime use of cocaine. In 1984, about 19.6% of the male sample and 12.7% of the female sample reported some prior cocaine use; by 1988 the respective figures were 32.6% and 21.2%. The observed increase in the initiation into cocaine use over this age range is consistent with previous studies (Kandel and Logan 1984; Raveis and Kandel 1987). The surprising finding is that the number of respondents who had used cocaine in the previous 30 days decreased between 1984 and 1988, whereas the number of people who had tried cocaine increased by approximately 66% over that period. The relatively high levels of lifetime cocaine use, compared to past 30 day use, imply that there were many individuals who experimented with cocaine but neither regularly used it nor became addicted to it.

Initiation into marijuana use largely ceased over the age range observed for this sample, as evidenced by the relatively small increase in the prevalence of lifetime marijuana use, and the dramatic decline in the number of respondents who reported using marijuana during the past 30 days, between 1984 and 1988.

The figures in Table 3.4 imply a general decline in illicit drug use consistent with the data from the recent National Institute on Drug Abuse (NIDA) household surveys. In general, marijuana use was much more common than cocaine use, and the proportion of users who reported relatively heavy marijuana use was much greater than the proportion reporting heavy cocaine use. It is also apparent that men had a greater frequency of use than women. Finally, the frequency distribution of illicit drug use for employed individuals (not shown) is very similar to that reported in Table 3.4 (Kaestner 1991).

The levels of reported drug use in the 1988 NLSY survey are very similar to those reported in the 1988 National Household Survey (NHS) on Drug Abuse (National Institute on Drug Abuse 1988). The sample of respondents used in this study had an age range of 23–32 in 1988, and 32.6% of the men in that sample reported having used cocaine at some time in their lives, slightly higher than the 32.3% figure reported in the NHS survey for a similarly aged (26–34) group of men.[11] 70.6% of the men in this sample reported having used marijuana at some time, compared to 68.1% of men in the NHS. Also consistent with the NHS results are the responses of women in the present sample. Of the women in this sample—who, like the men, were aged 23–32—21.2% reported having used cocaine at some time and 58.9% reported having used marijuana at some time, rates that closely match the corresponding figures of 21.0% and 56.2% for the 26–34-year-old women in the NHS. This finding raises questions about the extent of under-reporting in the NLSY, and particularly about whether there was in fact substantial under-reporting in 1984, as suggested by Mensch and Kandel (1988). Furthermore, Sickles and Taubman (1991) reported findings from an unpublished NLS study that suggest, contrary to Mensch and Kandel's criticism, that the self-reports in the NLSY are reliable.

For both marijuana and cocaine, five separate measures of drug use were used in the cross-sectional analyses: a linear measure of lifetime use that takes on values of 0–5, corresponding to the categories in Table 3.4; a linear measure of lifetime use that uses the midpoints of the categories observed in Table 3.4; two similar measures for past 30 day use; and a dummy variable indicating a relatively heavy amount of lifetime use and non-zero past 30 day use.[12] It should be noted that the intervals used to code the illicit drug use responses changed between the two surveys. The estimates for the drug use equations were obtained by OLS methods for the linear measures, and by a probit regression model for the dummy variable indicating heavy use.

For the longitudinal models, the coding intervals used to group the data according to lifetime drug use were standardized between the two years, and only the simple (non-midpoint) linear measures were used in the analysis.[13] These variables took on values from 0 to 4, indicating the following frequencies of use: 0, 1–9, 10–39, 40–99, and 100 or more times. In addition, a differenced version of this linear lifetime measure was created, and this variable took on values ranging from 0, for no change in use, to 4, for changes in reported lifetime use exceeding 99 (that is, in effect, reports of 100 or more instances of use in the past four years). Since lifetime drug use cannot decline, all analyses were estimated twice—once with consistency of response imposed on the data by using the 1984 value if the value reported in 1988 was below that in 1984, and a second time with no such adjustment of contradictory values. The results do not differ according to which method is used, and the results reported in the text are for data in which consistency of the response has been imposed.

As noted above, the grouped nature of the data limits the value of this differenced variable, since much of the variation in use over time is unobservable. For example, individuals who were in the highest category of use in 1984 will never be observed to have an increase in use. To better differentiate between types of users, two additional variables were created to be used in conjunction with this differenced measure of lifetime use. The first is a dummy variable indicating no reported use in either survey, and the second is a dummy variable indicating initiation into use between the two surveys.[14] Measures created for past 30 day drug use were similar, except that the two additional dummy variables were not used in the analysis of the effect of recent drug use.

CROSS-SECTIONAL RESULTS

One purpose of this paper is to use the 1988 NLSY survey year information to update the previous cross-sectional estimates of the effect of illicit drug use on wages. The model used to generate these estimates closely follows that in my 1991 study (Kaestner 1991), with only a few minor modifications.[15] Table 3.5 lists the parameter estimates of the effect of illicit drug use on the wage, and a full set of estimates is provided in the appendix. Five separate models were estimated for each gender group and both years of data. For example, lifetime cocaine use and past 30 day cocaine use were not entered into the same model,

Table 3.5

Cross-Sectional Estimates of the Effect of Illicit Drug Use on the Natural Logarithm of the Wage (Standard Errors in Parentheses)

Drug Type/Model		1984		1988	
		Men	Women	Men	Women
		Marijuana Use			
1	Lifetime Use	.042**	.022	.031	.044*
	(0,1,2,3,4,5)	(.022)	(.024)	(.028)	(.028)
2	Lifetime Use	.0002**	.0002	.001	.002
	(midpoints)	(.0001)	(.0002)	(.001)	(.001)
3	Heavy Use	.161	.166	.424**	.246
	(0,1)	(.123)	(.173)	(.192)	(.286)
4	Past 30 Day Use	.065*	.052	.034	.153
	(0,1,2,3,4,5,6)	(.003)	(.047)	(.060)	(.122)
5	Past 30 Day Use	.011+	.010	.006	.012
	(midpoints)	(.006)	(.008)	(.012)	(.017)
		Cocaine Use			
1	Lifetime Use	.096*	.124*	.046	.153***
	(0,1,2,3,4,5)	(.052)	(.066)	(.044)	(.051)
2	Lifetime Use	.001*	.002**	.003	.010**
	(midpoints)	(.001)	(.001)	(.002)	(.004)
3	Heavy Use	.012	.449	1.033**	−.361
	(0,1)	(.276)	(.364)	(.418)	(.509)
4	Past 30 Day Use	.313**	.515**	.315	.493
	(0,1,2,3,4,5,6)	(.142)	(.227)	(.221)	(.573)
5	Past 30 Day Use	.098**	.169**	.077*	.055
	(midpoints)	(.046)	(.079)	(.048)	(.144)
Observations		2852	2619	2907	2724

Notes: In all models the actual value of drug use is replaced by its predicted value. In models 1, 2, 4, and 5, the prediction method was an OLS regression. In model 3, a probit procedure was utilized, and the dummy variable was replaced by the predicted probability. All models include the inverse mills ratio associated with the Heckman two step sample selection correction.
*Statistically significant at the .10 level; **at the .05 level; ***at the .01 level.

due to the high degree of collinearity between the two predicted measures of illicit drug use. The same reasoning would also apply to the other models in which separate drug use measures were entered.

The parameter estimates associated with the 1988 survey year data are generally similar to those for 1984. In fact, the estimates of the effect of illicit drug use on the wage are large, positive, and frequently significant in both years, across both gender groups, and for both types of drugs. The only negative effect observed among the estimates is associated with heavy cocaine use (as defined in this paper) among the 1988 female sample. This coefficient has a very low level of significance, and its importance should be discounted accordingly. The coefficient on heavy cocaine use for men in 1988, however, has a somewhat unbelievably large, positive effect, which is statistically significant. In general, the results listed in Table 3.5 contradict prior expectations regarding the effect of illicit drug use on the wage, and are consistent with results that have been pre-viously reported. The results for the 1984 survey data are virtually the same as those I reported three years ago (Kaestner 1991), in the study that provides the framework for the analysis used here.

Respondents in the cross-sectional sample from 1988 were, on average, four years older than those in the 1984 sample. Therefore, if the detrimental effects of drug use are cumulative, the potential for observing a negative relationship between illicit drug use and wages should be greater in 1988 than in 1984. The results reported above, however, do not support this hypothesis. For men, the magnitude and significance of the results tend to diminish somewhat across years, but for women the opposite is true. Moreover, the changes in magnitude may be explained by slight differences between the units of measurement of the drug use variables in the two survey years. On the other hand, drug use may have adverse effects on wages that become noticeable only over a period longer than four years.

FIXED EFFECT ESTIMATES

The cross-sectional results are surprising, and most observers would probably consider them inadequate as a description of the true relationship between drug use and wages. The cross-sectional estimates are questionable primarily due to the possibility that there are unobserved characteristics that have been omitted from the analysis that are correlated with both drug use and the wage. To address this problem, I created a limited panel of data consisting of a matched sample of respondents present in both years and implemented a fixed effects estimator. The model used to generate these estimates is specified above, and is a relatively unrestrictive version of a model of first differences.

Before examining the fixed effects estimates, note that the cross-sectional mod-els of Table 3.5 were re-estimated using the matched sample. If attrition in the sample is an important source of potential bias, the cross-sectional results using the matched sample should differ from those reported in Table 3.5. On the other hand, if attrition is not a problem, the estimates from a cross-sectional analysis should be similar. In fact, when the cross-sectional models were re-estimated on the matched sample, the results (not shown) differed very little. The signs as-sociated with the drug use coefficients were identical, and the magnitudes of the drug effects were very close to those reported in Table 3.5. The standard errors associated with the estimates, however, were larger, and the effects were therefore reduced in significance.

There were two exceptions to these generalizations, and both involved the effect of past 30 day marijuana use on the female wage. In 1984 and 1988 the estimates of this effect were substantially smaller for the matched sample than for the full sample. Thus, to the extent that the cross-sectional and panel data estimates differ, that difference does not stem from changes in the sample, except possibly for the effect of past 30 day marijuana use on the wages of women.

Table 3.6
Fixed Effects Estimates of the Effect of Illicit Drug Use on the Natural Logarithm of
the Wage (Standard Errors in Parentheses)

		Cocaine Use		Marijuana Use	
Drug Type/Model		Men	Women	Men	Women
1	Lifetime Use 1984	−.224	.828*	−.079	−.277
	(0,1,2,3,4)	(.428)	(.428)	(.284)	(.277)
	Lifetime Use 1988	−.137	.607*	−.086	−.254
	(0,1,2,3,4)	(.275)	(.316)	(.219)	(.271)
2	Change in Lifetime	−.024	.276	−.093	−.250
	Use, 1988–84	(.155)	(.223)	(.208)	(.270)
3	Change in Lifetime	−.183	.538	−.032	−.129
	Use, 1988–84	(.317)	(.380)	(.219)	(.399)
	New User	−.225	.748	−.523	−.812
		(.586)	(.687)	(.530)	(.928)
	Never Used	−.274	.521**	.130	−.159
		(.338)	(.255)	(.238)	(.206)
4	Past 30 Day Use, 1984	−.106	.159	−.096	.024
	(0,1,2,3,4,5,6)	(.467)	(.343)	(.105)	(.130)
	Past 30 Day Use, 1988	−.094	.525	−.186	.086
	(0,1,2,3,4,5,6)	(.405)	(.700)	(.152)	(.252)
5	Change in Past 30	−.101	.166	−.051	−.002
	Day Use, 1988–84	(.409)	(.343)	(.106)	(.112)
Observations		1858	1623	1858	1623

Notes: In all models the actual value of drug use is replaced by its predicted value, and the prediction
    method was an OLS regression. Note that the signs associated with the 1984 drug variable
    coefficients have been reversed, since the regression package assumes that the model is additive.
    All models include the inverse mills ratio for each year.
*Statistically significant at the .10 level; **at the .05 level; ***at the .01 level.

Table 3.6 lists the parameter estimates associated with the illicit drug use
measures; a complete set of results is contained in the appendix. For simplicity,
the discussion of the results will be in terms of the effect of illicit drug use on
the level of the wage, even though the underlying model is of wage changes.

Drug Use by Men

All of the estimates of the effect of illicit drug use on wages of men are negative.
They are not statistically significant, however, and the large size of the standard
errors associated with the parameter estimates underscores the need to approach
these estimates cautiously. The magnitudes of these estimates are substantial, but
they are difficult to interpret given the way illicit drug use is measured. For
example, a one-unit increase in cocaine use over the preceding four-year period
would be expected to reduce an individual's wage anywhere from 2% (model 2)

to 22% (model 3 for a new user), and a one-unit increase in marijuana use would be expected to reduce the wage by between 9% (model 2) and 52% (model 3 for a new user).

The problem lies in the interpretation of what is meant by a one-unit increase, since the groupings into drug use categories were somewhat irregular. The specification of the illicit drug use variables in model 3 helps clarify the interpretation. For both marijuana and cocaine, an increase in use that is also associated with an individual's initiation into use has a more adverse impact on an individual's wage than an increase in use for a previous user.[16] In the case of cocaine, approximately 80% of all observed increases in use—531 male respondents, or 21.3% of the total male sample—were for people initiating use, with over half of these cases having a total reported use of only 1 to 9 times over the four-year period. For marijuana, approximately 40% of the observed increases in use—589 respondents, or 23.6% of the total male sample—were for individuals who initiated use during this period, and about a third of these cases were individuals who reported use of only 1 to 9 times during the period.[17]

It is not known whether the negative effect associated with the initiation measure of drug use is due primarily to the phenomenon of initiation itself, or to initiation into heavy use over a relatively short period of time. If the latter reason accounts for the negative effect, we would expect this effect to be greater in the case of marijuana, since a larger proportion of the individuals who started using marijuana than of those who started using cocaine became relatively heavy users. This expectation is in fact supported, as illustrated in Table 3.6.

There is, however, one anomalous result regarding the male sample. The wages of those men who never used cocaine is expected to be 27% lower than the wages of similar individuals who previously used cocaine, but did not increase their use during the four-year period between 1984 and 1988. Since most individuals reported a low level of lifetime use, this result implies that individuals who experimented with cocaine fared better than those who did not. Initiation into cocaine use over this period, however, does have a negative effect on the wage, as does an increase in use. Thus, those individuals who tried cocaine while relatively young, but did not increase their use afterward, are expected to have the highest wage, even compared to non-users.

Drug Use by Women

The findings for the female sample are qualitatively different from those for the male sample. Cocaine use appears to have had a large positive effect on women's wages. A one unit increase in cocaine use increased the wage by between 28% (model 2) and 75% (model 3, new user). These effects are extremely large, and in some cases reach commonly accepted levels of significance. The results obtain both for lifetime cocaine use and for past 30 day cocaine use. The model 3 estimates for women differ sharply from those for the male sample. These estimates suggest that the women who tried cocaine at a relatively young age tended to have a lower wage than women who either never used cocaine or initiated use between 1984 and 1988. Over 83% of all observed increases in use—447 respondents, or 14.1% of the total female sample—were individuals who first tried cocaine during this period, and over 60% of these individuals reported lifetime use of 1–9 times by 1988. Thus, very few of the observed increases in use are among relatively heavy users. Initiation into cocaine use during this period did not adversely affect women's wages.

The effect of marijuana use was negative for the female sample, although past 30 day marijuana use does have a positive coefficient. As was the case for the other estimates reported in Table 3.6, the standard errors associated with these estimates are large, and result in relatively low levels of significance.

CONCLUSION

This study has had two purposes: first, to update previous cross-sectional estimates of the effect of illicit drug use on the wage, using data from the 1988 wave of the NLSY; and second, using both the 1984 and 1988 NLSY, to provide a set of longitudinal estimates of the effect of illicit drug use on the wage. The longitudinal estimates are preferred, since in theory this methodology controls for potentially important unobserved individual characteristics that cause the cross-sectional estimates to be biased. I performed both analyses separately by gender.

In regard to the first objective, my estimates of the effect of illicit drug use on the wage using the 1988 NLSY data are consistent with those I obtained in 1991 using the 1984 NLSY data. Both sets of estimates indicate large, positive, statistically significant effects of illicit drug use on the wage, for both gender groups and for both marijuana and cocaine use.

These findings raise several disturbing questions related to drug prevention policy. Much time and money has been and continues to be invested in deterring and preventing drug use, and this investment is based on the proposition that illicit drug use adversely affects users. Few economists would be willing to argue that illicit drug use is somehow beneficial for young people, and is a characteristic that is rewarded in the labor market. Thus, an explanation of the cross-sectional results that would confirm our commonly held beliefs would be comforting. The most commonly invoked explanation of that kind has been that important unobserved characteristics that are positively correlated with both wages and illicit drug use underlie the empirical relationship found in cross-sectional models.

The longitudinal estimates presented in this paper, however, provide only partial support for that explanation. To some extent, the large standard errors associated with the fixed effects estimates can be interpreted to mean that there are really no effects of illicit drug use on the wage that are significantly different from zero. Unfortunately, the standard that must be imposed to draw that conclusion may be too stringent for this type of empirical analysis. If the sign and magnitude of the effects of illicit drug use on the wage are examined, the evidence is mixed. Among the male sample, illicit drug use tended to be negatively related to wages—a finding in accord with most people's expectations, and one that would support continued vigilance against drug use. Similarly, among the female sample, lifetime marijuana use appears to have been negatively associated with the wage; but recent marijuana use (use within the previous 30 days) had a positive effect, and, more important, cocaine use (both recent and lifetime) was positively related to the wage, and had quite a large impact.

There are two possible explanations for the results reported in this paper. The mixed nature of the preferred estimates—those obtained using the longitudinal data—implies that there is a wide range of wage effects among people who consume the same amount of drugs. Thus, illicit drug use may be a highly idiosyncratic phenomenon that has a variety of consequences that depend on the individual, the type of drug, or some combination of the two. The adverse physical and psychological consequences of drug use are known to be quite individual-specific, and a given level of use may therefore lead to a wide variety of labor market outcomes. Another possibility is that some drug users choose jobs in which their drug use has the least impact on their productivity, but others do not. In addition, the drug use measures incorporated in the analysis were extremely crude, and exactly what they measure may differ drastically from person to person. These considerations may explain why the observed wage effects of illicit drug use differ for men and women and are influenced by the type of drug and timing of its use.

The second possible explanation for the results obtained in this paper is that the current analysis, although a significant improvement on past work, is still inadequate. The fixed effects methodology used in this paper controls for characteristics that do not change over time, but among a sample of young adults in their twenties, there may be few characteristics that remain constant. These shortcomings of the analysis point to refinements that should be made in future studies to allow the identification of important personality traits and patterns of drug use that affect the wage.

I believe this study has taken an important new step in the analysis of the effect of illicit drug use. It is the first analysis to exploit longitudinal data, and therefore controls for unobserved person-specific effects that are important determinants of the wage. It has provided some important insight into the effect that these unobserved factors have on the relationship between illicit drug use and wages, and it has provided a foundation for future work on that subject.

NOTES

1. Kandel and Davies (1990) estimated a model in which the 1985 wage was the dependent variable, and all independent variables were measured as of 1984. Included among the independent variables were the 1984 wage and drug use, both of which were treated as exogenous. In addition, the authors made no attempt to correct for selection bias due to the labor force participation decision.

2. The two papers do not treat the problem in exactly the same way. In my 1991 study, I provided only a simple model similar to that found in Stigler and Becker (1977). In this model, the wage is simply the price of time used to produce consumption goods, including drug consumption. Gill and Michaels (1990) presented a much more detailed model, in which the role played by the wage, though similar, is more complex. In their model, drug time is being produced, and the wage becomes part of the full price.

3. This strategy is different from that found in Kaestner (1991). In that paper, I obtained the reduced from estimates of equation (2) using only employed persons, and a selectivity correction was applied to this equation as well as the wage equation (1). The results are little affected by which of these strategies is chosen.

4. In computing the standard errors for this model, it is important to take account of the fact that several of the right-hand-side variables (specifically, drug use and sample selection terms) are predicted values. Murphy and Topel (1985) outlined the procedure for calculating the exact standard errors for a simple version of this type of model. The current case is non-standard, given the inclusion of the selectivity terms. In the cross-sectional regressions, the standard errors are those that correct for the inclusion of the selection correction term, but ignore the fact that drug use is a predicted value. For the panel data estimates, in which there are two correction terms and two predicted drug use measures, the generalized correction for heteroscedasticity suggested by White (1980) is used to estimate the variance-covariance matrix. The latter procedure remains incorrect, but it should represent an improvement over OLS estimates.

5. To test the restrictions implied by equation (1c), I performed a series of Wald tests. The Wald test is appropriate in this case because the F-test assumes homoscedasticity. The variance-covariance matrix used for the Wald test incorporated the White (1980) correction for heteroscedasticity, and is only an approximation of the true estimate.

Although not all of the restrictions could be rejected, many were found to be invalid. In addition, the results of the Wald tests differed by gender, with more of the restrictions being rejected in the equations for women than in those for men.

6. The drug use measures are discrete, categorical variables, and taking first differences of these measures would also result in a discrete measure. The most appropriate estimation procedure for categorical variables of this type is an ordered probit (logit) model (Sickles and Taubman 1991; Kaestner 1991). In the cross-sectional model, this methodology is rejected, due to the severe collinearity between the predicted drug use categories that are used in the two step procedure; a person with a high probability of being a heavy cocaine user also has a high probability of being a moderate cocaine user. In the panel data analysis, a fixed effects model of an ordered categorical variable would need to be estimated, and that task is beyond the scope of this paper (Chamberlain 1984).

7. The standard errors reported in the text are from an OLS regression, and they ignore the fact that there are several predicted values among the right-hand-side variables.

8. The labor force participation model is estimated separately for each year, but includes all the exogenous variables in the model. For example, the respondent's education in both of the years under consideration will be included in the estimates of the probability of working in period 1. This specification can be interpreted as a reduced form version of the Chamberlain (1980) random effects probit model, and thus accounts for unobserved heterogeneity in the selection equation.

9. The 1988 NLSY survey limited the illicit drug use questions to include only marijuana and cocaine.

10. The empirical strategy is to use a Two Stage Least Squares (2SLS) estimation

procedure, and thus the drug use measures will be replaced by their respective predicted values. This procedure is appropriate due to both the simultaneity and measurement error problems.

11. The NHS numbers would be expected to be higher, since the NHS sample was somewhat older than the sample examined here, and therefore had a greater chance of having initiated use. In addition, the NLSY oversamples blacks and respondents from the South, two groups that have reported levels of illicit drug use below that of the entire population (Kozel and Adams 1985).

12. Heavy use of cocaine is defined as lifetime use of 40 or more times, and heavy use of marijuana is defined as lifetime use of 100 or more times.

13. The large intervals used in the NLSY make it difficult to use midpoints. There is little information on the nature of the true distribution of drug users within intervals, and any estimate of the mean within the interval would be ad hoc. In addition, estimating the mean of the open-ended interval would also be error-ridden. Because of these concerns, I used the untransformed data.

14. The predicted values of these variables are obtained by maximum likelihood probit methods. The probits are estimated independently of each other.

15. The differences are related to aspects of the sample, exogenous variables, and estimation strategy. First, in this study, individuals living in temporary quarters have been deleted, as have individuals with missing information related to the measure of self-esteem. Next, age and AFQT test score enter the model as quadratics. Finally, as mentioned in note 3, the reduced form drug estimates were obtained using the entire sample, as opposed to only the employed.

16. The coefficients on the change in use and initiation into use variables should be considered in an additive fashion when deriving the total wage effect of initiation into use. The total effect is not, however, the simple sum of the two estimates.

17. The figures on initiation into use of marijuana that are reported by the matched sample indicate that more initiation into marijuana use took place than is implied in Table 3.4.

REFERENCES

Center for Human Resource Research. 1990. *NLS Handbook 1990*. Columbus: Ohio State University.

Chamberlain, Gary. 1984. "Panel Data." In Zvi Griliches and Michael Intrilligator, eds., *Handbook of Econometrics*, Vol. 2. Amsterdam: North Holland, pp. 1248–1313.

———. 1982. "Multivariate Regression Models for Panel Data." *Journal of Econometrics*, Vol. 18, No. 1, pp. 5–46.

———. 1980. "Analysis of Covariance with Qualitative Data." *Review of Economic Studies*, Vol. 47, No. 2, pp. 225–38.

Gill, Andrew M., and Robert J. Michaels. 1990. "Drug Use and Earnings: Accounting for Self Selection of Drug Users." Working Paper 11–90, California State University–Fullerton.

———. 1992. "Does Drug Use Lower Wages?" *Industrial and Labor Relations Review*, Vol. 45, No. 3, pp. 93–105.

Goldstein, Avram, and Harold Kalant. 1990. "Drug Policy: Striking the Right Balance." *Science*, Vol. 249 (September 28), pp. 1513–21.

Gust, Steven W., J. Michael Walsh, Linda B. Thomas, and Dennis J. Crouch. 1991. *Drugs in the Workplace: Research and Evaluation Data*, Volume 2. Washington, D.C.: U.S. Department of Health and Human Services.

Hayghe, Howard V. 1991. "Survey of Employer Anti-Drug Programs." In Steven W. Gust, J. Michael Walsh, Linda B. Thomas, and Dennis J. Crouch, eds., *Drugs in the Workplace: Research and Evaluation Data*, Volume 2. Washington, D.C.: U.S. Department of Health and Human Services.

Heckman, James J. 1976. "The Common Structure of Statistical Models of Truncation, Sample Selection and Limited Dependent Variables." *Annals of Economic and Social Measurement*, Vol. 5, No. 4, pp. 475–92.

Kaestner, Robert. 1991. "The Effect of Illicit Drug Use on the Wages of Young Adults." *Journal of Labor Economics*, Vol. 9, No. 4, pp. 381–412.

———. 1994. "The Effect of Illicit Drug Use on the Labor Supply of Young Adults." *Journal of Human Resources*, Vol. 29, No. 1.

Kandel, Denise B., and Mark Davies. 1990. "Labor Force Experiences of a National Sample of Young Adult Men." *Youth and Society*, Vol. 21, No. 4, pp. 411–45.

Kandel, Denise B., and John Logan. 1984. "Patterns of Drug Use from Adolescence to Early Adulthood." *American Journal of Public Health*, Vol. 74, No. 7, pp. 660–66.

Kozel, Nicholas J., and Edgar H. Adams. 1985. *Cocaine Use in America: Epidemiological and Clinical Perspectives*. Washington, D.C.: U.S. Department of Health and Human Services.

Mensch, Barbara S., and Denise B. Kandel. 1988. "Underreporting of Substance Use in a National Longitudinal Youth Cohort." *Public Opinion Quarterly*, Vol. 52, No. 1, pp. 100–124.

Murphy, Kevin M., and Robert H. Topel. 1985. "Estimation and Inference in Two-Step Econometric Models." *Journal of Business and Economic Statistics*, Vol. 3, No. 4, pp. 370–79.

National Institute on Drug Abuse. 1986. *Drug Abuse in the Workplace*. Washington, D.C.: GPO.

———. 1988. *National Household Survey on Drug Abuse*. Rockville, Md.: U.S. Department of Health and Human Services.

———. 1991. *National Household Survey on Drug Abuse*. Rockville, Md.: U.S. Department of Health and Human Services.

Raveis, V. H., and Denise B. Kandel. 1987. "Changes in Drug Behavior from the Middle to Late Twenties: Initiation, Persistence, and the Cessation of Use." *American Journal of Public Health*, Vol. 77, pp. 607–11.

Register, Charles A., and Donald R. Williams. 1992. "Labor Market Effects of Marijuana and Cocaine Use Among Young Men." *Industrial and Labor Relations Review*, Vol. 45, No. 3, pp. 106–23.

Sickles, Robin, and Paul Taubman. 1991. "Who Uses Illegal Drugs." *American Economic Review*, Vol. 81, No. 2, pp. 248–51.

Stein, Judith A., Michael D. Newcomb, and P. M. Bentler. 1988. "Structure of Drug Use Behaviors and Consequences Among Young Adults: Multitrait Multimethod Assessment of Frequency, Quantity, Work Site, and Problem Substance Use." *Journal of Applied Psychology*, Vol. 73, pp. 595–605.

Stigler, George, and Gary Becker. 1977. "De Gustibus Non Est Disputandum." *American Economic Review*, Vol. 67, No. 2, pp. 76–90.

Chapter 4

Pre-Employment Drug Testing

Some studies have assessed the relationship between testing positive for marijuana on a pre-employment drug screening and subsequent job performance measured in terms of problem measures like absenteeism, turnover, disciplinary actions, and accidents. Unlike most of the controlled experimental research, this research deals directly with applicants for employment, so it is not as vulnerable to criticisms about external validity as is controlled experimental research. Further, the best of these studies (e.g., Zwerling et al., 1990) use urine screens or other methods to confirm marijuana use, thus avoiding the potential problems of using self-report data, which plague survey research on this topic. As noted in Table 4.2, studies using this methodology do not deal with attention, learning, memory, psychomotor skills, or motivation, so the discussion will focus directly on job performance.

JOB PERFORMANCE

Studies have examined a variety of outcome measures. However, involuntary turnover and on-the-job accidents have received the greatest attention.

Turnover

McDaniel (1988) examined self-reports of marijuana use by over ten thousand successful applicants to the four military services and collected data on the number subsequently discharged for "failure to meet minimum behavioral requirements" (McDaniel, 1988: 719–720). Respondents indicated their lifetime frequency of use and the age at which they began using marijuana. They combined these into a pre-employment drug use measure that was significantly related to the probability of discharge for unsuitability. Military recruits who tested positive for marijuana were 33% more likely to be discharged for unsuitability. Though the results were statistically significant because of the large sample size, marijuana use explained less that one half of one percent of the variance of the probability of discharge for unsuitability (McDaniel, 1988: 721–722).

Blank and Fenton (1989) analyzed turnover data for 482 male navy recruits who tested positive for marijuana when entering the service compared to a control group who did not. After 2½ years, 43% of those who had tested positive had separated from the navy while only 19% of the control group had. In this study, those who had tested positive were given counseling and in some cases subjected to random drug tests during this period. Since they may have been discharged for positive test results, potential criterion contamination may have contributed to the high number of discharges in the marijuana positive group.

Parish (1989), in a study involving 180 new employees, found that those who tested positive for any illicit drug were 28% more likely to be terminated than those who did not. However, the results for those testing positive for marijuana alone were not significant.

Normand, Salyards, and Mahoney (1990) examined 5,465 applicants to the U.S. Postal Service, 6.3% of which tested positive for marijuana. They found no significant relationship between positive test results and future involuntary turnover.

In summary, the body of evidence suggests that those who test positive for marijuana on pre-employment drug screens are more likely to turn over than those who do not. Estimates of the magnitude of this relationship vary considerably but the McDaniel and Blank and Fenton results suggest that marijuana users are one-third to twice as likely to separate from military service. The Normand et al. results suggest that the relationships may be much smaller in the postal service.

These results have lead some to argue that pre-employment drug testing is not cost-effective (Wish, 1990) and that it would be more cost-effective to use "impairment testing" in which the focus is on job impairment rather than drug use (Trice & Steele, 1995). Whether the results justify screening applicants for marijuana use depends on the cost of turnover in a particular job and the relationship between turnover and marijuana use in that specific job. If the employing organization invests heavily in training employees for a certain job, turnover would be expensive, and the use of pre-employment marijuana screens might be justified if marijuana use does predict turnover in that job.

Accidents

The second common dependent variable in these studies is workplace accidents. The study by Normand et al. (1990), cited above, examined workplace accidents in addition to turnover and found no significant relationship between positive results on a pre-employment drug screen for marijuana and number of accidents on the job.

In contrast, Crouch, Webb, Peterson, Buller, and Rollins (1989) showed that, among employees of a single company, Utah Power & Light, those who tested positive for marijuana, cocaine, and other drugs were five times more likely to have a reportable vehicle accident than a matched control group. Though their results were based on employees who used a variety of drugs, it is reasonable to assume that marijuana alone accounted for some increase in reportable vehicular accidents.

Zwerling, Ryan, and Orav (1990) conducted a study of the relationship between pre-employment urine tests for marijuana and adverse employment outcomes in over 2,500 postal employees, 7.8% of whom tested positive for marijuana. The results of the screen were not used in the employment decision or given to employees or their supervisors. Thus, it is unlikely that the study's findings were biased by differential treatment of those with positive drug tests by their supervisors or others. Employees with a preemployment drug screen positive for marijuana had 55% more industrial accidents and 85% more injuries. All these results were statistically significant though, as the authors observed, the effect sizes were small (Zwerling et al., 1990: 2643).

MacDonald (1995), used self-report data from a mail survey of 882 Canadian employees in a variety of jobs, 8.6% of which admitted to using marijuana. He found a significant positive relationship between marijuana use and workplace accidents. Those who used marijuana were approximately 2½ times more likely to be involved in accidents than those who did not. MacDonald also found that alcohol use and legal drug use had stronger relationships to accidents than use of illicit drugs. He concluded, "Overall, the results indicated that illicit drug use does not appear to be a major cause of job injuries" (MacDonald, 1995: 882).

In summary, the relationship between tests for marijuana use and accidents is ambiguous. Some studies have found significant relationships between testing positive and subsequent injuries but others have not. Some studies (Crouch et al., 1989; MacDonald, 1995) have estimated that marijuana users may be several times as likely as nonusers to experience accidents. Though these results are not conclusive, they support the use of pre-employment screens for marijuana in jobs where the costs of accidents may be very high or may involve loss of life (e.g., airline pilots).

METHODOLOGICAL ISSUES

There are problems with the use of pre-employment screening as a measure of the effects of marijuana in the workplace. First, a positive score on a urine test demonstrates only that the employee used marijuana at some time in the two to three weeks prior to the test. It does not provide any information on drug use during the period when the employee is in the job. Second, not all studies control for use of other drugs in addition to marijuana. Though some studies focus on those who tested positive *only* for marijuana, others include some who used marijuana and other drugs. In these studies, the relationship between marijuana and accidents may be contaminated by the effects of other drugs. Third, pre-employment drug screening may not identify all drug users but only those without the foresight or motivation to refrain from smoking marijuana for a sufficient time before the test. In many of these studies (e.g., Normand et al., 1990; Zwerling et al., 1990) the proportion of applicants or employees testing positive for marijuana is less than 9%, smaller than the estimates of the proportion of the general population who use marijuana. This suggests that not all of the users are being identified, perhaps because some have the foresight and motivation to prepare for the drug test.

Employees without foresight or motivation may be expected to have a greater number of employment problems whether or not they use marijuana. Therefore, this method may bias results toward a negative relationship. Nonetheless, even if positive test results are merely a marker for carelessness, it may be economically justified for employers to use them to screen out such employees.

This same logic does not, however, apply to attempts to reduce drug use in organizations or society as a whole. Unless marijuana actually *causes* performance declines, attempts to reduce its use may not have any economic benefits.

COMMENTS ON THE TWO STUDIES INCLUDED

We have included two studies of pre-employment drug use based on two different data collection methods. The first (McDaniel, 1988) uses self-report data and the second (Normand et al., 1990) makes use of urine samples.

In the McDaniel study, Table 2.2 shows that those who reported using marijuana were more likely to be discharged from military service as unsuitable and, in general, the probability of discharge was greater for those who used marijuana more frequently and began using marijuana at an earlier age. However, the reliability of the self-report data on marijuana use are suspect.

The Normand et al. study, conducted at the U.S. Postal Service, also examined involuntary separation and drug use. Table 4.10 shows no significant effect for marijuana use on involuntary turnover. The study also examined absenteeism and Table 4.4 shows no significant effect for marijuana use.

Thus, the two studies seem to impart different conclusions on the effects of pre-employment marijuana use. Possible reasons for the different results include differences in organizations studied (military vs. the postal service) and differences in methods of collecting data on drug use. Further, though McDaniel states that there was no criterion contamination, some of the people in his study were discharged for "alcohol and drug problems," which raises the possibility of criterion contamination.

Does Pre-Employment Drug Use Predict On-the-Job Suitability?

Michael A. McDaniel*

ABSTRACT

Drug testing is increasingly used in the screening of applicants for employment. Despite the growth of drug testing, there is little research that examines the value of pre-employment drug-use information in the prediction of post-employment suitability. This research, which was based on a sample of 10,188 young adults, examined the criterion-related validity of pre-employment drug-use information. For all drugs examined, the greater the frequency of use and the earlier the age at which the drug was first used, the greater the probability of a person being classified as unsuitable after hire. However, the operational validity of each drug variable was influenced by the base rate of drug use. The low base rates for some drugs make their operational validity of limited value. The operational validity of the marijuana frequency-of-use measure (.07) was approximately equal to that of less frequently used drugs (e.g., stimulants and depressants). No strong moderators of the validity of a drug-composite measure were found.

INTRODUCTION

Drug use in the work place is a subject of growing concern. It has been estimated that about one-half of work place injuries and nearly 40% of work place deaths

*The opinions expressed in this paper are those of the author and do not necessarily represent those of the author's employer or the Department of Defense. Earlier versions of this paper were presented at the Third Annual Conference of the Society for Industrial and Organizational Psychology, Dallas, Texas (1988), and the National Institute on Drug Abuse conference: Drugs in the Workplace: Research and Evaluation Data, Washington, DC (September, 1988). This paper has benefitted from comments of the editor and two anonymous reviewers. This article originally appeared in *Personnel Psychology*, Volume 41, pp. 717–729, 1988.

are attributed to drug or alcohol use. While compelling data are lacking, it is estimated that about two-thirds of the people entering the work force have used illegal drugs (Tyson & Vaughn, 1987). In response to concerns about drugs in the work place, pre-employment drug testing has become more prevalent among employers (Lindquist, 1988).

Although the reliability of drug-testing methods is receiving increasing attention (Council on Scientific Affairs, 1987), little research has examined the criterion-related validity of pre-employment drug use as a predictor of employment suitability. Kagel, Battalio, and Miles (1980; also see Miles, Battalio, Kagel, & Rhodes, 1975) examined the relationship between marijuana use and job performance in an "experimental microeconomy." The volunteer subjects lived and worked for 98 days in wings of a hospital facility where they earned money by performing manual labor tasks that were paid for on a piecework basis. Access to almost all consumer goods during the experiment, including food, was through income earnings.

Marijuana had no effect on work output or hours worked, although subjects preferred leisure time activities after marijuana use. Kolb, Nail, and Gunderson (1975) examined 903 navy enlisted personnel to determine the relationship between pre-employment drug use and in-service drug use and job performance. The subjects were drawn from those who had been granted amnesty from prosecution for illegal drug use and admitted to a drug rehabilitation center. After being admitted to the rehabilitation center, the subjects provided self-report data on their pre-service drug use. The subjects were provided assurances regarding the anonymity and confidentiality of the data provided. Those who reported pre-service drug use advanced less rapidly in pay grade, incurred more disciplinary actions, and were more likely to use heroin while in the military service. The findings of neither the Kagel et al. (1980) nor the Kolb et al. (1975) studies display much external validity for the question of the effects of pre-employment drug use on employment suitability. The former study did not measure pre-employment drug use and used an artificial work setting. The latter study suffered from subject selection contaminants and the collection of pre-employment drug use under anonymous conditions, which failed to mirror the testing conditions in a pre-employment situation. To attempt to address the research gap on the drug-use/suitability issue, the present study provides large-sample evidence addressing the usefulness of pre-employment drug-use information in predicting on-the-job suitability.

In the present research, self-report survey data were used as the source of the pre-employment drug-use information. The use of self-report data has a long history in personnel psychology, and these data have proven to be effective predictors for a variety of performance domains (Owens, 1976). Several authors have reviewed the accuracy of self-reported usage of illegal drugs (Brown, 1974; Brown & Harding, 1973; Harrell, 1985; Nurco, 1985; Rouse, Kozel, & Richards, 1985). To obtain accurate self-reported drug-use information, several conditions are necessary. First, the respondent must know what drug was consumed. Illegal drugs are often distributed using colloquial names (e.g., "black beauties" for amphetamines). If the drug names used in the self-report questions are not familiar to the respondent, an inaccurate response is probable. Furthermore, illegal drugs may be misrepresented (e.g., LSD may be sold as mescaline), such that the respondent does not know the name of the drug consumed. A second condition for accurate reporting is that the respondent must remember the drug-usage information solicited by the question. Respondents may not accurately recall the frequency of drug consumption or the age at which they began the use of a drug. Third, respondents must be willing to report illegal drug use. Respondents can be expected to minimize or deny their socially undesirable behaviors. While some authors have reported problems with respondents over-reporting their drug use (Petzel, Johnson, & McKillip, 1973), it is reasonable to expect that most job applicants would be motivated to under-report their drug use.

Self-report measures can be contrasted with physiological measures (e.g., urinalysis) of drug use. While the accuracy of physiological measures of drug use is a matter of continuing debate, clearly the effectiveness of physiological measures available at present is restricted to identifying recent (e.g., days or weeks) drug use that leaves residual chemical markers in the user's body (American Federation of Labor and Congress of Industrial Organizations, 1987; Rosen, 1987). Thus, the physiological measures available to date have no value in identifying historical patterns of drug use. While self-report drug-use measures are subject to the respondent's intentional and unintentional distortions, they represent the only available method of obtaining historical data on the respondent's use of drugs.

METHOD

The drug-use items were included in the military's Educational and Biographical Information Survey (EBIS) (Means & Perelman, 1984). During the spring of 1983, the EBIS was administered to approximately 34,800 applicants for the four military services. Those military applicants who entered the military service within one year of completing the EBIS were defined as the study sample ($N = 10,188$). Ten drug-use items were available. These items covered the age at which one first used (1) marijuana and (2) hard drugs, (3) whether one had been arrested or convicted of a drug-related offense, and the frequency with which one had used, without a prescription by a doctor, the following drugs: (4) marijuana, (5) heroin, (6) cocaine, (7) stimulants, (8) depressants, (9) other narcotics, and (10) other drugs. The two questions concerning age at first drug use had response alternatives of "age 14 or younger," "age 15–17," "age 18 or older," "I never did this," and "don't recall age." For this variable, the response option "don't recall age" was considered a missing datum. Response option "I never did this" was placed at the older end of the age scale. The drug-related arrest question had response alternatives of "never arrested," "arrested," and "convicted." The response scale for the seven drug-frequency items had six response categories ranging from "never used" to used "50 times or more."

The employment unsuitability measure was defined as discharge from military service for reasons classified as "failure to meet minimum behavioral or performance criteria" on or before September 30, 1987. This discharge category included

Table 4.1

Means, Standard Deviations, Percent Missing, and Reliability of Drug Measures

Variable	N	Mean	SD	% Missing	Reliability
Age marijuana use	9,411	3.24	1.05	7.6	.60
Age hard drug use	9,449	3.94	.31	7.3	.33
Drug arrest	9,456	1.02	.16	7.2	.73
Frequency of					
Marijuana	9,355	.86	1.38	8.2	.54
Heroin	9,207	.01	.12	9.6	-.01
Cocaine	9,224	.07	.40	9.5	.23
Stimulants	9,286	.23	.73	8.9	.41
Depressants	9,267	.09	.43	9.0	.25
Other narcotics	9,261	.03	.24	9.1	.16
Other drugs	9,262	.04	.31	9.1	.30
Unsuitability discharge	10,188	.16	.37	0.0	NA

Notes: For the age items, a response of "age 14 or younger" was coded 1; "age 15–17" was coded 2; "age 18 or older" was coded 3; "never used" was coded 4. A mean score on the age item near 3.0 indicates that the mean response was approximately "age 18 or older." For the drug-arrest item, a response of "never arrested" was coded 1; "arrested" was coded 2; "convicted" was coded 3. A mean score of 1 indicates that the average response was "never arrested." For the seven drug-frequency items, a response of "never" was coded 0; "1–4 times" was coded 1; "10–24 times" was coded 3; "25–49 times" was coded 4; and "50 or more times" was coded 5.

unsuitable discharges stemming from alcohol and drug problems, "discreditable incidents," and other discipline problems, as well as dismissal from military training programs. The unsuitable discharge category did not include discharge from the service for medical reasons, dependency or hardship, and pregnancy. The reliability of this dichotomous criterion is unknown. In this sample of military accessions, 16% were discharged for unsuitability. For those discharged, the mean number of days in the service was 451, while the median number of days was 346. Sixty-eight percent of those who received an unsuitable discharge received it between 48 and 939 days of service.

The study employed a predictive research design. The drug information collected from subjects using the EBIS survey was not used in making decisions regarding service entry. Thus, there was no direct range restriction on the predictor. In addition, there was no criterion contamination. Those who made decisions about unsuitability discharge did not have access to this drug-use data.

RESULTS

Table 4.1 presents the sample size, mean, standard deviation, percentage of missing data, and test-retest reliability for each item. The test-retest reliabilities were estimated from a subsample ($N = 754$) of individuals who completed the EBIS survey twice. The average test-retest time lapse was 38 days. The reliability for the frequency of heroin use item was $-.01$; this item was dropped from further

Table 4.2
Percentage of Respondents in Each Response Category who are Classified as
Unsuitable (Sample Size in Parentheses)

	Age at First Drug Use				
	< = 14	15--17	< = 18	Never	No response
Marijuana	21.0	18.2	16.6	14.6	19.6
	(150/715)	(395/2176)	(109/655)	(859/5865)	(152/777)
Hard drugs	30.4	26.0	18.7	15.9	19.6
	(7/23)	(38/146)	(23/123)	(1452/9157)	(145/739)

	Drug-related arrests and convictions			
	No arrest	Arrest-- no conviction	Arrest-- conviction	No response
Drug offense	15.8	32.2	27.0	21.0
	(1472 / 9329)	(29/90)	(10/37)	(154/732)

	Frequency of drug use (times used)						
	Never	1--4	5--9	10--24	25--49	> = 50	No response
Marijuana	14.2	16.4	18.8	21.1	15.9	23.7	22.1
	(800 / 5652)	(297/1808)	(119/634)	(117/555)	(40/251)	(108/455)	(184/833)
Cocaine	15.5	20.2	28.6	23.4	33.3	18.8	22.0
	(1358 / 8788)	(63/312)	(14/49)	(11/47)	(4/12)	(3/16)	(212/964)
Stimulants	15.0	18.9	21.5	23.1	29.2	31.7	22.5
	(1213/8107)	(133/704)	(41/191)	(36/156)	(19/65)	(20/63)	(203/902)
Depressants	15.2	22.2	30.3	31.4	28.6	46.7	22.9
	(1331/8784)	(70/316)	(24/80)	(16/51)	(6/21)	(7/15)	(211/921)
Other narcotics	15.5	24.3	31.6	21.4	50.0	60.0	22.9
	(1402/9067)	(37/152)	(6/19)	(3/14)	(2/4)	(3/5)	(212/927)
Other drugs	15.5	23.0	25.0	26.9	20.0	33.3	22.8
	(1391/9000)	(41/178)	(11/44)	(7/26)	(1/5)	(3/9)	(211/926)

analysis. The reliabilities of the remaining drug variables range from .16 to .73.
While the reliabilities of some of the items are low, such levels of reliability are
not uncommon for single-item measures. The percentage of missing responses
ranges from 7.2% to 9.6%.

Table 4.2 presents the percentage of persons in each response category in nine
drug variables who were classified on the criterion as unsuitable. While there are
some departures from linearity, in general the younger one begins to use drugs
and the more one uses drugs, the greater is the probability of being unsuitable
for employment. Those who refused to respond to the drug items had unsuitability
rates similar to those who reported drug use. Note that although the unsuitability

rates for those who used drugs at an early age, those who were arrested or con-victed for drugs, or those who frequently used drugs were always higher than the rates for those who reported no drug use, the number of persons who reported using drugs, particularly drugs other than marijuana, was small.

Two drug-use composite measures were calculated. Drug-Use Composite Num-ber 1 was calculated by summing the drug questions with the two age questions being reversed scored. That is, those who first tried using a drug early in life would tend to score higher on the drug-composite scale than those who first used drugs later in life or who had never used drugs. Given that the nonresponders resembled the drug users in their unsuitability rates, nonresponders were scored as drug users in calculating the drug composite variable. For the two age-at-first-use questions, the nonresponders were scored as beginning drug use at age 14 or younger. For the arrest-and-conviction item, the nonresponders were scored as being convicted for drug use, and for the six drug-frequency items, the nonres-ponders were scored as using the drug 50 or more times. In brief, the higher the Drug-Use Composite Number 1 score, the higher one's involvement with drugs through early use, drug-related law contacts, or greater frequency of drug use. Those who refused to respond to the drug questions also scored high on the Drug-Use Composite Number 1. Drug-Use Composite Number 2 was calculated in the same manner as the first composite except that nonresponders were counted as missing data. To obtain a score on Drug-Use Composite Number 2, the applicant needed to provide usable responses to each of the nine drug-use items.

Table 4.3 displays the observed correlations between the drug use items, the two drug-use composites, a measure of general cognitive ability (AFQT), and the suitability criterion. Also listed is the percentage of persons, by item, who had used the drug at least once. For the drug arrest or conviction item, the listed statistic is the percentage of persons who had been either arrested or convicted for a drug-related offense. Although the drug-use measures were not used in selection, the variance on all but one of the drug measures was slightly greater in the applicant pool than in the subset of the applicant pool who entered the service. The variable age at first marijuana use had a slightly higher variance in the study sample than in the applicant pool. Table 4.3 lists the observed validity coefficients and, in parentheses, the coefficients corrected for range restriction.

The validity of the Drug-Use Composite Number 1 was analyzed to determine if it covaried with any of four moderators. The results of these analyses are pre-sented in Table 4.4. The first potential moderator was testing condition. About half of the subjects were told that their responses were for research purposes only and would not be used in screening decisions. The remaining applicants were permitted to infer that their responses could be used in screening. The validity of the drug composite was not strongly moderated by testing condition. There were no differences in the mean reported drug-use levels between the groups.

The second potential moderator was cognitive ability. One might argue that the more intelligent applicants would be less likely to report illegal drug use, and the resulting inaccuracy would lower the validity for the more intelligent appli-

Table 4.3
Validity of Pre-Employment Drug-Use Measures for Predicting On-the-Job
Suitability

Variable	N	r		% Used at least once
Age at first use of marijuana	9,411	-.05	(-.05)	38
Age at first hard drug use	9,449	-.04	(-.04)	3
Drug arrest/conviction	9,456	.05	(.06)	1
Frequency of drug use:				
Marijuana	9,355	.07	(.07)	31
Cocaine	9,224	.04	(.04)	5
Stimulants	9,286	.07	(.07)	13
Depressants	9,267	.07	(.08)	5
Other narcotics	9,261	.05	(.06)	2
Other drugs	9,262	.04	(.04)	3
Drug-Use Composite Number 1	10,188	.08	(.09)	49
Drug-Use Composite Number 2	8,461	.08	(.08)	40
AFQT percentile	10,188	-.06	(-.06)	NA

Notes: For the drug arrest/conviction item, the listed statistic is the percentage of persons who were
either arrested or convicted for a drug-related offense. The coefficients in parentheses have been
corrected for range restriction (range enhancement in the case of the age at first marijuana use).
The Drug-Use Composite Number 1 treated nonresponders as drug users. The Drug-Use Composite Number 2 treated nonresponders as missing data. To obtain a score on Drug-Use Composite Number 2, nonmissing responses were needed on all nine drug items.

cants. Although the validity varied across cognitive ability groups, no clear mon-
otonic moderating effect was evident. The mean reported drug-use levels did vary
monotonically with cognitive ability, with the most intelligent applicants reporting the least drug use.

The third and fourth potential moderators were sex and race. While there was
no compelling argument to expect either variable to moderate the validity of
drug-use measures, the potential moderators were examined in deference to federal testing guidelines (i.e., "Uniform Guidelines," Equal Employment
Opportunity Commission et al., 1978). Sex was not a strong moderator of the
validity of the drug composite, although females reported lower levels of drug use
than did males. Race also was not a strong moderator of the validity.

DISCUSSION

Table 4.2 indicates that employment suitability rates vary with drug-use patterns. Those who have not used drugs before hire are less likely to be judged
unsuitable on the job. In general, the earlier one begins to use a drug, the greater
is the probability of being classified as unsuitable. Those who have never been
arrested for drug offenses have substantially lower unsuitability rates than those
who have been arrested. For those who have been arrested for a drug offense,

Table 4.4

Moderator Analyses of the Validity of Pre-Employment Drug-Use Composite
Number 1 for Predicting On-the-Job Suitability

		N	r	Mean drug use	SD drug use	% Unsuitable
Total sample		10,188	.08	50.0	10.0	16
Testing condition:						
Operational		5,515	.07	50.0	9.9	17
Research		4,673	.09	50.0	10.1	16
AFQT category						
(high	I	610	.02	49.0	8.1	9
ability)	II	3,045	.09	49.0	8.2	14
	IIIA	2,067	.06	49.4	9.2	18
	IIIB	3,324	.07	50.6	10.8	17
(low	IV	986	.10	52.5	12.9	18
ability)	Below IV	156	.12	54.4	14.5	12
Sex						
Male		8,927	.08	50.2	10.2	17
Female		1,261	.07	48.4	7.8	14
Race						
White		7,432	.08	49.7	9.4	17
Black		1,989	.08	50.9	11.6	15
Hispanic		423	.09	49.7	10.4	14
Asian		96	.06	53.1	13.5	8

Notes: Drug-Use Composite Number 1 is expressed as a t score. High score indicates frequent drug
    use.

there is no meaningful difference in unsuitability rates for those who are convicted and those who are not convicted. In general, for all drugs, the more times
one uses the drug, the greater the probability of being classified as unsuitable.

Although those who report substantial drug use are much more likely to be
discharged from the service for unsuitability than those who do not report drug
use, the base rate for drugs, except marijuana, is low. These low base rates contribute to the low predictive validity of the drug measures. For applicant pools
where the base rate of nonmarijuana drugs is higher than in the present sample,
one can expect the validity of the drug measures to increase. For applicant populations where the base rate of self-reported drug use for nonmarijuana drugs is
low, however, such drug measures will have little usefulness in employee screening. In this sample, marijuana has a moderately high base rate (31% to 38%),
yet its validity is low (.07). Used alone as a predictor of suitability, self-reported
marijuana use has positive utility but may be less useful than other predictors of
unsuitable employee behavior.

A contributing factor to the low validities of the drug-use measures is their low reliability. Although the magnitude of the reliabilities is not uncommon for single-item measures, when compared with other personnel selection tools, these reliabilities are very low. In future research, it may be possible to raise the reliability of self-report measures of drug use by assessing the usage with multiple items. For example, the items may request information on the use of a drug in different settings (e.g., work, school) or over different time periods (e.g., during high school, during the last six months).

Those persons with high cognitive skills as measured by the AFQT are less likely to receive an unsuitability discharge. However, the relationship is small ($-.06$). Since the correlation between general cognitive ability and job performance is about .50 (Hunter & Hunter, 1984), the low correlation between AFQT and the suitability criterion may indicate that the criterion measures a performance domain that is substantially different from those assessed by supervisor ratings or work samples. Thus, the small correlations between the self-reported drug-use measures and unsuitability may also be a function of the dissimilarity between unsuitability discharge and more common forms of employee performance measurement.

Although the validities were low, it is useful to consider the possible reasons for the extent of the validity. At least two hypotheses can explain the relationship between pre-employment drug use and on-the-job suitability. These hypotheses are similar to two perspectives on the relationship between drug use and delinquency ("drugs cause crime" and "common cause" models) as reviewed by Watters, Reinarman, and Fagan (1985). First, pre-employment drug use may cause lasting physiological and behavioral changes. Some of these physiological and behavioral changes may cause on-the-job performance decrements that increase the probability of being classified as unsuitable. The second hypothesis posits that the relationship between drug use and on-the-job suitability is spurious and that a number of social and psychological factors (e.g., family and school factors, psychological adjustment) cause both drug use and employment unsuitability.

Although none of the validities were substantial, some drugs had stronger relationships with on-the-job suitability than did other drugs. Although the base rates and reliabilities of the measures affect the magnitude of the validities, the differences in relationship magnitude may also be explained by either of the two hypotheses relating drug use and unsuitability. First, some drugs, more than others, are likely to cause severe physiological and behavioral changes that more adversely affect employment suitability. Second, those applicants whose employment suitability has been adversely affected by social and psychological factors may be more likely to use one drug over another. For example, those with severe life-adjustment problems may be more likely to use nonmarijuana drugs, while those with fewer life-adjustment problems may be more likely to limit drug use to marijuana.

The limited operational validity of pre-employment drug-use measures found in the present research suggests that employers who now rely solely on drug-use measures as predictors of on-the-job suitability will be doing less than an optimal job of applicant screening. Any predictor with a low operational validity will screen in many applicants who prove unsuitable after hire while screening out many applicants who would perform well once hired. For a suitability screening program based solely on pre-employment drug use, the screening errors will be predominantly of two types. First, since use of nonmarijuana drugs is relatively low, many screening errors will result from hiring applicants who do not report drug use yet who prove unsuitable once hired. Second, given that the base rate of marijuana is relatively high, yet the relationship between marijuana use and suitability is low, additional screening errors will result from rejecting applicants who have used marijuana but who, if hired, would be judged suitable.

To minimize selection errors, employers who at present rely solely on drug-use measures for screening applicants for suitability should consider supplementing or replacing their drug-screening programs with selection systems that more optimally predict employee unsuitability. For predicting unsuitability discharge from the military, the predictive power of the high-school graduation dichotomy is higher than the drug-use measures found in the present research. Typically, the discharge rate for non-high-school graduates is approximately twice that of those with high-school diplomas (Cheatham, 1978; Elster & Flyer, 1981; Flyer, 1959; Flyer & Elster, 1983; Means & Laurence, 1984; Sinaiko, 1977). Also research on several paper-and-pencil employee reliability measures (Betts & Cassel, 1957; Gough, 1971, 1972; Haymaker, 1986; Hogan, 1986; Loudermilk, 1966; Paajanen, 1986; Personnel Decisions, Inc., 1986) show useful levels of validities. Such measures may provide better prediction of employee unsuitability than drug-use measures because they tap a wider range of background and personal characteristics predictive of unsuitability.

LIMITATIONS OF THE PRESENT STUDY

While this study makes a contribution to cumulative knowledge on the effects of pre-employment drug use on subsequent employment suitability, the limitations of the study should be made explicit and the effect of the study's limitations on the results should be estimated. Five caveats are offered.

First, the questions are self-report measures of illegal acts. One can expect some systematic distortion of the respondents' answers. For example, it appears that the missing data are not random. In this study, those who provided missing or nonusable responses were consistently more likely to be classified as unsuitable. For those who provide nonmissing responses, it is reasonable to expect more of the responses to be underestimates rather than overestimates of pre-employment drug use. The effect of this pattern of distorted responses is to limit the variance of the questions and, thus, to underestimate the true relationship between pre-employment drug use and subsequent employment suitability. Note that a correction of correlation coefficients for unreliability in the drug measures would not correct for this underestimation if the respondents were consistent in their response distortion.

Second, the unsuitability criterion is of unknown reliability and is potentially subject to systematic error. While data on this issue are nonexistent, it is thought that military discharge categories are sometimes selected on the basis of administrative ease rather than the accuracy of their descriptions. Thus, it may be possible that an unsuitable recruit may be discharged with a fully honorable discharge if it hastens the recruit's separation from the service. This unestimated error may cause the validities to be underestimates of the true relation between pre-employment drug use and on-the-job suitability.

Third, the base rate of the criterion (16%) is very low. Criteria with low base rates are difficult to predict with almost any measure. For example, although measures of cognitive ability typically show substantial validity for predicting many performance criteria, the cognitive ability measure (AFQT) available in this study had a very low validity.

Fourth, military occupations have important differences from civilian occupations. For example, in the civilian sector, failure to follow the instructions of one's supervisor may result in some adverse action (e.g., reprimand, firing). In the military, the same action may result in a court martial and a prison sentence. Conversely, in civilian firms strongly motivated by profit making, marginally suitable employees may be fired. In the military, a person with a similar level of suitability may be reassigned to a position of less responsibility. In contrast to the civilian sector, where one may quit one's job, military personnel who wish to leave service may have difficulty quitting. A military recruit who would not normally engage in irresponsible behavior may engage in such behaviors with the intent of facilitating a discharge from the service.

Fifth, this study's sample is drawn from a population that differs systematically from other populations of interest. The population of military recruits is young, predominantly male, and seldom has education beyond high school. These sample characteristics may limit the generalizability of the findings.

These data and study design limitations precluded the examination of a critical issue that warrants future research attention: the effect of recency of drug use on employment suitability. One might expect that drug use occuring 10 years ago will have less effect on employee suitability than drug use occuring last week. Given the increasing use and debate over drug testing for employment screening and the lack of research on the topic, personnel psychologists should devote more attention to this area.

REFERENCES

American Federation of Labor and Congress of Industrial Organizations. (1987). *Drugs and alcohol testing on the job*. (Publication No. 177). Washington, DC: Author.

Betts G.L., Cassel R.N. (1957). *Manual: Life experience inventory*. Cincinnati, OH: Author.

Brown G.H. (1974). *Drug usage rates as related to method of data acquisition.* (HumRRO-TR-74–20). Alexandria, VA: Human Resources Research Organization.

Brown G.H., Harding F.D. (1973). *A comparison of methods of studying illicit drug usage.* (HumRRO-TR-73–9). Alexandria, VA: Human Resources Research Organization.

Cheatham C.W. (1978). *The high school graduate, an indicator of a quality Marine?* Unpublished master's thesis. Fort Leavenworth, KS: U.S. Army Command and General Staff College.

Council on Scientific Affairs, American Medical Association. (1987). Scientific issues in drug testing. *Journal of the American Medical Association, 257,* 3110–3114.

Elster R.S., Flyer E.S. (1981). *A study of the relationship between educational credentials and military performance criteria* (BDM/M-TR-0018–81). Monterey, CA: Naval Postgraduate School.

Equal Employment Opportunity Commission, Civil Service Commission, Department of Labor, Department of Justice. (1978). Adoption by four agencies of uniform guidelines on employee selection procedures. *Federal Register, 43,* 38290–38315.

Flyer E.S. (1959). *Factors relating to discharge for unsuitability among 1956 airman accessions to the Air Force* (WADC-TN-59–201). Lackland Air Force Base, TX: Personnel Research Laboratory.

Flyer E.S., Elster R.S. (1983). *First term attrition among non-prior service enlisted personnel: Loss possibilities based on selected entry factors.* Monterey, CA: Naval Postgraduate School.

Gough H.G. (1972). *Manual for the Personnel Reaction Blank.* Palo Alto, CA: Consulting Psychology Press.

Gough H.G. (1971). The assessment of wayward impulse by means of the Personnel Reaction Blank. *Personnel Psychology, 24,* 669–667.

Harrell A.V. (1985). Validation of self-report: The research record. In Rouse BA, Kozel NJ, Richards LG (Eds.), *Self-report methods of drug use: Meeting current challenges to validity* (pp. 12–21; NIDA Research Monograph 57). Rockville, MD: Division of Epidemiology and Statistical Analysis, National Institute on Drug Abuse (DHHS Publication Number [ADM] 85–1402).

Haymaker J.C. (1986). *Biodata as a predictor of employee integrity and turnover.* Presented at the 94th annual convention of the American Psychological Association, Washington, DC.

Hogan R. (1986). *Hogan personality manual.* Minneapolis, MN: National Computer Systems.

Hunter J.E., Hunter R.F. (1984). Validity and utility of alternative predictors of job performance. *Psychological Bulletin, 96,* 72–98.

Kagel J.H., Battalio R.C., Miles C.G. (1980). Marihuana and work performance: Results from an experiment. *Journal of Human Resources, 15,* 373–395.

Kolb D., Nail R.L., Gunderson E.K.E. (1975). Pre-service drug abuse as a predictor of in-service drug abuse and military performance. *Military Medicine, 140,* 104–107.

Lindquist V.R. (1988). *The Northwestern Lindquist-Endicott Report, 1988.* Evanston, IL: Placement Center, Northwestern University.

Loudermilk K.M. (1966). Prediction of efficiency of lumber and paper mill employees. *Personnel Psychology, 19,* 301–310.

Means B., Laurence J.H. (1984). *Characteristics and performance of recruits enlisted with general education development (GED) credentials* (FR-PRD-84–6). Alexandria, VA: Human Resources Research Organization.

Means B., Perelman L.S. (1984). *The development of the Educational and Background Information Survey* (FR-PRD-84–3). Alexandria, VA: Human Resources Research Organization.

Miles C.G., Battalio R.C., Kagel J.H., Rhodes G.F. (1975). The effects of cannabis and negotiated wage rate changes on income and job performance in an experimental token economy. In Miles CG (Ed.), *Experimentation in controlled environment: Its implications for economic behaviour and social policy making* (pp. 57–69). Toronto: Alcoholism and Drug Addiction Research Foundation of Ontario.

Nurco D.N. (1985). A discussion of validity. In Rouse BA, Kozel NJ, Richards LG (Eds.), *Self-report methods of drug use: Meeting current challenges to validity* (pp. 4–11; NIDA Research Monograph 57). Rockville, MD: Division of Epidemiology and Statistical Analysis, National Institute on Drug Abuse (DHHS Publication Number [ADM] 85–1402).

Owens W.A. (1976). Background data. In Dunnette MD (Ed.) *Handbook of industrial psychology* (pp. 609–644). Chicago: Rand-McNally.

Paajanen G.E. (1986). *Development and validation of the PDI employment inventory.* Presented at the 94th annual convention of the American Psychological Association, Washington, DC.

Personnel Decisions, Inc. (1986). *PDI employment inventory: Summary of findings—retail industry.* Minneapolis, MN: Author.

Petzel T.P., Johnson J.E., McKillip J. (1973). Response bias in drug surveys. *Journal of Consulting and Clinical Psychology, 40,* 437–439.

Rosen T.H. (1987). Identification of substance abusers in the workplace. *Public Personnel Management, 16,* 197–298.

Rouse B.A., Kozel N.J., Richards L.G. (1985). *Self-report methods of drug use: Meeting current challenges to validity* (NIDA Research Monograph 57). Rockville, MD: Division of Epidemiology and Statistical Analysis, National Institute on Drug Abuse (DHHS Publication Number [ADM] 85–1402).

Sinaiko H.W. (Ed.). (1977). *First term enlisted attrition. Volume I: Papers* (TR-3). Arlington, VA: Office of Naval Research.

Tyson P.R., Vaughn R.A. (1987, April). Drug testing in the work place: Legal responsibilities. *Occupational Health and Safety,* pp. 24, 26, 34, 36.

Watters J.K., Reinarman C., Fagan J. (1985, Fall). Causality, context, and contingency: Relationships between drug abuse and delinquency. *Contemporary Drug Problems,* pp. 351–373.

APPENDIX B

An Evaluation of Preemployment Drug Testing

Jacques Normand, Stephen D. Salyards, and John I. Mahoney,
U.S. Postal Service, Washington, DC

ABSTRACT

As part of a blind longitudinal study, 5,465 job applicants were tested for use of illicit drugs, and the relationships between these drug-test results and absenteeism, turnover, injuries, and accidents on the job were evaluated. After an average 1.3 years of employment, employees who had tested positive for illicit drugs had an absenteeism rate 59.3% higher than employees who had tested negative (6.63% vs. 4.16% of scheduled work hours, respectively). Employees who had tested positive also had a 47% higher rate of involuntary turnover than employees who had tested negative (15.41% vs. 10.51% respectively). No significant associations were detected between drug-test results and measures of injury and accident occurrence. The practical implications of these results, in terms of economic utility and prediction errors, are discussed.

INTRODUCTION

The use of illicit drugs has been a matter of growing concern in the United States. According to the latest National Household Survey on Drug Abuse (Staff, 1989), 32% of 18- to 25-year-olds; (the age group now entering the workforce) had used illicit drugs in the past year. The survey also indicated that although the general prevalence of drug use has begun to decline, the prevalence remains quite high. Estimates of the cost of such drug use to employers and employees typically amount to several billion dollars annually (e.g., Harwood, Napolitano, Kristiansen, & Collins, 1984).

In response to employee drug use and its associated costs, an increasing number

This article originally appeared in the *Journal of Applied Psychology*, Volume 75, pp. 629–639, 1990.

of employers have adopted drug testing and employee assistance programs (EAPs). Drug screening, usually in the form of urinalysis, has become common in Fortune 500 companies (Walsh & Hawks, 1988) and several government agencies (Willette, 1986). A recent employer survey conducted by the U.S. Department of Labor's Bureau of Labor Statistics showed (1989) that the larger the establishment, the more likely it was to have a drug-testing program or an EAR. Forty-three percent of the nation's largest business establishments (those having more than 1,000 workers) had drug-testing programs but only about 2% of the smallest establishments (those having fewer than 50 workers) did. The survey also revealed that about 85% of the business establishments with drug-testing programs targeted job applicants.

Despite the popularity of drug-screening programs, a number of technical, practical, and legal concerns have surfaced regarding their role in reducing the negative impact of employee drug abuse (e.g., Crown & Rosse, 1988; Dogoloff & Angarola, 1985; Wrich, 1988). One criticism of particular concern has been the lack of systematic evaluation of the efficacy of drug-screening programs. The scientific base of information currently used to justify the implementation of these programs has come largely from laboratory and self-report studies. For example, in several controlled laboratory studies, the ingestion of drugs impaired basic cognitive and psychomotor skills relevant to job performance (e.g., Chait, Fischman, & Schuster, 1985; Fischman, Kelly, & Foltin, 1989; Herning, Glover, Koeppl, & Jaffe, 1989; Murray, 1986; Yesavage, Leirer, Denari, & Hollister, 1985). In empirical self-report studies, low to moderate correlations have been observed between drug use and work-related variables, such as job separation, job instability, and vandalism at work (e.g., Kandel & Yamaguchi, 1987; McDaniel, 1988; Newcomb, 1988).

The relationship between preemployment urinalysis test results and job outcomes has been investigated in very few studies. Blank and Fenton (1989) analyzed demographic and turnover data for 482 male navy recruits who tested positive for marijuana at accession and for a comparable group who tested negative at the same time. Though retained by the navy, recruits who tested positive were warned, counseled, and in some cases subjected to regular drug testing. If subsequent tests were positive for any illicit substance, the recruit was discharged from the navy and sent home. (All recruits were subject to occasional random testing about three times a year.) Turnover data revealed that 43% of the recruits who tested positive for drug use, but only 19% of those who tested negative had separated from the navy after 2½ years. This difference in turnover may have been somewhat spurious, however, because of potential criterion contamination. At least some of the observed turnover appeared to be a direct consequence of subsequent drug test results. Because of the criterion contamination issue, Blank and Fenton's (1989) study is inconclusive with respect to the relationship between preemployment drug-test results and turnover.

Levy (1983) reported results of a study, conducted in a hospital setting, in which 500 routine preemployment urine toxicology examinations were performed. The prevalence of confirmed positive tests was 2.61%. On the basis of these findings,

Levy concluded that routine toxicology screens in a preemployment examination may not be cost effective. However, because Levy did not mention the method used to confirm the initial test results, the true positive results for these limited drug types is unknown and thus the accuracy of the reported prevalence of positive drug tests (2.61%) is uncertain. Furthermore, the toxicology screen did not test for the presence of the most prevalent illicit drugs (i.e., marijuana and cocaine). Therefore, given these inherent limitations, Levy's conclusion that preemployment drug testing is not cost effective is unsubstantiated.

More recently, Parish (1989) attempted to assess the effectiveness of preemployment drug testing. Twelve percent of 180 newly hired employees (i.e., 22) tested positive for drugs at the time of their preemployment physical. The job performance characteristics of employees who tested positive were compared with those who tested negative. The positive group had a 28% higher turnover rate and a 64% higher rate of disciplinary warnings than the negative group. However, one should be very cautious in interpreting these results because of the low power of the statistical tests used.

Finally, results from a retrospective study conducted at the Georgia Power Company (Winkler & Sheridan, 1989) have shown that individuals testing positive in a "for-cause" drug testing program used more medical benefits each year, were absent more often each year, and were involved in more vehicular accidents than were matched control groups. Because of the nature of the testing program (i.e., for-cause testing), these results do not directly reflect on the ability of preemployment drug-test results to predict important job outcomes.

In summary, the lack of sound empirical research directed at estimating drug-use-job-outcome relationships is evident. The present large-scale longitudinal study was designed to evaluate the relationship between drug-test results and job performance indicators. More specifically, the primary purpose was to estimate the relationship between preemployment drug-test results and absenteeism, turnover, injury, and accident criteria. Another objective was to evaluate the practical significance of preemployment drug testing as assessed by a utility analysis.

METHOD

Subjects

All persons who applied for permanent positions with the U.S. Postal Service and had their preemployment medical examination performed by a U.S. Postal Service medical officer in one of 21 sites across the country submitted a urine sample at the time of their medical examinations. Specimens were collected between September 14, 1987 and May 27, 1988. Four selection criteria were used to identify the participating sites. First, employment sites that had a formal preemployment drug-testing program in place were excluded. Second, only sites with computerized personnel data bases were considered. This prerequisite was imposed so that participants' Postal Service careers could be accurately monitored from existing computer records, without any local monitoring. To ensure that a

Table 4.5
Demographic Characteristics of New Employees

Characteristics	No.	% of sample
Sex		
Male	2,630	59.8
Female	1,765	40.2
Data missing	1	
Ethnicity		
White	2,168	49.4
Black	1,439	32.8
Other	783	17.8
Data missing	6	
Age (in years)		
<26	732	16.7
26 to 30	1,083	24.6
31 to 35	959	21.8
36 to 40	702	16 0
41 and older	920	20.9

demographically heterogeneous sample of applicants was obtained, we selected diverse geographic locations. All participating sites had to have a Postal Service medical officer perform the medical examinations in the context of which the urine samples would be collected. Of the 21 sites that met the selection criteria, 6 were located on the East Coast, 8 were in the central part of the country, and 7 were on the West Coast.

Drug-test results were obtained from 5,465 job applicants. A total of 4,396 of these job applicants were eventually hired and made up the study sample. This 80% hiring rate resulted from other selection hurdles that were used to determine whether or not job applicants were fit for duty. Suitability for employment in the Postal Service is based in part on various preemployment evaluation procedures, including a review of previous work and criminal records, as well as a medical evaluation performed by a licensed physician. In addition, before reaching the suitability-for-employment selection stage, most applicants had to successfully pass a written examination.

The demographic characteristics of the sample are given in Table 4.5. Breakdowns are provided for sex, age, and ethnicity. The analyses presented below are based on employees who had an average job tenure of 1.3 years.

Procedure

Data collection. Before the study was initiated, participating physicians and representatives of the human resources office from each site attended 1-day briefing sessions. During these meetings, each attendee was provided with a detailed documentation package that described the study's methodology and data-collection protocol. Physicians were informed that neither they nor any other local personnel would have access to the drug-test results. The individual drug-test results were made available only to the research team at U.S. Postal Service headquarters to ensure the objectivity of the study's results and the privacy of the individuals involved. To further protect the confidentiality of study participants, we obtained a confidentiality certificate issued by the National Institute on Drug Abuse (NIDA) under the authority vested in the Secretary of Health and Human Services. This certificate legally protects the privacy of research subjects from any private or governmental access (e.g., courts). In the orientation, physicians were reminded that they should follow normal medical protocol when determining whether an applicant was fit for duty and to include their own separate drug test only if they would normally have requested such a diagnostic test. It was clearly communicated to them that they should not, as a result of the study, deviate from their normal protocol when performing their medical examinations.

Although no individual personnel action was taken as a result of the drug-test results, it was still deemed essential that proper control mechanisms (i.e., chain of custody and standard collection protocol) be followed to ensure the accuracy of the data recorded. Physicians were already collecting urine specimens from job applicants as part of the standard medical procedure for the preemployment physical examination; we asked them to transfer a sufficient quantity of urine (approximately 50 ml.) to the toxicology laboratory's collection bottle immediately after collecting the specimen and before performing the standard multitest stick for albumen, sugar, and blood. All collected specimens were then sent to the contracted toxicology laboratory via express mail.

In addition to collecting urine specimens, physicians were required to complete a personal-history form (PHF) for all job applicants. The information collected on the PHF consisted of demographic information (e.g., name, sex, and age) and personal-history data (e.g., use of medication). Physicians were instructed both verbally during the briefing sessions and in writing (i.e., in the collection-protocol documentation package) to investigate thoroughly the applicant's prior use of medication when completing the "Current Medication Used" section of the PHF. We used the information about the use of over-the-counter drugs or prescription medicine to identify justified true positives (i.e., applicants whose positive test results could have been caused by the legitimate use of medication) and to properly code these applicants' drug-test results for statistical analysis. Assistance from toxicologists at NIDA was obtained to ensure that all justified true positives were accurately identified. We coded as negative only those positive drug-test results that could have been due to the legitimate use of prescribed or over-the-counter medication.

Most applicants were informed at the time of their medical examinations that drug tests would be performed, but at some study sites (those that hired large numbers of applicants) job applicants were informed well in advance (e.g., 2 to 5 days). In addition, the medical-evaluation form (a portion of which is completed and signed by applicants) notified participants in writing that a urine sample would be collected and that part of the specimen would be used for a drug test. Physicians were also provided with standard language to read aloud to applicants, informing them of their participation in a drug study. The PHF, which was partially completed by applicants, also contained language indicating the purpose of the data collection and how the information would be used.

Quality-control study. Finally, 5 of the 21 sites were randomly selected to serve as quality-control sites. To evaluate the reliability and accuracy of the toxicology laboratory, we submitted 250 quality-control urine samples "blind" (i.e., without the laboratory's knowledge) via the quality-control sites. Fifty blank (i.e., drug-free) samples, 100 samples containing cross-reactive agents, 50 samples spiked with drug metabolites at concentration levels just below the cutoff levels, and 50 samples spiked with drug metabolites above the cutoff levels were purchased. Each quality-control site was given detailed instructions to ensure that these quality-control samples would be submitted blind to the toxicology laboratory.

Measures

Drug tests. Urine samples were initially screened with the enzyme multiplied immunoassay technique (EMIT). All specimens identified as positive at the initial screening were confirmed with the gas chromatography/mass spectrometry (GC/MS) technique. For a technical description of the EMIT, the reader is referred to Morgan (1984) and Moyer, Palmen, Johnson, Charlson, and Ellefson (1987). Schwartz and Hawks (1985) and Hawks (1986) provide detailed discussions of the GC/MS technique.

All specimens were tested for eight drug types at predetermined levels of sensitivity. A list of the individual drug types, along with their associated drug metabolites and the required cutoff levels for positive screening and confirmation test results are provided in Table 4.6. Quantitative GC/MS readings were reported for all specimens that were identified as positive at the initial screening, regardless of the concentration level detected at confirmation. These cutoff scores were selected to ensure that this study's cutoff scores complied with those recommended by the U.S. Department of Health and Human Services (1988).

Four independent drug-test variables were used for this study. The first variable, *overall test*, was defined as positive if, according to the GC/MS, the urine specimen contained one or more of the drugs or metabolites of the eight drug-type categories at predetermined concentration levels. Specimens that contained none of the drugs or metabolites at the confirmation stage were defined as negative. This operational definition is consistent with that used by most organizations that have implemented urinalysis drug-testing programs.

Three independent variables were used to assess the effect of individual drugs. The variable *marijuana* was defined as positive only if a urine specimen was

Table 4.6
Drugs and Cutoff Levels for EMIT Screening and GC/MS Confirmation Tests

Drug type	Drug or metabolite	Cutoff levels (In ng/ml)	
		EMIT	GC/MS
Amphetamines	Amphetamine	1,000	300
	Methamphetamine		
Barbiturates	Amobarbital	300	300
	Butabarbital		
	Pentobarbital		
	Phenobarbital		
	Secobarbital		
Benzodiazepines	N-Desmethyldiazepam	300	300
	Nordiazepam		
	Oxazepam		
Cocaine	Benzoylecgonine	300	150
Marijuana	THC-COOH	100	15
Methadone	Methadone	300	300
Opiates	Codeine	300	300
	Morphine		
Phencyclidine	Phencyclidine	25	25

Notes: EMIT = enzyme multiplied immunoassay technique; GC/MS = gas chromatography/mass spectrometry.

confirmed to contain THC-COOH metabolites and no other drug-type metabolites. Marijuana was defined as negative if no drug metabolites were confirmed to be present in the urine sample.

The *cocaine* variable was defined as positive only if benzoylecgonine metabolites or THC-COOH and benzoylecgonine metabolites in combination were found at concentrations equal to or exceeding the GC/MS cutoff levels. The cocaine variable was defined as negative if no drug metabolites were confirmed by GC/MS. The rationale used to define cocaine as positive if the urine specimen also contained THC-COOH was based on pharmacological and theoretical considerations. First, because cocaine is metabolized so much more rapidly than marijuana, a cocaine-positive result is more likely to indicate recent and possibly dependent use. Second, cocaine is a harder drug than marijuana and, according to the progressive theory of drug use, indicates that a higher stage has been reached on the drug-involvement continuum (Kandel, 1975). Therefore, people who test positive for both cocaine and marijuana resemble cocaine positives more than marijuana positives and should be grouped accordingly because they have progressed to similar stages of drug involvement.

Finally, the measure *other* was defined as positive if the specimen contained confirmed levels of one or more of the remaining drugs or combinations of any of the drugs except for the marijuana-cocaine combination. If the specimen was confirmed to be drug free, the other variable was said to be negative.

Absenteeism. The first outcome measure to be investigated in this phase of the longitudinal study was absenteeism. For the purpose of this study, absenteeism was operationalized as a function of three different types of leave: sick leave, leave without pay (LWOP), and absent without official leave (AWOL). This definition automatically excluded annual leave (vacation), administrative leave, and the like. The total hours of sick leave, LWOP, and AWOL taken were used to compute an absenteeism index for each employee participating in the study—the ratio of total hours absent (i.e., the sum of sick leave, LWOP, and AWOL) to total scheduled work hours (i.e., the sum of sick leave, LWOP, AWOL, and hours worked).

Turnover. To determine overall turnover, we divided employees into two categories: those whose employment with the Postal Service was terminated, regardless of reason, and those who had not experienced any break in service and were still active employees. In addition to overall turnover, more refined analyses were carried out by type of turnover (voluntary or involuntary; Abelson, 1987); turnover was defined as voluntary if an employee resigned or was transferred to another agency and was defined as involuntary if the employee was fired.

Injuries. Individuals who had experienced an injury recorded on Form CA-1 (U.S. Department of Labor, Employee Standard Administration, Office of Workers' Compensation Program, 1986) were said to have had a work-related injury. Each individual's injury record was updated bimonthly to capture the frequency of injuries. Those participants whose injury records did not contain injury information, as recorded by Form CA-1, were coded as not having experienced a work-related injury. Those individuals with a single injury were coded as having experienced one injury, whereas those employees with multiple injuries were grouped into a distinct multiple-injury category.

Accidents. All study participants who experienced a work-related accident recorded on U.S. Postal Service Form 1769 (U.S. Postal Service, 1984) were said to have had an accident. Individual records were updated bimonthly to capture all accident occurrences. Employees who had experienced a single accident were coded as having one accident. Employees with multiple accidents were grouped into a multiple-accident category. Employees whose records did not contain any accident information were coded as not having experienced a work-related accident. In addition to the number of accidents, each individual's accident record contained information on the type (i.e., motor vs. industrial), cause (i.e., fault vs. no fault), and severity (i.e., severe vs. not severe) of each accident.

Analyses

First, basic descriptive statistics for all pertinent variables were obtained. Although all selected sites had computerized personnel records, some of the applicants whose medical examinations were performed at those sites were assigned to working sites that did not have computerized systems. This logistical constraint prevented the retrieval of certain types of information (e.g., absenteeism records) for 1,326 employees.

Permanent employment with the U.S. Postal Service is contingent on successful completion of a 90-day probationary period. After the probationary period, the employee's job performance is evaluated and he or she is retained or fired on the basis of that performance. For this reason, the probationary period represents a rather atypical phase of a new employee's Postal Service career. For example, during the probationary period, employees are encouraged not to use any leave and are generally expected to be on their "best behavior." It was determined that analyzing only the leave usage of employees who had completed the probationary period would result in more stable absenteeism estimates and consequently provide more meaningful results. Therefore, all study participants who did not survive the probationary period ($n = 359$) were eliminated from absenteeism analyses.

To ensure the integrity and accuracy of the remaining 2,711 leave records, we contacted personnel administrators at sites having individuals with absence rates in excess of 10% and asked them to provide an explanation for the unusual absence records of these individuals. The number of employees who had absence rates in excess of 10% was 298. Four employees were found to have inaccurate leave records resulting from clerical or administrative errors; these four cases were also omitted from the absenteeism data base.

An inspection of the resulting absenteeism distribution revealed that traditional measures of association and their respective statistical tests should not be performed on the continuous absenteeism measure. The skewness and kurtosis values for the absenteeism distribution were 4.54 and 27.76, respectively, indicating a substantial departure from normality. We therefore decided to partition the absenteeism distribution into meaningful class intervals before performing the statistical-relationship analyses.

What was of interest organizationally was not moderate but excessive leave use. Therefore, we used two class intervals that would categorize employees as either moderate leave users or heavy leave users. To identify an adequate break point, we examined annual sick leave rates for the last few years. The annual sick-leave rate in the Postal Service has typically been 3.0% of total work hours scheduled and in 1988, it was 3.1%. Therefore, 3.0% was used as the break point; 64.8% of the participants were placed in the moderate leave (0%–3%) category and 35.21%, in the heavy leave (above 3%) category.

Differences in mean absence rates between the positive and negative drug-test groups were also considered highly informative. We used a t test to investigate the disparity in mean absence rates because of the test's robustness against violations of the normality assumption (Holden & Overall, 1987).

Measures of association. The chi-square test of independence was used to assess the significance of the association between drug-test results and the outcome measures of job absence, turnover, injuries, and accidents.

One measure of association that is not a function of chi-square and is insensitive to marginal distributions is the odds ratio. This measure of association allows the researcher to determine the strength of the relationship after having determined with a chi-square test that the two characteristics being studied are not independent. Advantages of using the odds ratio instead of other measures have been illustrated by Mosteller (1968). Some researchers (see Fleiss, 1973) considered the advantages to be so great that they recommended that only the odds ratio or functions of it be used to measure association in 2×2 contingency tables.

Another positive feature of the odds ratio is that it constitutes the basic building block of the logistic model, which we used to assess the predictive ability of drug-test results. A measure of association that is a function of the odds ratio and consequently shares its strengths is Yule's Q. The values of this measure range from -1.0 to $+1.0$, with 0 implying statistical independence. When chi-square tests revealed the presence of a significant association, we used both the odds ratio and Yule's Q to reflect the strength of the association.

Predictive models. Because the use of discrete dependent variables does not meet the underlying assumptions of the linear regression model, we used the logistic regression model to investigate the predictive efficiency of individual drug-test results. Because previous research suggests that sex, race, age, and occupational group are related to both drug use and the outcome measures of interest, we used these demographic variables as control variables in the predictive models (e.g., Flanagan, Strauss, & Ulman, 1974; Hedges, 1973; Nicholson, Brown, & Chadwick-Jones, 1977; Steers & Rhodes, 1979; U.S. Postal Service, 1987). The inclusion of these covariates allowed more efficient tests of significance for the coefficient associated with drug-test results. This investigation was not concerned with the magnitude of the individual effect size of the independent variables relative to one another. The main question of interest was whether or not drug-test results were viable predictors of the outcome measures being investigated, that is, turnover, absenteeism, injuries, and accidents. The predictive ability of the models was assessed with the SAS Logist procedure (Harrell, 1986).

Utility analyses. To apply the Brogden-Cronbach-Gleser paradigm to this organizational intervention (Brogden, 1949; Cronbach & Gleser, 1965), we used modifications introduced by Schmidt, Hunter, and Pearlman (1982). Schmidt et al. (1982) showed that the total gain in utility resulting from an organizational intervention program can be written as:

$$\Delta U = (TN_1 d_1 Sd_y) - NC,$$

where ΔU is the dollar value of the intervention program; T is the number of years duration of the effect of the intervention program on the job-performance measure (i.e., the tenure of the average selectee); N_1 is the total number of yearly applicants affected by the program; d_1 is the average gain in performance due to the intervention in standard score units (i.e., the difference in average performance between employees who tested positive and employees who tested negative for drug use expressed in standard deviation units of the combined [pooled] group); SD_y is the standard deviation of the job-performance measure in dollars in the combined group;[1] N is the total annual number of job applicants submitted to the intervention (i.e., testing); and C is the average cost of testing a new employee.

Because this utility model and subsequent modifications of it are based on the implicit assumption that the criterion measure is continuous, application of the model was limited to the continuous absenteeism measure. Although the absenteeism distribution was skewed, no transformations were performed because implementing the utility equation did not entail inferential testing. Furthermore, to prevent the loss of valuable information, researchers should avoid modifying the shape of the original performance distribution when conducting utility analyses (Raju, Burke, & Normand, 1990). The dichotomized nature of the turnover measure prevented us from using this utility model to assess the financial savings accrued from the turnover results. The economic impact of the observed reduction in involuntary turnover resulting from the organizational intervention was assessed with a technique recommended by Cascio and McEvoy (1984). With this approach, the number of potential turnovers the intervention avoids is multiplied by the estimate of the turnover cost per employee.

The utility estimates were not adjusted for such economic considerations as discounting, variable costs, and taxation. These economic considerations are rarely incorporated into economic utility analyses of operational selection programs (Burke & Frederick, 1986). A projected multiple-cohort analysis also was not included in the utility analysis because U.S. Postal Service management deemed the gross utility estimates for a single cohort appropriate to determine the efficacy of preemployment drug testing. As discussed later, including economic considerations in the utility analysis would lower the gross utility estimates. However, other study factors (also described later) have already created downward (conservative) biases in the gross utility estimates, and, as noted by several researchers (e.g., Burke & Frederick, 1986; Hunter, Schmidt, & Coggin, 1988), there is no "correct" definition of payoff (e.g., gross utility, net present value).

RESULTS

Prevalence

Ten percent of all eligible job applicants tested positive for drugs at the time of their medical examinations (see Table 4.7). Sixty-five percent of these applicants tested positive for marijuana, 24% tested positive for cocaine, and 11% tested positive for one or more of the other drugs.

Slightly fewer new employees than eligible applicants tested positive for drug use in the various categories. Nine percent of the new employees tested positive overall; 68% of those tested positive for marijuana, 23% tested positive for cocaine, and 9% tested positive for one or more of the other drugs. The data

Table 4.7
Drug-Test Results for Applicants and New Employees

Drug type/result	Applicants		New employees	
	No.	%	No.	%
Overall				
Positive	544	10.0	395	9.0
Negative	4,921	90.0	4,001	91.0
Marijuana				
Positive	356	6.7	268	6.3
Negative	4,921	93.3	4,001	93.7
Cocaine				
Positive	130	2.6	92	2.2
Negative	4,921	97.4	4,001	97.8
Other				
Positive	58	1.2	35	0.9
Negative	4,921	98.8	4,001	99.1

presented in Table 4.7 also indicate that 27% of the eligible applicants who tested positive were not hired, compared with 19% of those who tested negative.

An analysis of drug-test results by race, sex, and age group showed that the odds of testing positive were higher for Blacks, men, and people between the ages of 25 and 35. More specifically, the percentage of Black new employees testing positive for drug use (15.01%) was significantly higher than the percentage of White new employees testing positive (7.15%), χ^2 (1, N = 3,607) = 57.92, $p \leq .01$. Moreover, Blacks were more than six times as likely as Whites to test positive for cocaine and almost twice as likely to test positive for marijuana. In addition, although significantly more men (10.04%) than women (7.42%) tested positive overall, χ^2 (1, N = 4,395) = 8.84, $p \leq .01$, and for marijuana (7.25% for men vs. 4.83% for women), χ^2 (1, N = 4,268) = 10.20, $p \leq .01$, no such difference was observed for cocaine. Approximately the same proportion of men and women tested positive for cocaine (2.27% and 2.21% respectively). Of the applicants 25 years old or younger, 8.06% tested positive for overall drug use; of applicants 26 to 30, 31 to 35, 36 to 40, and 41 and older, 10.34%, 12.83%, 8.97%, and 4.13% tested positive, respectively. The overall chi-square test revealed that these percentages were significantly different from one another, χ^2 (1, N = 4,396) = 47.01, $p \leq .01$.

Quality-Control Study

The results of the double-blind quality-control study revealed that the laboratory analysis of blank specimens and cross-reactants resulted in the reporting of no false-positive results even though the cross-reactants produced 19 presumptive positives on the initial immunoassay screening (i.e., EMIT). GC/MS

Table 4.8
Associations Between Absenteeism and Drug-Test Results

Drug type/ absence category	No. who tested negative	No. who tested positive	χ^2	df	Odds ratio	Yule's Q
Overall test						
Moderate	1,607	139	29.27	1	1.97	.33
Heavy	821	140				
Marijuana						
Moderate	1,607	107	7.11	1	1.50	.20
Heavy	821	82				
Cocaine						
Moderate	1,607	21	34.91	1	4.29	.62
Heavy	821	46				

Notes: All chi-square values are significant at $p \leq .01$. Employees whose total hours of sick leave, leave without pay (LWOP), and absence without official leave (AWOL) constituted 3% or less of their total scheduled work hours were classified as moderate leave takers; employees whose total sick leave, LWOP, and AWOL hours constituted more than 3% of their total scheduled work hours were classified as heavy leave takers.

confirmation by the laboratory correctly declined every false positive result indicated in the initial screening test. Laboratory analysis of the spiked positive specimens yielded four false negative results: one for phenobarbital, two for morphine, and one for marijuana. Quality-control studies are designed to favor false-negative errors because of the adverse consequences that may be associated with false-positive results, so that a finite but low false-negative rate is generally considered acceptable by the forensic science community (Finkle, Blanke, & Walsh, 1990).

Absenteeism

The mean absence rate of 6.63% of total work hours scheduled for employees who tested positive for drugs was significantly different from the rate found for the negative drug-test group (4.16% of hours scheduled). The t statistic was computed under the assumption of unequal variances by using Satterthwaite's formula for approximation of the degrees of freedom (SAS Institute, 1985), t (316) $= -3.77$, $p \leq .01$. The positive drug test group had a 59.3% higher absence rate than the negative drug-test group. Furthermore, as indicated by the odds ratio, employees who tested positive were 1.97 times more likely than employees who tested negative to use leave heavily (see Table 4.8). The results of the chi-square test of independence revealed that drug-test results were significantly related to job absence, χ^2 (1, $N = 2,707$) $= 29.27$, $p \leq .01$. The magnitude of the association was estimated, by Yule's Q, to be .33.

When these analyses were carried out separately for individual drug type, an enlightening pattern emerged (see Table 4.8). Employees who tested positive

Table 4.9
Logistic Regression Model for Job Absence

Variable	Regression coefficient	χ^2	df
Overall model		166.91*	5
Intercept	-0.0265	0.02	1
Overall test	0.6403	23.46*	1
Age	-0.0303	30.60*	1
Sex	0.6123	51.22*	1
Race			
White vs. Black[a]	-0.2929	23.77*	1
White vs. Other[b]	0.3085	14.44*	1

Notes: Somer's D = .30; Goodman-Kruskal γ = .30.
[a]White = 1, Other = 0, and Black = −1; [b]White = 1, Other = −1, and Black = 0.
*$p \le .01$.
*$p \le .01$.

for marijuana were 1.50 times more likely to be heavy leave users than employees who tested negative for drug use. Employees who tested positive for cocaine were more than 4 times as likely as employees who tested negative to be heavy leave users.

The results of the logistic regression analysis of absenteeism, presented in Table 4.9, indicate that the postulated absence model is viable. The results also reveal that the overall drug test contributed significantly to the predictive power of the job absence model.

Turnover

The results of the chi-square test of independence for test results revealed no significant relationship between drug-test results and overall turnover or between drug-test results and voluntary turnover. However, as illustrated in Table 4.10, a significant association was found between the overall drug test and involuntary turnover, χ^2 (1, N = 3,693) = 7.66, $p \le .01$. The odds ratio indicated that for applicants testing positive, the odds of being fired were 1.55 times those of applicants testing negative. The degree of this relationship was reflected by Yule's Q, which was 22. Another way of expressing this disparity is that employees who tested positive for drug use had a 47% higher rate of involuntary separation than those who tested negative. A summary of the chi-square tests of independence and the respective measures of association between involuntary separation and drug type are presented in Table 4.10. As was observed with the absenteeism results, the magnitude of the relationship was strongest for cocaine.

The results of the logistic regression model used to determine whether or not the overall drug test was a significant predictor of involuntary turnover are pre-

Table 4.10
Associations Between Involuntary Separation and Drug-Test Results

Drug type/ separation category	No. who tested negative	No. who tested positive	χ^2	df	Odds ratio	Yule's Q
Overall test						
Not separated	2,997	291				
Fired	352	53	7.66*	1	1.55	.22
Marijuana						
Not separated	2,997	203				
Fired	352	30	1.28	1	--	--
Cocaine						
Not separated	2,997	65				
Fired	352	18	10.52*	1	2.36	.40

Notes: The odds ratio and Yule's Q were not calculated for the marijuana test because the chi-square value was not significant.
*$p \le .01$.

sented in Table 4.11. The proposed model was viable, χ^2 (6, N = 3,693) = 77.50, $p \le .01$. Furthermore, the results show that the overall test contributed significantly to the involuntary-turnover predictive model.

Injuries

The chi-square test of independence revealed no statistically significant relationship between drug-test results and number of injuries. Furthermore, after job type was controlled in the logistic regression analysis, test results were not a significant contributor to the predictive model.

Accidents

No statistically significant relationship was detected between drug-test results and number of accidents. The logistic regression analysis revealed that even after job category was controlled, test results did not contribute significantly to the prediction of work-related accidents. Furthermore, no significant relations were detected when separate analyses were performed by accident type (motor vs. industrial), cause (fault vs. no fault), or severity (severe vs. not severe).

Economic Utility

To apply Equation 1, we first needed to estimate d_1 (the observed gain in performance in standard score units), which is equal to $(Y_e - Y_c)/SD_p$, Y_e (the mean absence rate of the positive drug-test group) was 0.0663; Y_c (the mean absence rate of the negative drug-test group) was 0.0416; and SD_p (the standard

Table 4.11
Logistic Regression Model for Involuntary Separation

Variable	Regression coefficient	χ^2	df
Overall model		77.50*	6
Intercept	-2.9419	189.41*	1
Overall test	0.5494	12.94*	1
Job category			
Distribution clerk [a]	0.6164	6.93*	1
Carrier [b]	1.1604	27.34*	1
Mail handler [c]	-0.0300	0.01	1
Race			
White vs. Black [d]	0.1245	2.35	1
White vs. Other [e]	-0.1126	1.56	1

Notes: Somer's D = .24; Goodman-Kruskal γ = .36.
[a]Distribution clerk = 1, carrier = 0, mail handler = 0, and miscellaneous = 0. [b]Distribution clerk = 0, carrier = 1, mail handler = 0, and miscellaneous = 0. [c]Distribution clerk = 0, carrier = 0, mail handler = 1, and miscellaneous = 0. [d]White = 1, Other = 0, and Black = -1. [e]White = 1, Other = -1, and Black = 0.
*$p \leq .01$.

deviation of absence rates for the combined group) was 0.0841. This yielded a d_t parameter estimate equal to 0.294.

The value of SD_y, the variability of the absenteeism measure (in dollars) in the combined group (negative and positive drug test groups pooled), was estimated to be $3,320. This parameter estimate was obtained by linearly transforming the individual absence rates to a dollar value and then computing the standard deviation of that transformed absenteeism value. More specifically, the total annual hours of leave used by each study participant was obtained by multiplying each subject's absence rate by 2,000 hours (i.e., the total number of regular work hours in a postal year). These individual leave hours were then multiplied by the cost associated with one hour of leave for that person's job category. These hourly rates were obtained from the Postal Service's National Payroll Summary Report (U.S. Postal Service, 1989). Once an absenteeism dollar value was obtained for each subject, the standard deviation of the absenteeism dollar distribution was computed.

The N_t parameter is equal to the annual number of new employees that would be affected by the drug-testing program. We expected that, nationally, approximately 9% of the 61,588 applicants normally hired would be screened out and replaced by applicants who test negative for drug use. Therefore, we expected the drug-testing program to affect 5,543 new employees annually. N is the total number of applicants who would submit to the drug test annually, which we estimated to be approximately 180,000. The total annual cost © of testing per applicant is $11.

Finally, the T parameter is the duration in years of the drug-testing program's effect on performance. Because d_1, the observed absenteeism effect, reflects the disparity in absence rates (in standard units) for the first year only, and because the observed effect for one cohort was expected to be constant over the tenure of that cohort, the average tenure of Postal Service employees (10 years) was used as an estimate of T.

The unadjusted absenteeism cost-savings estimate for the first year of implementation would be approximately $3.43 million dollars, with subsequent years resulting in savings of approximately $5.41 million. The annual turnover cost savings were obtained by first estimating the rate of excess firings (i.e., 15.41% minus 10.51%) that would result from hiring those who tested positive for illicit drugs. The annual number of new employees affected by the drug-testing program (5,543) was then multiplied by this excess firing rate (4.90%) to obtain the number of avoidable firings (272). The procedure used to estimate the average cost per employee turnover was based on two separate estimates: turnover savings and turnover costs. The turnover savings were derived by estimating the productivity gain during the employment period of those employees involuntarily separated and then subtracting from that amount the turnover cost estimates. Turnover cost included the following components: testing, separation, training, productivity loss, accidents, uniform allowance, and unemployment compensation. The resulting average turnover cost per employee was estimated to be $2,303. The cost per involuntary separation would translate into an annual savings of approximately $626,416 dollars for one cohort of new employees.

When the absenteeism savings estimated with Equation 1 ($52,124,114) were added to the turnover savings ($626,416), the total estimated cost savings obtained by screening out job applicants who test positive for drug use was approximately $52,750,000 for one cohort of new employees. The absenteeism cost-saving estimate does not take into account certain incidental costs associated with job absences. Such costs might include supervisors' compensation for time spent per day dealing with all the problems stemming from employee absenteeism (e.g., production, instructing replacement employees, checking on performance of replacements), overtime premiums, and so forth. Furthermore, the savings presented above for one cohort of new employees do not reflect the compounding of savings derived by the cohorts of new employees added each year the program is in existence. These considerations create downward biases in the gross utility estimates.

Discussion

The observed prevalence of positive drug tests among new employees (9.0%) was somewhat lower than what previous surveys of working adults led us to anticipate (e.g., Cook & Harrel, 1987). However, this relatively low prevalence may be attributed in part to our operational definition of drug use and to the components of the Postal Service's selection process. Our prevalence estimates were based on urinalysis drug-test results, whereas most prevalence figures reported in the literature are based on self-report survey data. As a rule, prevalence figures based on urinalysis results tend to be much lower than those based on self-report measures of drug use (U.S. Department of Labor, Bureau of Labor Statistics, 1989). One reason may be that the potential risks associated with disclosing one's use of illicit drugs in a confidential research survey are not nearly as great as testing positive for drugs when applying for a permanent position with an organization. Some applicants in this study were informed of the drug test well in advance of the medical examination (either through official channels or by word of mouth) and some of those using drugs may have chosen not to show up or managed to curtail their use of drugs prior to the examination. Anecdotal evidence from medical personnel at various study sites suggests that such a deterrence effect may have contributed to the relatively low prevalence of positive drug tests in this study.

Furthermore, the results revealed that eligible job applicants who tested positive for drug use (i.e., those who survived the first selection hurdle) were less likely to be hired in this blind study (27% were disqualified) than those who tested negative (19% were disqualified). Here again, a closer look at the nature of the remaining selection components that all eligible applicants must pass prior to being hired may partially explain why a greater percentage of applicants who tested positive were disqualified. The first of these remaining selection hurdles is a personal suitability check. This basically consists of a review of prior work and criminal records. The last selection component consists of a fitness-for-duty medical examination. A number of researchers have concluded that drug involvement may represent only one facet of a deviance-prone lifestyle that is typified by nonconformist attitudes and problem behavior (e.g., Castro, Newcomb, & Cadish, 1987; Donovan & Jessor, 1985; Kandel & Yamaguchi, 1987; Newcomb, 1988; Stein, Newcomb, & Bentler, 1988). It is therefore quite likely that applicants who tested positive for illicit drugs exhibited, through their criminal, medical, or work histories, certain deviant lifestyle characteristics that served to disqualify them at a higher rate than those testing negative.

The proportion of applicants disqualified also varied by drug type, with a greater proportion of those who tested positive for harder drugs being disqualified. The proportion of applicants who were disqualified was 25% for those who tested positive for marijuana, 29% for those who tested positive for cocaine, and 40% for those who tested positive for other drugs or for more than one drug.

The patterns of drug use found for various demographic groups in this study are similar to those reported by other researchers. Men have a higher drug-use rate than women (e.g., Cook & Harrel, 1987; Johnston, O'Malley, & Bachman, 1987); the drug-use rates of Blacks are higher than those of Whites (cf. Blank & Fenton, 1989; Newcomb, 1988); and workers under 35 years of age have higher rates than older workers (e.g., Cook & Harrel, 1987). It is therefore not unexpected to see these demographic patterns reflected in urinalysis drug-test results. It was surprising, however, that the difference observed between men and women for the overall drug-use test and the marijuana test did not hold for cocaine. In addition, the proportion of Blacks testing positive for cocaine was triple that of Whites. These findings may be related to the increase in popularity and availability of cocaine in recent years among women and Blacks/Hispanics (Washton & Gold, 1987).

Given the observed sex, race, and age-group differences in the prevalence of positive drug tests, it would be informative from a selection perspective to examine the effect of a preemployment drug-testing program on the hiring rates of various population subgroups. As shown in the **Results** section, these differences were statistically significant. Another standard traditionally used to assess such differences is the four-fifths rule, promulgated in the Uniform Guidelines on Employee Selection Procedures (Ledvinka, 1982). The prevalence of positive drug tests observed among men (10.04%) and women (7.42%) translates into an 89.96% selection rate for men and a 92.58% selection rate for women for this selection component. The calculated impact ratio (the selection rate for a group divided by the selection rate for the highest group) is 97.17%, which is well above the four-fifths (or 80%) threshold. The same conclusion is reached when the impact ratio is calculated for Blacks and Whites. The ratio of the Black selection rate to that of Whites is substantially higher (91.53%) than four-fifths and does not indicate adverse impact. With regard to age-group differences, only individuals between the ages of 40 and 69 are protected under the Age Discrimination in Employment Act (1967). The reported age-group prevalence data clearly show that people between 40 and 69 would not be adversely affected by the implementation of a preemployment drug-testing program. Nevertheless, one should keep in mind that a court's subjective notion of what constitutes a "substantial disparity" may be the final determinant of whether differences in selection rates are large enough to indicate adverse impact (see, e.g., Gold, 1985; Morris, 1978).

Drug-test results were significantly associated with both job absence and involuntary separation. The degree of association was .33 for absenteeism and .22 for involuntary separation. In addition, drug-test results also contributed significantly to the prediction of absenteeism and involuntary separation as measures of job performance after pertinent covariates were controlled.

The magnitude of these relationships may be underestimated because of the misclassification of individuals. Both false-positive and false-negative classification errors can potentially contribute to this underestimation. With regard to this study's drug test measures we determined through the quality-control study that the only errors observed were due to false-negative classifications. Similar quality-control findings have been reported elsewhere (Frings, Battaglia, & White, 1989) and are to be expected in drug-testing programs complying with established professional standards. In fact, the detection of a single false-positive result at any time by government regulators can result in a laboratory's having its certification revoked (U.S. Department of Health and Human Services, 1988).

With regard to the injury and accident results, various factors may have contributed to the nonsignificant findings. First, given the low observed base rate (approximately 10% for both injuries and accidents), any meaningful disparity in injury or accident rates between the positive and negative drug-test groups would require a larger number of positive cases than was available in this study. Furthermore, the relatively short tenure of study participants (1.3 years) at the time the analyses were performed may have contributed to these low base rates. As the tenure of participants increases, the accident and injury rates are expected to increase, which will permit us to more efficiently detect any true differences.

Finally, the practical meaningfulness of a preemployment drug-testing program may be assessed in light of two criteria: the type of employment errors that would result from such a program and the economic utility of such a prediction system. When performed by a competent laboratory, the GC/MS confirmation test has an essentially zero rate of false-positive classification, as we found with this study's quality-control evaluation. This is in contrast to personnel-selection tests that attempt to predict low base-rate phenomena (e.g., an integrity test intended to predict infrequent deception; Murphy, 1987). The virtual absence of false-positive drug-test results makes this highly controversial type of employment error extremely unlikely; in other words, the probability of rejecting applicants who erroneously test positive and would have performed satisfactorily on the job had they been hired is very low. In a drug testing program that complies with professional standards, there can be little doubt that individuals who test positive have recently used illicit drugs. The real question is whether this information will help reduce employment error. The results of this study show that preemployment drug tests do provide information that contributes significantly to the prediction of such outcomes as absenteeism and turnover.

The cost savings derived by implementing a drug-testing program may also be used to evaluate the usefulness of drug-test results as a viable selection device. Our estimates of the amount of lost productivity associated with hiring job applicants who test positive indicated that the U.S. Postal Service could save approximately $4,000,000 in undiscounted and unadjusted Productivity costs in the first year and that the accrued savings for one cohort of new employees over their tenure would be about $52,750,000. Although these cost estimates are not adjusted for economic considerations, such as discount rates and variable costs, the estimated losses in productivity associated with involuntary separation and job absence nevertheless represent significant costs that could be avoided through the use of a sound drug testing program. However, there are important facts that should be kept in mind when examining the absence-related cost savings. First, these costs are underestimates of gross utility. They do not take into account certain incidental costs associated with absenteeism. As noted previously, such costs might include supervisors' compensation for time spent per day dealing with all the problems stemming from employee absenteeism (such as scheduling, lowered productivity, instructing replacement employees, and checking on performance of replacement employees), overtime premiums, and so forth. Moreover, these cost savings were based on only two outcome measures (i.e., absenteeism and turnover); other outcome measures may reflect additional savings. Second, because the average tenure of the study participants was only 1.3 years, the observed difference in absenteeism rates between the positive and negative drug-test groups (2.47%) may be an underestimate of the real difference in absence rates in the population. We anticipate that the discrepancy in absence rates between the two groups will increase as participants gain tenure. Finally, the savings presented are for one cohort of new employees. Assuming that the drug program would be used every year for screening new applicants, a more accurate estimate of the savings would have to account for the compounding effect of adding a new cohort every year.

In summary, the results of this study establish an empirical relationship between preemployment drug-test results and various work-related outcome measures in an applied setting. The practical significance of these relationships was demonstrated with a decision-theoretic utility model. This study represents a first step toward building a scientific data base exploring drug-use-job-performance relationships. Further investigation of drug-test results and other outcome measures (e.g., performance appraisals, grievances, disciplinary actions) is encouraged.

NOTE

1. When the purpose is to evaluate a selection procedure, the group is made up of employees selected without the use of the test being evaluated; that is, the appropriate SD_y is the value for the (unrestricted) applicant group, the group with which the selection procedure is actually used. In this study, such a group consisted of all new employees regardless of test results (i.e., the pooled group).

REFERENCES

Abelson, M. A. (1987). Examination of avoidable and unavoidable turnover. *Journal of Applied Psychology, 72,* 382–386.

Age Discrimination in Employment Act of 1964, 621, 29 U.S.C. (1967).

Blank, D. L., & Fenton, J. W (1989). Early employment testing for marijuana: Demographic and employee retention patterns. In S. W Gust & J. M. Walsh (Eds.), *Drugs in the workplace: Research and evaluation data* (pp. 139–150). Rockville, MD: National Institute on Drug Abuse.

Brogden, H. E. (1949). When testing pays off. *Personnel Psychology, 2,* 171–183.

Burke, M. J., & Frederick, J. (1986). A comparison of economic utility estimates for alternative SD_y estimation procedures. *Journal of Applied Psychology, 71,* 334–339.

Cascio, W. E., & McEvoy, G. M. (1984, August). Extension of utility analysis research to turnover reduction strategies. Paper presented at the 92nd Annual Convention of the American Psychological Association, Toronto, Canada.

Castro, E. G., Newcomb, M. D., & Cadish, K. (1987). Lifestyle differences between young adult cocaine users and their nonuser peers. *Journal of Drug Education, 17,* 89–111.

Chait, L. D., Fischman, M. W., & Schuster, C. R. (1985). "Hangover" effects the morning after marijuana smoking. *Drug and Alcohol Dependence, 15,* 229–238.

Cook, R. E., & Harrel, A. V. (1987). Drug abuse among working adults: Prevalence rates and recommended strategies. *Health Education Research*, 2, 353–359.

Cronbach, L. J., & Gleser, G. C. (1965). *Psychological tests and personnel decisions.* Urbana: University of Illinois Press.

Crown, D. F., & Rosse, J. G. (1988). A critical review of the assumptions underlying drug testing. *Journal of Business and Psychology*, 3, 2241.

Dogoloff, L. I., & Angarola, R. T. (1985). In S. C. Price (Ed.), *Urine testing in the workplace* (pp. 5–31). Rockville, MD: American Council for Drug Education.

Donovan, J. E., & Jessor, R. (1985). Structure of problem behavior in adolescence and young adulthood. *Journal of Consulting and Clinical Psychology*, 53, 890–904.

Finkle, B. S., Blanke, R. V., & Walsh, J. M. (1990). *Technical, scientific, and procedural issues of employee drug testing.* Rockville, MD: National Institute on Drug Abuse.

Fischman, M. W., Kelly, T. H., & Foltin, R. W. (1989, September). Residential laboratory research: A multidimensional evaluation of the effects of drugs on behavior. Paper presented at the National Institute on Drug Abuse conference on Drugs in the Workplace: Research and Evaluation Data, Bethesda, MD.

Flanagan, R. J., Strauss, G., & Ulman, L. (1974). Worker discontent and work place behavior. *Industrial Relations*, 13, 101–123.

Fleiss, J. L. (1973). *Statistical methods for rates and proportions.* New York: Wiley.

Frings, C. S., Battaglia, D., & White, R. M. (1989). Status of drugs-of-abuse testing in urine under blind conditions: An AACC study. *Clinical Chemistry*, 35, 891–894.

Gold, M. E. (1985). Griggs' folly: An essay on the theory, problems, and origin of the adverse impact definition of employment discrimination and a recommendation for reform. *Industrial Relations Law Journal*, 7, 429–598.

Harrell, E. E. (1986). The logist procedure. In *SUGI Supplemental library user-guide, Version 5 Edition* (pp. 269–292) [Computer program manual]. Cary, NC: SAS Institute.

Harwood, H. J., Napolitano, D. M., Kristiansen, P. L., & Collins, J. J. (1984). *Economic costs to society of alcohol and drug abuse and mental illness: 1980.* Research Triangle Park, NC: Research Triangle Institute.

Hawks, R. L. (1986). Analytical methodology. In R. L. Hawks & C. N. Chiang (Eds.), *Urine testing for drugs of abuse* (pp. 30–42). Rockville, MD: National Institute on Drug Abuse.

Hedges, J. N. (1973). Absence from work: A look at some national data. *Monthly Labor Review*, 96, 24–30.

Herning, R. I., Glover, B. J., Koeppl, B. S., & Jaffe, J. H. (1989, September). Cocaine and workplace performance: Inferences from clinical studies. Paper presented at the National Institute on Drug Abuse conference on Drugs in the Workplace: Research and Evaluation Data, Bethesda, MD.

Holden, K. L., & Overall, J. E. (1987). Tests of significance for differences in counts of rare events in two treatment groups. *Educational and Psychological Measurement*, 47, 881–892.

Hunter, J. E., Schmidt, E. L., & Coggin, T. D. (1988). Problems and pitfalls in using capital budgeting and financial accounting techniques in assessing the utility of personnel programs. *Journal of Applied Psychology*, 73, 522–528.

Johnston, L. D., O'Malley, P. M., & Bachman, J. G. (1987). *National trends in drug use and related factors among American high school students and young adults, 1975–1986.* Rockville, MD: National Institute on Drug Abuse.

Kandel, D. B. (1975). Stages in adolescent involvement in drug use. *Science*, 190, 912–914.

Kandel, D. B., & Yamaguchi, K. (1987). Job mobility and drug use: An event history analysis. *American Journal of Sociology*, 92, 836–878.

Ledvinka, J. (1982). *Federal regulation of personnel and human resource management*. Boston, MA: Kent Publishing Co.

Levy, R. (1983). Preemployment qualitative urine toxicology screening. *Journal of Occupational Medicine*, 25, 579–580.

McDaniel, M. A. (1988). Does pre-employment drug use predict on-the-job suitability? *Personnel Psychology*, 41, 717–729.

Morgan, J. P. (1984). Problems of mass urine screening for misused drugs. *Journal of Psychoactive Drugs*, 16, 305–317.

Morris, E. C. (1978). *Current trends in the use (and misuse) of statistics in employment discrimination litigation (2nd ed)*. Washington, DC: Equal Employment Advisory Council.

Mosteller, E. (1968). Association and estimation in contingency tables. *Journal of the American Statistical Association*, 63, 1–28.

Moyer, T. R., Palmen, M. A., Johnson, R., Charlson, J. R., & Ellefson, (1987). Marijuana testing—How good is it? *Mayo Clinic Proceedings*, 62, 413–417.

Murphy, K. R. (1987). Detecting infrequent deception. *Journal of Applied Psychology*, 72, 611–614.

Murray, J. B. (1986). Marijuana's effects on human cognitive functions, psychomotor functions, and personality. *Journal of General Psychology*, 113, 23–55.

Newcomb, M. D. (1988). *Drug use in the workplace: Risk factors for disruptive substance use among young adults*. Dover, MA: Auburn House.

Nicholson, N., Brown, C. A., & Chadwick-Jones, J. K. (1977). Absence from work and personal characteristics. *Journal of Applied Psychology*, 62, 319–327.

Parish, D. C. (1989). Relation of the pre-employment drug testing result to employment status: A one year follow-up. *Journal of General Internal Medicine*, 4, 44–47.

Raju, N. S., Burke, M. J., & Normand, J. (1990). A new approach for utility analysis. *Journal of Applied Psychology*, 75, 3–12.

SAS Institute. (1985). *SAS user-guide—Statistics, Version 5 Edition* [Computer program manual]. Cary, NC: Author.

Schmidt, E. L., Hunter, J. E., & Pearlman, K. (1982). Assessing the economic impact of personnel programs on workforce productivity. *Personnel Psychology*, 35, 333–347.

Schwartz, R. H., & Hawks, R. L. (1985). Laboratory detection of marijuana. *JAMA: The Journal of the American Medical Association*, 245, 788–792.

Staff (1989, August). Highlights of the 1988 national household survey on drug abuse. *National Institute on Drug Abuse Capsules*, C-86–13, pp. 1–4.

Steers, R. M., & Rhodes, S. R. (1979). Major influences on employee attendance: A process model. In R. M. Steers & L. W. Porter (Eds.), *Motivation and work behavior* (pp. 326–340). New York: McGraw-Hill.

Stein, I. A., Newcomb, M. D., & Bentler, R. M. (1988). Structure of drug use behaviors and consequences among young adults: Multitrait, multimethod assessment of frequency, quantity, worksite, and problem substance use. *Journal of Applied Psychology*, 73, 595–605.

U.S. Department of Health and Human Services. (1988). Mandatory guidelines for federal workplace drug testing programs; final guidelines; notice. *Federal Register, 53*, 11970–11989.

U.S. Department of Labor, Bureau of Labor Statistics. (1989). *Survey of employer anti-drug programs*. Washington, DC: Author.

U.S. Department of Labor, Employee Standard Administration, Office of Workers' Compensation Programs. (1986). *Form CA-1*. Washington, DC: Author.

U.S. Postal Service. (1984). *Accident report. PS Form 1769*. Washington, DC: Author.

U.S. Postal Service. (1987). *A study of turnover among part-time flexible employees*. Washington, DC: Author.

U.S. Postal Service. (1989). *National payroll hours summary report—PFY 1989*. Washington, DC: Author.

Walsh, J. M., & Hawks, R. L. (1988). *Employee drug screening and detection of drug use by urinalysis*. Rockville, MD: National Institute on Drug Abuse.

Washton, A. M., & Gold, M. S. (1987). Recent trends in cocaine abuse as seen from the "800 COCAINE" hotline. In A. M. Washton & M. S. Gold (Eds.), *Cocaine: A clinician's handbook*, (pp. 10–22). New York: Guilford Press.

Willette, R. E. (1986). Drug testing programs. In R. L. Hawks & C. N. Chiang (Eds.), *Urine testing for drugs of abuse* (pp. 5–12). Rockville, MD: National Institute on Drug Abuse.

Winkler, H., & Sheridan, J. (1989, September). An examination of behavior related to drug use at Georgia Power Company. Paper presented at the National Institute on Drug Abuse conference on Drugs in the Workplace: Research and Evaluation Data, Bethesda, MD.

Wrich, J. T. (1988). Beyond testing: Coping with drugs at work. *Harvard Business Review, 66*, 120–130.

Yesavage, J. A., Leirer, V., Denari, M., & Hollister, L. E. (1985). Carry-over effects of marijuana intoxication on aircraft pilot performance: A preliminary report. *American Journal of Psychiatry, 142*, 1325–1329.

Chapter 5

Ethnographic Field Research

Three anthropological studies of marijuana use and its effects have been conducted; one in Costa Rica (Carter, 1980), one in Greece (Stefanis, et al., 1976), and one in Jamaica (Dreher, 1982). These studies illustrate the strengths and potential weakness of this approach to inquiry. Researchers lived in or near the communities and observed the ways marijuana was "woven into the fabric of working-class life" (Dreher, 1982: 197) in each country. This approach to inquiry produces a more complex understanding of the role of marijuana in work life within a small population. It is impossible to capture the richness of the findings of these studies in a brief review, so only their findings with respect to variables examined in experimental and survey research will be discussed here.

ATTENTION, LEARNING, MEMORY, AND PSYCHOMOTOR SKILLS

The Costa Rican study did include tests of attention, learning, and memory as well as psychomotor skills. The author summarizes the results as follows:

Although some users reported that marijuana was impairing their short-term memory processes, this was *not* confirmed by the neuropsychological battery. Lack of agreement between the test results and user perception may be attributable to the fact that users were reporting their *acute* reactions whereas the test battery was designed and administered to measure *chronic* effects. No hard data were obtained regarding the effect of marijuana use on driving ability. However, some of the user subjects did earn their living by driving trucks, buses, or taxis, and some preferred to drive while under the influence of the drug. (Carter, 1980: 202)

MOTIVATION

Regarding the relationship between indices of motivation to achieve and level of marijuana consumption, Carter observed, "The heaviest users had the highest incomes, the least unemployment, and the most stable job histories of the entire user group. They also more frequently reported that their preferred activity while intoxicated was to work. As with Jamaicans who used the drug primarily as a work adjunct, Costa Rican users did not usually report the 'high' sought by American recreational users" (Carter, 1980: 202). Page (1983) and Page, Fletcher, and True (1988) found few differences in the symptoms of amotivational syndrome between cannabis users and nonusers in a Costa Rican sample, a result which is consistent with Carter's (1980) observations.

JOB PERFORMANCE

In the second of these studies, conducted among agricultural laborers in Jamaica (Dreher, 1982), data were collected on earnings and other measures of performance. These performance measures showed no consistent differences between smokers of marijuana and nonsmokers in job performance at low-skill harvesting jobs, but there was some evidence that nonusers fared better than users (Dreher, 1982: 173–185). Dreher suggests the following explanation for this divergence, "While there is little evidence to indicate that differences in worker productivity—measured in dollars and tons—can be successfully related to ganja (marijuana) use, there is strong indication that the attitudes of managerial staff toward ganja use do affect worker performance. If nonsmokers are consistently selected on the basis of alleged reliability or manageability over smokers for the most lucrative jobs, it would be surprising if they failed to produce and earn more" (Dreher, 1982: 191). This suggests that relationships observed between marijuana and productivity as measured by wages may be influenced by cultural (and subcultural) attitudes toward marijuana use.

Dreher's study was criticized by Nahas (1985) on the grounds that sampling biases accounted for the failure to find any negative effects of marijuana on health or productivity and on the grounds that observer biases account for the positive motivational effects of marijuana observed.

One interesting finding of both the Carter and Dreher studies is that the *perception* of the effects of marijuana on work performance is much different among the Jamaican and Costa Rican study participants than it is among people in the U.S. Members of the working class and agricultural laborers who used marijuana in both Costa Rica and Jamaica believed that it could *facilitate* work performance. One ganja user in Dreher's study remarked, "For the man that have the workin' spirit, it let him work more" (Dreher, 1982: 173). A later ethnographic study in Jamaica confirmed this perception (Broad & Feinberg, 1995).

Similar attitudes are found in India, in that marijuana has a reputation as the "herb of concentration" dating back at least 3,400 years to the Vedic scriptures.

Among some subcultures it is seen as an aid to concentration in meditation and work (Aldrich, 1977; Morningstar, 1985: 157). This belief seems incompatible with the common view in the U.S. that marijuana reduces concentration and motivation. However, among some subcultures of users, the belief that marijuana increases concentration is more common. Sussman et al. (1996) reported that 15% of a group of continuation students in the U.S. expressed this belief (which the authors call a myth).

The fact that members of different cultures and subcultures have radically different perceptions of marijuana's effects on performance suggests that these effects may be largely socially mediated. It may be that perceived effects of marijuana vary from one country to the next *or* that members of the working class in each culture have different perceptions of marijuana's effects than do members of the middle class.

METHODOLOGICAL ISSUES

The great strength of ethnographic field research is that it allows researchers to probe a phenomenon in depth and to identify the variables that are most important in explaining this phenomenon. Typically, such research is conducted without explicitly stated hypotheses, and researchers are open to information that may come from unexpected findings and exploratory inquiry. However, the lack of specific hypotheses to guide research makes it necessary for researchers to engage in ex post facto explanation (Kerlinger, 1973: 390–391).

In anthropological field studies, researchers typically live with or near their subjects and collect a great deal of information on the way practices like marijuana use are integrated into their day-to-day life. However, in this process it is difficult to ensure that researchers' prior biases do not affect their collection or interpretation of information. For these reasons, it is safer to use this sort of research for hypothesis generation rather than hypothesis testing.

COMMENTS ON THE DREHER STUDY

The example of ethnographic field research we have chosen to include is from the book *Working Men and Ganja* by Melanie Dreher. This study deals with the use of marijuana by Jamaican agricultural laborers involved in harvesting sugar cane on three separate farms under the direction of three separate supervisors or "bushers." The study, reported in detail in her book, describes the roles marijuana plays in working-class life in rural Jamaica and how it is connected with kinship and neighborhood ties as well as group and political affiliations. Social relationships, in which ganja plays a part, influence the organization of labor and patterns of cooperation and competition and the stabilization of each worker's place in a basically unstable labor scheme.

Ganja smoking is well integrated with work and leisure activities in this setting to the point that those who avoid smoking ganja under some circumstances risk offending other members of the community. Thus, in this community, marijuana smoking is not a sign of deviance or alienation. In fact, the opposite appears to be true. As one of Dreher's informants commented, "Those who don't smoke are set apart; they are most despairing. When men smoke together they are united; they stand for socialism [sociability]" (Dreher, 1982: 201). The circumstances under which men in rural Jamaica decide to smoke and with whom they choose to smoke are not random choices; nor are they based only on a desire to share the drug experience. Rather, they reflect social and economic conditions and limitations of the local environment.

As part of the study, Dreher collected information on various measures of worker performance at sugar cane harvesting including back pay, wages, bonuses, and tons of sugar cane harvested in two periods. These data are presented in the table contained in the excerpt.

The data show an interesting divergence between performance measures related to compensation (back pay, wages, and bonuses) and those related to production (tonnage harvested in the first and second periods). Though none of the differences were statistically significant, an examination of the means shows that when the results for the three farms were summed, smokers had lower back pay, wages, and bonuses though they harvested more cane than nonsmokers. The description of the management practices at the three farms provides information that explains this divergence as well as the differences in productivity between the three farms. Thus, this excerpt demonstrates the value of the ethnographic approach to research on the issue of marijuana use and job performance.

We would like to draw the reader's attention to the differences between cane production between the three farms and suggest that a reanalysis of the data might show that the differences in cane production between users and nonusers were significant, at least for the first period. Professor Dreher used a t-test to assess the significance of the difference in tonnage between the smokers and nonsmokers. The t-test is essentially a ratio of the difference (or variance) between smokers and nonsmokers divided by the variance attributable to all other factors that may influence performance, including the variance due to the farm on which the individuals worked. From the table, we can see that there were large differences in productivity between the different farms. Indeed, the differences between farms are so large that they swamp the differences between smokers and nonsmokers. In the chapter, Dreher explains the reasons for these differences between farms.

Instead of using a t-test to assess the differences between smokers and nonsmokers, the author could have used a two-way Analysis of Variance (ANOVA) to control for the variance between farms. This analysis would have included the data for smokers and nonsmokers at each farm and would have assessed the significance of the differences between farms and the significance of the difference between smokers and nonsmokers separately. By removing the variance between farms from the calculation of the significance of the difference between smokers and nonsmokers, the two-way ANOVA would have shown that the differences between smokers and nonsmokers in the first period approached statistical significance.

A simpler nonparametric technique called the sign test (Siegel, 1956: 68–75) can be used to show that the marijuana users did, in fact, harvest significantly more cane than the nonusers. The table shows that smokers harvested more cane than nonsmokers at all three farms in both the first and second periods. Thus, all of the six possible comparisons favored smokers. The sign test shows that the probability of this occurring by chance is .016, well below the standard cutoff of .05 used to assess statistical significance. In other words, using the sign test, we can say that the difference between smokers and nonsmokers is significant at $p < .016$.

As noted earlier, there is a divergence between actual productivity and financial rewards for smokers versus nonsmokers. This is due to policies on the part of the supervisers of the farms that have the effect of favoring nonsmokers over smokers. This serves to emphasize the importance of a point we will discuss further in the concluding chapter of this book. Beliefs about the effects of marijuana on job performance may become self-fulfilling prophesies. If employers believe that marijuana users are poor workers, and establish employment policies favoring nonusers, then users may in fact become poorer workers.

This reading gives insights into the potential value of a single well-conducted piece of ethnographic field research on a very complex topic like the role of marijuana in the workplace. Admittedly, the study involved only one type of job in a specific setting (rural Jamaica) and a relatively small number of subjects, all of whom were men of working age. Therefore, it would not be wise to generalize these results to all types of jobs. However, this study raises many questions and suggestions for future controlled experiments, surveys, and field research.

One of the most important contributions of this study has to do with the questions it raises about the "amotivational syndrome," which marijuana is believed to produce. Users claim that the use of ganja actually *increases* motivation to work hard. As noted earlier, there is some evidence to suggest that marijuana users may harvest more cane than nonusers, though the effects of marijuana use are confounded with age (smokers tend to be younger than nonsmokers). At a minimum, we would have to say that the study provides no support for the claim that users are less motivated than nonusers. Whether or not marijuana increases individual productivity as users claim, Dreher's study shows that it often provides the impetus for both individuals and groups to accomplish work. It appears to enhance the social relationships necessary for productivity. Woodward (1962) noted the importance of sociotechnical systems in work productivity in British coal mines and it would appear that marijuana influences these systems in this type of agricultural labor in Jamaica as well.

Dreher notes that her cross-cultural research exposes the ethnocentrism of much of the research on marijuana done in America and Europe. One of the greatest problems created by this ethnocentrism is that it tends to narrow the focus of research on the phenomenon of marijuana use to individual variables at the expense of variables relating to the social context. She suggests that this focus has affected the choice of methods, the units of analysis, and the theoretical models used to interpret results. Despite the fact that marijuana cannot be understood without understanding its place in a social context, much of the past research on marijuana has focused on the marijuana experience and characteristics of the individual user rather than the society and social context within which marijuana is used. This research focus helps explain why marijuana use has been linked to such individual characteristics as deviance and rebellion and why its use is seen as a way of relieving boredom and as a stepping stone to harder drugs.

Dreher argues that two models have dominated research in this area and that each is based on its own assumptions about the role of culture. Both models, however, take a simplistic view of culture that does not stand up to more detailed examination in ethnographic studies. She calls these models the *predisposing background model* and the *deviant subculture model* (Dreher, 1982: 198–199).

Research within the predisposing background model focuses on common characteristics of marijuana users thought to influence users' initial use of marijuana and their later patterns of use. Given the availability of marijuana, some individuals are predisposed to use it and continue to use it because of psychological, social, and cultural characteristics expressed in their individual behavior. The "cultural milieu" is considered important because it provides the situation in which marijuana smoking is permitted, but cultural factors are addressed mainly as background characteristics of individuals. Thus, the role of social context is sometimes neglected. In much of the survey research, for example, populations are surveyed and explanations are derived from statistical associations between amount or pattern of use and individual demographic characteristics, expressed beliefs and features of the individuals' lifestyles. According to this model, subpopulations maintain different patterns of marijuana use because of the psychological or sociological characteristics of their members. The focus on marijuana use and the separation of marijuana smoking from other aspects of his or her social behavior often lead to overly simplistic explanations of the relationship of marijuana use to workplace behavior. Marijuana use is explained in terms of one or a few variables related to characteristics of the individual.

In contrast, the deviant subculture model stresses the influence of the marijuana-using group or subculture in promoting individual use of the drug. According to this model, a group of individuals who share an activity considered deviant by society develop a group identity based on marijuana use. New users are encouraged to adopt this identity as part of the process of socialization into the group. Survey and field research based on this model tends to focus narrowly on relationships and behaviors that directly involve marijuana use, rather than looking at the wider social context and the ways individuals' roles in the marijuana-using subculture fit with other roles they play in society.

In the Jamaican sample studied by Dreher, the sort of survey research she criticizes would have yielded results consistent with what is already known about users but far less helpful than the results her study produced. If the standard survey of individual smokers had been done instead of the detailed ethnographic study she performed, researchers would have found that 99% of heavy smokers were from the lowest socioeconomic groups, 98% were functionally illiterate, 80% do not attend church, and 68% live in substandard housing. Most would be Afro-Jamaicans, and the heaviest users would be between 25 and 45 years of age. These results, however, would give us little understanding of the dynamics of marijuana use or the reasons why these individuals use the drug.

According to Professor Dreher, formal interviews and surveys based on the predisposing background model and the deviant subculture model tend to analytically separate the individual from his or her socioeconomic environment through the use of previously designated, researcher-formulated variables. She feels that, though this approach is methodologically rigorous, it often leads researchers to ignore significant social and cultural data that would be more likely to be discovered using community-based institutional analysis. Needless to say, survey researchers do sometimes ignore significant social and cultural data, but when they do, this is due to the limitations of the researchers rather than fundamental flaws in the research method. One of the purposes of this book is to argue for the incorporation of insights from ethnographic methods into survey (and laboratory) research, thereby overcoming this potential weakness of survey research.

Dreher's study shows that the ethnographic method can correct misleading assumptions that might develop from correlations between variables used in survey research. For example, Dreher's study confirmed the results of survey research showing that poorer men were more likely to smoke marijuana than middle-class men. One conclusion that might be drawn from this fact is that marijuana use is a means of escape from the problems associated with poverty. However, Dreher's study showed that ganja smoking was most prevalent when employment opportunities were abundant and the men had greater amounts of money. Further, of the three separate communities she studied, marijuana smoking was most prevalent in the community where the laboring class was most socially and economically stable.

Her results also showed a correlation between marijuana use and anti-social and violent behavior on the Deerfield Estate. This might lead to the conclusion that marijuana use promotes anti-social behavior and violence. However, upon closer observation, she found that the smoking and exchange of ganja were often attempts to deal with a highly charged and competitive work environment (Dreher, 1982: 200). It may be that this type of research is the only way to sort out the complex relationship between marijuana use and social behaviors. Without such in-depth exploration of the use of marijuana in a social context, researchers may tend to accept simplistic explanations of the causal role of the drug in work and social life.

According to Dreher, (1982: 202–204) both the predisposing background model and the deviant subculture model suggest that individuals' values determine whether or not he or she will smoke marijuana and that the existence of these values in a culture determine the extent to which marijuana use will be present in this culture. Thus, these models suggest that reducing the use of marijuana in a culture is a relatively straightforward (though not necessarily simple) matter of changing the values among members of the society. However, these models are based on assumptions of cultural uniformity and do not account for situational and developmental variations in the expression of marijuana-related values in a culture.

Her study shows that social and institutional circumstances will strongly influence the expression of values related to marijuana use. For example, in response to the labor problems involved in harvesting cane, farmers sometimes set aside their values regarding marijuana use. Though they do not use ganja themselves and forbid their children to use it, they will sometimes procure and distribute ganja to their workers. Despite their claim that ganja makes workers difficult to manage, supervisors recognize the value of ganja in expediting production under some circumstances and will promote its use among workers as well as attempting to reduce police enforcement of laws against ganja smoking. Values related to the use of ganja sometimes conflict with other values so that compromise is required.

Further, individuals may change their values with respect to the use of ganja when they moved to new communities or jobs. She cites examples of community leaders who strongly condemn the use of marijuana but who were once among those who not only smoked it but cultivated and sold it as well. Their change in values make sense when you understand that social and economic mobility may be initiated by ganja use but maintained by criticizing marijuana use.

Thus, while individual beliefs and values may play a role in the decision to smoke ganja, the data from Dreher's study shows that the relationship between beliefs about marijuana and behavior related to marijuana is much more complex than is implied in the simple theory that individuals make decisions and take actions in accordance with their basic values. Values linked to marijuana use are not formed in a vacuum but shaped in a particular social context that may either support or reject marijuana. In the Jamaican working class, marijuana use is a well-established institution. Therefore, any interpretation of ganja use must include the structure and organization of the community or neighborhood, work group cohesion, relationships between partners, and the necessity of maintaining and reinforcing group identity.

Dreher observes that the mode of consumption of marijuana in these communities is very important in evaluating its appropriateness. For example, she observed men who were negative about smoking marijuana in the form of chillum but who smoked up to fifteen spliffs a day. She argues that the mode of consumption has symbolic significance that determines whether marijuana use is acceptable or not. When marijuana assumes symbolic significance, individual drives and perceptions centered on properties or effects of the substance become less useful in explaining consumption and its effects as well as the degree of marijuana use in society. Marijuana consumption in Jamaica rarely moves outside institutionally defined limitations to the point where it was used primarily for personal relief.

Dreher argues that simply asking smokers why they smoke is insufficient. Ethnographic research of the type she conducted also involves asking nonusers why they chose not to use the drug. She feels that until community-based studies of marijuana use are conducted in several North American contexts, with subjects selected because they are representative of society in general rather than because of their level of marijuana use, it will be difficult to establish the role of marijuana use in the work lives and social lives of American users. Such research is essential in determining the extent to which the findings of ethnographic studies conducted in other cultures apply in the United States. To our knowledge, no such studies have been conducted in the United States. Thus, we will end this chapter with a call for ethnographic studies on the role of marijuana use in the American workplace that focus on how marijuana use is integrated into the social lives of workers and the functions it serves in helping individuals adjust to the demands of work life.

APPENDIX A

Ganja and Worker Performance

Melanie Creagan Dreher

Routine smokers of ganja in all three communities believe that ganja enhances their ability to work. According to popular belief, ganja affects the ability to work in two ways. First, smoking reportedly produces an immediate surge of energy. An informant in Leyburn claims, for example, that when he has a large piece of work to do, such as weeding or clearing a field, he first sits down, smokes a spliff, and within fifteen minutes is ready to begin the task. Other typical comments include:

> When crop is on I "eat" the weed. It mek I (lets me) feel workish. (Deerfield).
>
> It mek I be powerful to work; it give I courage. (Buckland).
>
> During crop me ha fe for breakfast, lunch and, dinner. (Deerfield).
>
> It give me a different change of personality; it mek I feel stronger, work calmly, give a longer breath. (Leyburn).
>
> For the man that have the workin' spirit, it let him work more. (Buckland).

The second way in which ganja enhances the ability to work is through the regular consumption of ganja teas and tonics. A majority of informants, including both smokers and non-smokers, endorse ganja teas and tonics as being efficacious in promoting strength and physical stamina. As one Leyburn farmer claimed, "Come November (a labor-intensive month in Leyburn), me drink the tonic before bed and me can work on just a few hours sleep."

Excerpted from Melanie Dreher, *Working Men and Ganja: Marijuana Use in Rural Jamaica*, Philadelphia, ISHI Press, 1982, pp. 173–196.

Likewise, men scheduled for farm work abroad, anticipating continuous manual labor in a comparatively cold climate, may begin a regimen of ganja tea or tonic a few months prior to departure.

The strength of this belief is reflected by the seasonal variations in the amount of ganja smoking, particularly in Deerfield. Because workers increase their consumption of ganja with the objective of augmenting their productivity, smokers and vendors uniformly reported burgeoning ganja activity when the "crop is on." To a somewhat lesser extent, the same is true of Leyburn farmers whose heaviest smoking periods take place in July and August and again in November and December. In both these communities the periods of increased ganja activity coincide with labor intensive mounts in which there is increased cash available for routine ganja purchases. These seasonal fluctuations in ganja use, typical of Leyburn and Deerfield, are for the most part absent in Buckland. A notable exception to the more consistent pattern of ganja consumption in this community are those men, including loading crews and some cane farmers, who are directly or indirectly related to the cane industry. For example, Frank Davies, from Buckland, farms a small cane piece, has a part-time job during crop time cleaning the boilers in the sugar factory, and increases his volume of trade as a carpenter during reaping season; he uses ganja more frequently during this active time, claiming, "When me need strength, it help de body more." However, for the majority of workers in Buckland, temporal variation in ganja activity is on a weekly rather than seasonal basis with a spurt of ganja purchasing on Friday, which is pay day. This weekly cycle is also evident if in Deerfield, though during reaping season heightened ganja activity extends from pay day through Saturday and Sunday; the overtime differential in pay on the weekend stimulates increased worker performance.

These community-level differences in the relationship between ganja and work also apply to the apportionment of daily ganja consumption between work and leisure. Thus, Leyburn smokers report and were observed consuming more ganja during work hours than in leisure time. In Buckland, however, where the reverse pattern is evident, men tend to reserve their supply of ganja for recreational purposes after working hours. As one Buckland laborer explained, "The work not dat strivin' again like first time" (when Windsor Farms was planted in cane). Except for a few casual laborers who gather and husk coconuts for small farmers, most laborers on the properties in Buckland are paid on a daily rather than task basis. Thus, workers no longer feel the intense pressure to step up productivity. Buckland's major ganja vendor confirmed the difference in ganja activities, claiming that though the volume of his business has not decreased, it is evidently organizationally different. He no longer goes into the fields to sell weed to laborers as he did to cane cutters; nor do workers call at his yard early in the morning to purchase ganja on their way to work. Now his heaviest business transpires in the afternoon and evening when men are on their way home from work.

Predictably, ganja activity in Buckland shifts contexts with the season. When the crop is on, cane workers, paid by the task, smoke more ganja in the work context than in the recreational. During dull season, however, these same men emphasize leisure smoking. It is significant that their dull season jobs generally consist of "day work" for the sugar estate or the surrounding banana and coconut estates, following a system of payment similar to that of Buckland.

Because Buckland men place less emphasis on the use of ganja for stimulating production, they are considerably more lenient in their assessment of non-smokers. Though regular users insist that ganja enhances their own work performance, comments to the effect that non-smokers are less efficient workers than smokers are rare. In Leyburn, on the other hand, smokers regularly distinguish themselves from non-smokers in terms of their capacity for work. Non-smoking men are frequently regarded as hard-working or men who "c'yan keep up" to the difficult tasks of farming. Since the men in Leyburn who earn a living solely through wage labor for other farmers also tend to be non-smokers, this commonly held belief receives empirical support. When names of productive, non-smoking farmers were mentioned to challenge this belief, regular users were quick to claim that when these farmers were doing their hardest work—five or ten years earlier—they consumed ganja regularly. Accordingly, now that they have grown sons to assist them and don't have to supplement their farm income with off-farm labor, the work is less taxing; therefore they were able to succumb to social pressure and relinquish ganja smoking. To further substantiate this position, it is often pointed out that most of these more senior farmers have continued to consume ganja in the form of tea or tonic.

Similar beliefs are common among cane workers in Deerfield, and it is not unusual to hear claims such as "Herb users work harder" and "Dem (non-smokers) c'yan keep up to the work me do when me smoke it." In both Leyburn and Deerfield, contingent beliefs and values rationalize the performance of those men who are obviously poor workers and who also happen to be regular smokers. Explanations include theories that poor workers did not eat enough food ("Weed is a t'ing dat require plenty good food"), that they smoke in the hot sun, or on an empty stomach; sometimes the fault lay in some characteristic of the user himself—his brains are "too weak," or he is too young, inhibiting the "conscious" use of ganja.

In most rural Jamaican communities, where agricultural tasks vary daily and are performed in multifarious settings, the difficulties of establishing quantifiable units of productivity, or even ascertaining base line data pertaining to work performance, are almost insurmountable. Consequently, the claims of ganja users that smoking enhances their ability to work are as difficult to challenge as to sustain. The general progress of any own-account farmer is influenced by so many factors outside his control—weather conditions, market fluctuations, availability of land room and so forth—that his success, or lack of it, is not a fair or sufficient means of evaluating his productivity. The acute effects of ganja smoking on productivity have been objectively examined by Schaeffer (Rubin and Comitas, 1975: 63–79). In a rural Jamaican community not unlike Leyburn, Schaeffer analyzed the immediate effects of smoking in terms of energy expended and work accomplished. However, even that carefully executed study carried a note of caution that the results did not provide a basis for projection of productivity over a season, or a year, or in a different context.

In Deerfield, however, where the tons of cane cut and the number of days worked by each man are carefully recorded for payroll tabulation, at least it is possible to measure output in tons and dollars, and compare smokers with non-smokers in this regard. Unlike Schaeffer's analysis, which concentrated on the immediate effects of smoking on productivity, the figures pertaining to tonnage and earnings reported here are not indicative of the amount of cane a worker can cut within a given period of time.[1] The difficulties of measuring work performance in this sense, even on a sugar estate where production is carefully calculated, have been reviewed by Davidson (1973: 132–133) in his report on the labor force of the Jamaican sugar industry:

> In the first place it becomes clear on every estate that it is virtually impossible, given the present organization of the industry, to keep any kind of accurate check on the number of hours spent by a cutter in the field. The work may be half finished by the time the overseer arrives, a system of time clocks would be quite impractical and serve no useful purpose anyway. The fact is that hours are not homogeneous—the amount that a man can cut between 4:30 and 6:00 A.M. is quite different from his potentiality between 11:00 A.M. and 12:00 noon when the sun is blazing into the cane field. A measure of hours spent without reference to the period of the day would be of little use, even if the information could be obtained, which it cannot at present.

Thus, the tabulation of tonnage and earnings for Deerfield cane laborers reveals how a particular worker compares with other workers doing the same task in terms of tons cut and dollars earned over a given season. While it may not be feasible to talk about physical productivity per se, it is possible to compare workers with regard to their continued performance as earner-producers and relate that performance to their dispositions toward ganja.

The three reaping gangs selected for comparison are from Wilmington, Ipswich, and Dover. All three are mechanical-loading gangs and all represent premium employment opportunities for estate laborers. The Wilmington farm, with over eight hundred acres planted in cane,[2] was the first farm on the estate to institute mechanical loading. Prior to this change, Wilmington required a large reaping crew and experienced severe problems in attracting and keeping laborers for the duration of the reaping season. So successful was the transition from hand to mechanical loading in alleviating the critical labor shortages suffered each year, that within two years Ipswich, with thirteen hundred acres planted in cane,[3] was also converted to mechanical loading.

Before the elimination of hand loading, these farms had to depend on men from outside the area who migrated annually or permanently to provide a sufficient quantity of cutters. According to bushers, local men worked irregularly, and when they did work, preferred to load rather than to cut cane. Most of the men who were indigenous to Deerfield had additional occupational responsibilities, such as cultivation, fishing, and various small commercial and trade ventures which encroached on their performance as cane workers. Laboring for the estate was viewed as the most accessible but least desirable source of income and was readily relinquished for more promising opportunities when they appeared. As occupational pluralists, the needs of local men were more effectively met by loading than cutting. Complex and reciprocal arrangements established within spells permitted individual members to continue other vocational pursuits during crop time without losing a day's pay or bonus time. After completing the twenty weeks necessary to qualify for the crop bonus,[4] many of these men went back to their other work and were not seen again by the busher until the beginning of the next crop.

In contrast, men from outside the district had few, if any, sources of revenue other than cane work. For the most part they resided in company housing strategically located adjacent to the cane fields, and thus were always available to management. Many of these men, having little incentive to return to the parishes from which they came, remained in Deerfield through the dull season. Without access to land on which to cultivate, they relied solely on estate day work to tide them over to the next crop, and hence were in a position to develop an intensive year-round Association with the busher. Consequently, when hand loading was phased out, the remaining positions on the gang were awarded to those men whom the bushers felt had demonstrated their faithfulness by returning each year to do the least desirable tasks. At the time of the selections, local men complained bitterly of favoritism but had no recourse other than to seek work on one of the less desirable farms. Currently, only twenty-one percent of workers on Wilmington and eight percent on Ipswich are indigenous to the area, though many have established domestic unions with local women, moved out of worker housing, and become well integrated with community life.

Since the conversion to mechanical loading, which took place five years earlier on Wilmington and three years before on Ipswich, the process of attrition, accompanied by a policy of minimal replacement, has produced two reliable and comparatively small reaping gangs. Dover farm is the most recent flat-land farm to implement mechanical loading, the conversion taking place during the period of field work. Though this farm has roughly the same acreage planted in cane as Wilmington (eight hundred acres), only about three-fourths of this acreage are suitable for mechanical loading. The remainder continues to be loaded by a hand loading gang on the same farm. Though the manager of Dover refused to take any new men, his gang is currently large in proportion to the size of the farm. However, he expects that attrition will eventually produce a small stable gang similar to those in Ipswich and Wilmington. The Dover gang has the highest proportion of indigenous men (30 percent), many of whom had worked previously on Ipswich or Wilmington before hand loading was eliminated. There are no barracks on the Dover farm, though several men and their families live in government subsidized housing, built approximately twenty years earlier and situated on the hills that surround the Dover cane piece. As mechanical loading gangs, Wilmington, Ipswich, and Dover represent the three best employment opportunities for estate field laborers in Deerfield. While other gangs must reap hillside cane under hand-loading procedures, or work on low lands which restrict production to the first six weeks of reaping season, Ipswich, Dover, and Wilmington are almost entirely flat-land farms with an elevation that leaves production comparatively unaffected by rains.

Both smokers and non-smokers are found on all three gangs, but in varying proportions. As indicated in Table 5.1, Ipswich men are fairly evenly distributed between the two categories with 53 percent smokers and 47 percent non-smokers. The Dover gang, on the other hand, has almost twice as many smokers as non-smokers (65.5 percent and 34.1 percent), while Wilmington has just the opposite (34.6 percent are smokers and 65.4 are non-smokers). These differences in the prevalence of ganja smokers from farm to farm are often invoked by management to account for differences in productivity and manageability. Dover, with its high proportion of ganja smokers, is consistently cited as a managerial trouble spot where performance is low, disputes about pay checks are rampant, and where cutters often refuse to work, quarrel with the tractor drivers, and complain to the headmen. Wilmington and Ipswich, on the other hand, with the lowest rates of ganja use for the entire estate, are regarded as the most "polite" and "hard working" gangs.[5]

In order to evaluate the performance of workers, data were collected from the payroll stubs of 151 cutters on Dover, Ipswich, and Wilmington. Since payroll tabulations were made available for research purposes only after the reaping season had been completed, when the information was no longer of any use to the estate, some of the payroll information had been lost or destroyed. Therefore, a worker was included in the study only if data could be obtained for at least three of the five designated variables. Using this criterion, the sample presented here comprises at least 80 percent of the men on each of the three gangs though the N's are different for each variable, reflecting the missing data.

The averages compiled in Table 5.1 summarize the quantitative comparison of smokers and non-smokers for all farms and for individual farms by age, earnings, and production. Independent t-tests were performed on each variable to compute the levels of significance for differences between smokers and non-smokers. Because managers and head-men frequently report that younger men are faster workers and have a greater capacity for productivity than older men, the mean ages for smokers and non-smokers were computed for all farms and for individual farms. Independent t-tests revealed that while there was a significant difference in the mean age of smokers compared with non-smokers for all farms, the differences in mean ages between smokers and non-smokers on individual farms was not found to be significant.

The dependent variable, worker performance, comprises two major categories:

the first is earnings represented by "backpay," "wages," and "bonus"; the second is production represented by tons of cane cut during two selected three-week intervals ("first period" and "second period"). The relationship between the amount of cane a worker cuts and the amount of pay he receives is complex and varies from farm to farm. While cutters were compensated at a rate of sixty-six cents for each ton of cane, their pay also reflects compensation for cane cut during premium time, for "bad cane"[6] or for additional reaping tasks such as building the fire guard, setting up field tents, burning cane, and so forth. Thus a man's tonnage alone is not an adequate indicator of his performance as a worker for he may have been pulled from cutting to do less well-paying work or he may have run into bad cane. On the other hand, an excess of premium cane may serve to inflate the wages of a cutter who may actually be a low producer. Therefore, to obtain a more comprehensive picture of worker performance, both earnings (dollar) data and production (tonnage) data were extracted from payroll tabulations.

Earning Performance

Three separate indicators—"backpay," "wages," and "bonus"—were selected to measure different aspects of estate earnings. "Backpay" pertains to the additional wages received by each worker in settlement of a strike held mid-crop in which estate workers were awarded an increase for specific reaping tasks, most notably a four cent increment for cutting cane. As such, backpay is the earning indicator which is most strongly correlated with production as measured by tons of cane cut. Since the workers were paid retroactively from the beginning of the crop, the "backpay" figure represents the worker's earning performance on reaping tasks in the first twelve weeks of the season. "Wages" constitutes the average weekly paycheck for cutters during the first three months of the reaping season. It was calculated for each cutter by dividing his total gross wages paid for that period of time by the number of weeks he worked. This dollar figure reflects not only the cutter's regular and premium time tonnage but also a "soap money" allotment and additional compensation for any other work performed for the estate. The third earning indicator, "bonus," is the sum paid to those laborers who worked a minimum of twenty weeks of the reaping season. The amount of the bonus varies annually, and for the season in question it amounted to 12.5 percent of the gross earning for all work done on the estate throughout the reaping season. Thus while "backpay" and "wages" measure worker earning performance for the first half of the season when production peaks, "bonus" money measures earning performance throughout the entire season.

Backpay: Data on backpay were collected for 128 workers. The amounts ranged from seven dollars to twenty-seven dollars with the mean backpay for all workers being $16.16. The difference in backpay between the sixty-four smokers ($15.92) and the sixty-four non-smokers ($16.41) was not significant (p > .5). Ipswich workers (N = 49) received an average backpay of $18.96 in a range of $10.00 to $27.00. Ganja smokers on Ipswich (N = 26) averaged $18.54 which was not

Table 5.1
Summary of Worker Performance

Summary Findings for All Farms

	Mean Age (N=151)	Mean Backpay (N=128)	Mean Wages (N=128)	Mean Bonus (N=117)	Mean Cane Production First Period (N=128)	Mean Cane Production Second Period (N=47)
All persons	45.5 years	$16.16	$13.79	$37.38	59.8 tons	60.0 tons
Smokers	42.9 years (N=76)	$15.92 (N=64)	$13.53 (N=53)	$36.07 (N=56)	67.0 tons (N=65)	60.2 tons (N=63)
Non-smokers	48.1 years (N=75)	$16.41 (N=64)	$14.00 (N=66)	$38.59 (N=61)	57.6 tons (N=63)	59.7 tons (N=62)
P-values	(p < .01)	(p > .52)	(p > .44)	(p > .34)	(p > .26)	(p > .87)

Summary Findings for Ipswich Farm

	Mean Age (N=55)	Mean Backpay (N=49)	Mean Wages (N=44)	Mean Bonus (N=39)	Mean Cane Production First Period (N=49)	Mean Cane Production Second Period (N=125)
All persons	46.4 years	$18.96	$15.27	$50.28	76.2 tons	67.4 tons
Smokers	45.6 years (N=29)	$18.54 (N=26)	$14.70 (N=20)	$50.11 (N=18)	76.7 tons (N=27)	79.6 tons (N=25)
Non-smokers	47.3 years (N=26)	$19.43 (N=23)	$15.75 (N=24)	$50.43 (N=21)	75.7 tons (N=22)	65.0 tons (N=22)
P-values	(p > .63)	(p > .47)	(p > .34)	(p > .94)	(p > .89)	(p > .41)

152

Table 5.1 (continued)

Summary Findings for Dover Farm

	Mean Age (N=44)	Mean Backpay (N=38)	Mean Wages (N=34)	Mean Bonus (N=37)	Mean Cane Production First Period (N=39)	Mean Cane Production Second Period (N=37)
All persons	41.5 years	$13.41	$12.97	$26.65	49.4 tons	48.7 tons
Smokers	39.9 years (N=29)	$13.34 (N=26)	$12.71 (N=21)	$26.21 (N=24)	51.0 tons (N=26)	49.6 tons (N=25)
Non-smokers	44.7 years (N=12)	$12.92 (N=12)	$13.38 (N=13)	$27.46 (N=13)	46.2 tons (N=13)	46.7 tons (N=12)
P-values	(p > .12)	(p > .69)	(p > .53)	(p > .69)	(P > .27)	(p > .51)

Summary Findings for Wilmington Farm

	Mean Age (N=52)	Mean Backpay (N=41)	Mean Wages (N=41)	Mean Bonus (N=41)	Mean Cane Production First Period (N=40)	Mean Cane Production Second Period (N=37)
All persons	47.9 years	$15.56	$12.88	$34.80	49.9 tons	61.6 tons
Smokers	43.7 years (N=18)	$15.83 (N=12)	$13.00 (N=12)	$34.92 (N=14)	52.6 tons (N=12)	62.4 tons (N=13)
Non-smokers	50.1 years (N=34)	$15.45 (N=29)	$12.83 (N=29)	$34.72 (N=27)	48.7 tons (N=28)	61.2 tons (N=28)
P-values	(p > .06)	(p > .72)	(p > .85)	(p > .94)	(p > .28)	(p > .73)

153

significantly different (p > .4) than the average backpay of the non-smokers on Ipswich (N = 23) which was $19.43. On Dover, the average backpay for workers (N = 38) ranged from $8.00 to $19.00 with a mean of $13.21. Ganja smokers on Dover (N = 26) received an average backpay of $13.34 compared to $12.92 for the non-smokers (N = 12). As on Ipswich, this difference was not significant (p > .6). Backpay amounts for Wilmington workers (N = 41) ranged from $7.00 to $21.00 with a mean of $15.83 compared to $15.45 for non-smokers (N = 29). Once again this difference was not significant (p > .7).

Wages: Data on average weekly wages were collected on 119 workers among the three farms. The wages ranged rom $6.00 to $24.00 with the mean for all workers being $13.79. The difference in mean wages between the fifty-three smokers ($13.53) and the sixty-six non-smokers ($14.00) was not significant (p > .4). Salaries for Ipswich workers ranged from $6.00 to $23.00 with a mean of $15.27. The average weekly salary of ganja smokers on Ipswich (N = 20) was $14.70 compared to $15.75 for the twenty-four non-smokers. The difference between them was not significant (p > .3). Nor was there a significant difference (p > .5) in average weekly wages on Dover between the twenty-one smokers ($12.71) and the thirteen non-smokers ($13.38). The range on Dover was $8.00 to $24.00 with a mean for all workers of $12.97. For Wilmington men (N = 41) the range in average weekly salary was $7.00 to $17.00 with a mean of $12.88. The average weekly salary for the twelve ganja smokers was $13.00, while for non-smokers (N = 29) it was $12.83. As with Ipswich and Dover, the difference between smokers and non-smokers on Wilmington was not significant (p > .8).

Bonus: Data on the third earning performance indicator, "bonus" were collected for 117 workers. Bonuses varied a great deal, ranging from $13.00 to $75.00 with the average bonus for all workers being $37.38. The average bonus of the ganja smokers (N = 56) was $36.07, while for non-smokers (N = 61) it was $38.59. The difference in bonus between smokers and non-smokers was not significant (p > .3). Bonuses for Ipswich workers (N = 39) ranged from $25.00 to $75.00 with a mean of $50.28. Ipswich smokers (N = 18) averaged a $50.11 bonus which was not significantly different (p > .9) than the average bonus for Ipswich non-smokers (N = 21) which was $50.43. On Dover, bonuses for all workers (N = 37) ranged from $13.00 to $45.00 with a mean of $26.65. Ganja smokers (N = 24) averaged $26.21 compared with $27.46 for non-smokers (N = 13). This difference was not significant (p > .6). Finally, on Wilmington (N = 41) bonuses ranged from $15.00 to $58.00 with a mean of $34.80. The average bonus for Wilmington smokers (N = 14) was $34.92 compared to $34.74 for the non-smokers (N = 27). Once again, this difference was not significant (p > .9).

Production Performance

Because of the many and various factors which influence production, the amount of cane cut in any one week is not an adequate indicator of ongoing productivity. Therefore, two three-week periods were specified to constitute the production performance variable. They comprise the fourth, fifth, and sixth weeks and the tenth, eleventh, and twelfth weeks of the reaping season. During these periods there were no inclement weather conditions or labor disputes to prevent the workers from being out in full force. Thus, "cane production/first period" and "second period" refer to the average per man tonnage over two three-week periods of time. They are the only performance measures which do not include any other work performed for the estate.

The comparison of smokers and non-smokers in production performance is consistent with earning performance. Data on the quantity of cane cut were collected for 128 workers in the first period and 125 workers in the second period. The average amount of cane cut per man was 59.8 tons and 60.0 tons respectively. In the first period ganja smokers (N = 65) averaged 67.0 tons, while the mean for non-smokers (N = 63) was 57.6. In the second period, smokers (N = 63) produced on the average 60.2 tons of cane compared with non-smokers (N = 62) who cut an average of 59.7 tons. In both periods the slightly better performance of smokers over non-smokers was not statistically significant in the first period (p > .2) or in the second period (p > .8).

Turning to the individual farms, Ipswich workers averaged 76.2 tons in the first period (N = 49) and 67.4 tons in the second period (N = 47). Smokers (N = 27), with a mean of 76.7 tons, were only one ton higher than non-smokers (N = 22) who averaged 75.7 tons during the first period. In the second period Ipswich smokers (N = 25) averaged 79.6 tons compared with a mean of 65 tons produced by non-smokers (N = 22). These differences were not significant in either the first period (p > .8) or the second period (p > .4).

On Dover, 39 workers averaged 49.4 tons in the first period and 37 workers averaged 48.7 tons in the second period. The mean for ganja smokers (N = 26) in the first period was 51 tons compared with 46.2 tons for non-smokers (N = 13), while in the second period the twenty-five smokers averaged 49.6 tons compared with 46.7 tons for the twelve non-smokers. The differences between smokers and non-smokers were not significant in either instance (p > .2 and p > .5).

The figures from Wilmington continue the same pattern established on Ipswich and Dover. The mean cane production for forty Wilmington workers was 49.9 tons in the first period with smokers (N = 12) averaging 52.6 tons and non-smokers (N = 28) averaging 48.7 tons. In the second period the average cane production for all workers (N = 41) was 61.6 tons with smokers (N = 13) producing 62.4 tons and non-smokers (N = 28) producing 61.2 tons. Once again these differences were not statistically significant (p > .2 in period one and p > .7 period two).

Summarizing the results of both earning and production variables, independent t-tests performed on the data from each farm indicate that there are no significant differences between smokers and non-smokers on Ipswich, Dover, or Wilmington in age, backpay, average weekly wages, bonus payments, or tons of cane cut during two three-week periods. Shifting, however, from intra-farm comparisons of smokers and non-smokers to inter-farm comparison, a one way analysis of variance revealed that there are significant differences among and between Ipswich, Dover, and Wilmington in each of the five variables measuring worker performance. A priori contrasts show that Ipswich workers are significantly higher than Dover and Wilmington workers in backpay (p < .001 for both), wages (p < .001 for both), bonus (p < .001), and cane production/first period (p < .001 for both). In cane production/second period the difference between Ipswich and Dover continues to be significant at p < .001, while the difference between Ipswich and Wilmington was just not significant (p > .07). A priori contrasts further reveal that Wilmington workers are significantly higher than Dover workers in backpay (p < .01), bonus (p < .05), and cane production/second period (p < .001). Differences in salary and cane production/second period follow the same trend but are not significantly different.

For estate administration, these inter-farm differences overshadow the more subtle distinctions between smokers and non-smokers within each farm and lend confirmation to the opinion that the low ganja use gangs—Ipswich and Wilmington—are generally harder working than the high ganja use Dover farm. A comparison of reaping operations on the three farms, however, suggests an alternative explanation for the differences in worker performance and exposes the context in which ganja and productivity are often linked. As mechanical loading gangs, reaping flat-land farms, Ipswich, Dover, and Wilmington are technologically similar. Nevertheless, each gang functions within a distinct managerial framework in which administrative policies and strategies are determined to a great extent by the individual busher. The influence of management on worker performance is clearly addressed in Davidson's report on the sugar industry in Jamaica (1973: 132) in which he cautions that variations in worker output from estate to estate may be the responsibility of managerial decision-making as well as worker capabilities. On Deerfield Estate, where farm administration is highly decentralized and individualistic, Davidson's note of caution regarding comparisons among estates is equally applicable to comparisons among the various farms.

IPSWICH AND MR. PIEDMONT

One of the primary influences on the amount of cane a worker can cut is the policy held by each busher regulating the ratio of laborers to the work to be done.[7] Despite having the largest amount of acreage to reap, Mr. Piedmont, the manager of Ipswich, prefers to employ a small reaping gang of sixty men. On the first day of the season, he announced to this gang, "Na carry, na bring come," indicating that the cutters must select their partners from within the existing gang. When one of the younger workers protested that he would not work with "old men," Mr. Piedmont replied that every year "the company" pressures him to employ seventy-five men for the Ipswich gang but that he is holding to sixty for the benefit of the workers. According to the busher, small gangs are more easily managed because the men earn more money and worker satisfaction is high: "They will say, 'Piedmont the most baddest man,' but the Ipswich gang made more money last crop than any other gang."

While it is acknowledged among workers throughout the estate that "Mr. Piedmont gang a money gang," it is also recognized that one must work much harder for money earned on Ipswich because of Mr. Piedmont's policy of not reaping bad cane. Contending that the additional cost in time and money required to cut a small section of cane that is thick with vines is out of proportion to its value, Mr. Piedmont instructs the men to leave it standing and work around it. If laborers worked continuously and had unlimited cane to cut, this policy would be to their advantage. However, because individual assignments are restricted to certain rows each day, workers usually find that, by leaving out bad cane, their rows are shortened and their daily tonnage rates affected. On the other hand, if they proceed to reap the cane, as many do, they can expect to work much harder without the additional compensation that would be awarded on other gangs. Hence workers on Ipswich frequently complain that Mr. Piedmont "prefer cane styan up in de field. . . . Him na wan fe see we mek money." Mr. Piedmont also holds over-time production in check through minimal burning of fields on Friday and Saturday evenings. According to an Ipswich headman, "Busher na give anyt'ing. Him save de estate money and get bonus.[8] Him look pleasin' and nice, but no' him. . . . Him bring starvation to the people."

Finally, to accomplish the additional tasks that accompany reaping operations such as burning cane or building the fire guard, Mr. Piedmont routinely selects men from a pool of six favored cutters. Because these men are often required to interrupt their cutting in order to perform this other work, they are awarded the privilege of marking off their rows on the next piece of cane before they have completed the one in which they are working, in advance of the other men. Since they are thus almost always assured of good rows, these favored workers can secure their regular tonnage as well as increase their earnings through the performance of additional tasks.

DOVER AND MR. FURGUSON

At the other extreme, Mr. Furguson, the manager of Dover, employs fifty-eight men to cut cane on approximately six hundred acres—a ratio of ten acres per man on Dover compared with twenty acres per man on Ipswich. Unwilling to interfere with existing partner relations or show partiality in his selection of men from the former hand-loading gang, Mr. Furguson has tried to accommodate as many of the workers as possible in Dover's recent conversion to mechanical loading. Hence the amount of work each laborer can be assigned is necessarily limited in comparison with Ipswich. Unlike Mr. Piedmont, Mr. Furguson does not cut back on weekend production and many of his cutters weigh in nearly as much cane on Sunday and Monday morning as they do for the entire week. Furthermore, he directs the men to reap bad cane and then pays additional compensation. The more lenient position of this busher in regard to premium time and bad cane imposes additional costs on the estate which he justifies as compensation for the limited work assignments that accompany a large gang in transition.

Mr. Furguson is the most popular busher with the workers. Though the men often complain that they don't make much money on Dover, they praise Mr. Furguson regularly for his fairness and impartiality. As one worker commented, "Busher Furguson de best busher. To him every man is just a man." In contrast to Mr. Piedmont, Mr. Furguson tries to avoid situations in which he might be accused of favoritism, contending that it kindles resentment among the men and encumbers management. For example, he does not request specific workers to leave their cutting in order to perform other reaping tasks. Rather, he employs three men as year-round workers who do all the special procedures that Piedmont distributes among six favored cutters for extra income. Ironically, however, in his attempts to be fair, Mr. Furguson has increased the potential for conflict on his gang. By distributing the quantity of work among as many workers as possible, all are slightly dissatisfied with their pay. By authorizing the reaping of bad cane— a more equitable policy from the worker's viewpoint—Furguson endorses an activity that is very difficult to administer. Differences in opinion between the cutters and the headman in estimating the proportion of bad cane in a cutter's work, errors made in the field both in recording and reporting, or in the accounting department or computer are a constant source of complaints from workers, voiced at the Friday paybill. Thus, despite the overwhelming popularity of Busher Furguson, the Dover gang is the most irascible and difficult to manage.

WILMINGTON AND MR. DARRITY

The manager of Wilmington, Mr. Darrity, uses a strategy that is unique from the other two bushers. Currently employing sixty-six men to cut approximately eight hundred acres, Mr. Darrity's ratio of men to land (one to twelve) is only slightly better than that of Dover. However, in contrast to Furguson who is temporarily trying to accommodate as many workers as possible, Mr. Darrity is highly selective. His first consideration is not productivity, but manageability. According to this busher, "Young boys only want to make enough money to buy weed and sport themselves on Friday night. They complain all the while and if you try to talk to them, them black up with ganja and curse you off." In his efforts to eliminate "rude boys" from Wilmington, there are only nine of his fifty-five cutters who have not passed their fortieth birthday. Darrity prefers to have a gang of "manageable" men over age forty than thirty young, high producers who create "botheration" for him.[9] Because older men do not demand large work assignments, Darrity maintains a proportionately large gang without encountering the problems with worker satisfaction typical of Dover. Similar to Piedmont, Darrity delegates additional reaping tasks to certain cutters. He does not, however, permit them to select their next rows in advance. Thus on Wilmington these tasks are not regarded as extra income opportunities but rather as unwelcome assignments reserved for those with the least seniority. Darrity also holds premium production in check; thus, while tonnage rates are slightly greater than those on Dover, per man earnings on the two farms are similar. Wilmington men are well aware of their busher's position on age and manageability and occasionally complain that he takes unfair advantage of them. During a minor dispute over poorly burned cane, one cutter objected, "Oonoo (you) must treat we good because young men won't do this work and we dead soon and then oonoo must plant all ganja instead of cane."

It is evident from this brief comparison that the three farms provide vastly different opportunities for workers to earn and produce. Policies governing the ratio of laborers to land, premium time production, and assignment of additional reaping tasks all influence the performance of workers. Obviously, the fact that Mr. Piedmont employs the same number of men to cut over twice as much acreage almost guarantees that Ipswich workers will be stronger performers over the season. Cutters on Ipswich are seldom turned away because not enough cane has been burned to accommodate all the men who report to work, while on Wilmington and Dover this is a routine occurrence. The disparity in earning potential among the three farms is manifested in the differences in bonus payments which measure earnings over an entire season: the average bonus on the Ipswich gang was $50.28, while for Dover and Wilmington it was only $26.25 and $34.80.

Managerial policies are also linked to labor relations, manageability, and the extent to which workers express their dissatisfaction. Both Piedmont and Furguson are agreed that an earning gang is a manageable gang. However, their operational strategies to meet this objective differ. Piedmont puts the onus of responsibility on the worker to cut more cane, while Furguson shifts responsibility to the estate to pay more money. Thus, while their total earnings are less, Dover men are actually compensated at a higher rate than Ipswich men for work accomplished. Yet on Dover, with its high proportion of young workers, its absence of selection criteria, and its policies for additional reimbursement that invite resentment and dissatisfaction, labor skirmishes are routine. Piedmont minimizes labor disputes through a managerial logic—by eliminating potential sources of conflict (for example, compensation for bad cane) or by turning liabilities for workers into advantages as in the assignment of additional reaping tasks. In contrast to Piedmont and Furguson, Darrity reasons that an old gang is a manageable gang and selects men who are less likely to object to small work assignments and limited premium cane. However, while it is true that the older men on Wilmington and, to some extent, Ipswich tend to be less vocal in expressing their dissatisfaction, they are also sensitive to the competition for places on their gangs, regarded as the two best employment opportunities for unskilled labor on the estate. Thus, while they are quick to criticize their bushers' frugal policies among themselves, even the young men on Ipswich and Wilmington are hesitant to jeopardize their jobs in a confrontation with either Darrity or Piedmont.

This review of administrative strategies employed on the three farms further suggests the extent to which managers themselves are responsible for the inter-farm variations in worker performance which they commonly attribute to the use of ganja. Although none of the farm managers approve the use of ganja by workers, they vary considerably in their tolerance of ganja smoking at the work site. Mr. Piedmont neither supports nor contests the smokers' position regarding the effects of ganja on productivity. He is, however, fully aware of the significance of ganja smoking among working class men and regards it as one of the routine problems which accompany labor administration. During a discussion with the manager of Chelsea farm, Piedmont facetiously remarked that the only way to get hillside cane reaped was to "plant one entire hill in ganja and let them (the laborers) in there when the cane done." Though Ipswich workers do not hide their ganja when Piedmont enters the cane piece, they generally "show respect" by "outing" a lighted "spliff" before approaching him directly.

Despite Mr. Piedmont's existential view of ganja smoking, all but one of the men whom he has selected for extra income tasks are non-smokers. Though undeniably members of the laboring class, these workers approach middle class standards of respectability, being legally married, church-going, and literate, as well as abstaining from ganja smoking. Though they are not particularly fast workers compared with other men on the gang, the additional tasks and secure tonnage raise their earnings until they are commensurate with or even surpass the leading cutters on the gang. For example, we can see from Table 5.1 that while the differences are not significant, non-smokers are consistently lower in tonnage than smokers. Yet they are higher than smokers in dollars for each earning category. Of the seven Ipswich men who represented the upper range in average weekly wages (over $20.00 per week), five are non-smokers and all five are in Piedmont's exclusive group. Furthermore, of the six men who received the highest backpay settlement, four were favored cutters whose payment was based on the performance of tasks in addition to cutting, while the backpay of the two non-smokers was based completely on cutting performance.

In contrast to Ipswich men, Dover workers were observed not only to address Mr. Furguson with ganja in hand but jokingly to ask if he wanted a draw or if he would bring them some weed to smoke. When asked about Mr. Furguson's position on ganja, one of the men commented typically, "Him just jocular . . . Busher sit down next to we . . . him seh, 'well boys, we ain't got any rum but we got a little tot.' . . . Busher tek two spliff from him shirt pocket and give to we." Though he does not believe ganja to be harmful, Furguson is also not convinced that it really steps up productivity. He attributes the extensive use of ganja among his workers to an over-rated faith in the efficacy of the drug, "Since they believe it will make them work, it does." As with Ipswich, the highest ranges in tonnage are consistently occupied by smokers, but unlike Ipswich there is apparently little discrimination against smokers in the day to day operations on Dover; therefore, the relationship between tonnage and earnings is fairly uniform across the two categories of workers. The somewhat higher average weekly earnings and bonus payments for non-smokers, despite their lower tonnage, reflects the wages of one cutter who worked in the factory at night; thus, his cutting production was understandably less. If the average weekly earnings and bonus payment of this cutter were eliminated from the calculations, the means for average weekly wages and for bonus payment would drop to 12.5 and 26.1 respectively, thus conforming to the pattern of the other figures for Dover.

Despite his casual, accepting, even encouraging approach to the use of ganja among workers, five of the six men whom Furguson promoted to assist the loader operator as "scrappers" were non-smokers. According to this busher, these men were promoted to this highly desired employment opportunity because they were the most "reliable," "conscientious," and "polite" workers on the gang, though their behavior did not differ noticeably from other workers.

Of all three managers, Mr. Darrity is the most rigid and negative with regard to the workers' use of ganja. He maintains that during the labor shortages of hand loading days he was forced to employ ganja-smoking boys on his gang and contend with their disruptive behavior. Now that he can be selective, however, he prefers older, non-smoking workers. Wilmington is the only farm where smoking men ordinarily hide their ganja from the busher when he enters the field. One such smoker commented, "Busher na like fe see a man enjoy him likkle weed . . . a fe no outlaw on the Wilmington gang." While the difference between smokers and non-smokers on Wilmington, as on the other farms, is not statistically significant, the consistently superior performance of smokers is of interest in an employment context where youth and ganja are negatively sanctioned in the selection of workers. To be retained as cutters on Wilmington, given Mr. Darrity's antagonism toward youthful, ganja-smoking employees, they must clearly demonstrate their proficiency as workers.

While there is little evidence to indicate that differences in worker productivity—measured in dollars and tons—can be successfully related to ganja use, there is strong indication that the attitudes of managerial staff toward ganja use do affect worker performance. If non-smokers are consistently selected on the basis of alleged greater reliability or manageability over smokers for the most lucrative and secure jobs, it would be surprising if they failed to produce and earn more. Mr. Piedmont's selection of his non-smoking political associates for additional work, Mr. Furguson's preference for "well-mannered" men for scrapper jobs, and even Darrity's general exclusion of young, ganja-smoking men from his gang are just a few examples of the ways in which bushers reinforce their own values through their actions. Thus while management will often argue that the two gangs which are highest in per-man production, Ipswich and Wilmington, are lowest in ganja use, they are also the two farms on which optimal conditions exist both for worker productivity and worker satisfaction.

In spite of management's essentially skeptical view of the effects of ganja on productivity, it generally acknowledges the role of ganja in providing the necessary motivation for laborers to face the arduous task of reaping cane. As such, ganja has been accepted as a necessary evil. For example, the primary issue of a parish-wide management meeting was a new sergeant of police who was conducting a series of small ganja raids, searching and arresting workers on their way to the cane fields. Discussion centered on the best way to approach the parish constabulary in order to limit police molestation of workers.

Not only do bushers passively acknowledge and permit the use of ganja, they are known to distribute it in order to attract and encourage workers. Early in the crop, bushers generally have no trouble obtaining labor; having accumulated debts during the dull season, men are usually anxious to work. Later in the season, however, when debts are paid, the weather is hot, and the twenty weeks necessary to qualify for a bonus have been completed, workers may become more scarce. Loaders in particular often leave the estate after their bonus commitment has been fulfilled and work for one of the private transport contractors, who pay considerably higher.[10] Moreover, because loaders are generally younger and have fewer domestic responsibilities, they are less interested in working as long as possible. This situation has been relieved to a large extent through the introduction of mechanical loading and the gradual phasing out of hand loaders. However, it is not unusual to find hillside cane left standing in the field at the end of the season because there were not enough workers to reap it. Bushers were reported to drive through the district in the evening during labor shortages, seeking out workers and buying them rum in the shop or distributing ganja to some of the more influential laborers as an inducement to work. Likewise, if production appeared to be lagging, as it often does during the middle of the week, bushers were reported to procure ganja for the men to motivate them to work faster and harder.

An illustrative incident involving Mr. Furguson and the Dover laborers occurred in the season previous to the field work used in this study. Less than two months into the season, one of the loaders, ironically called "Peace-and-Love," "cursed off" the busher at Friday payroll during a dispute over extra pay for "heading" cane.[11] In order not to appear manipulated by Peace-and-Love, Furguson told him not to report for work for three days, which meant missing the premium days for the next work week. The three other men in his spell stated that they would not return to work either, and would take the matter to the union. On Saturday, the entire loading staff of the Dover gang stayed home. Mr. Bellamy, the union official residing in Dover, reviewed the issue but indicated that in this situation the union could not support the workers. He advised them to go back to work so that their bonus pay would not be affected.

Sunday morning the loaders arrived in the cane piece between 7:00 and 7:30—a full two hours later than their ordinary arrival, particularly for a Sunday. By this time, according to Dover workers, there were "all fifteen hundred ton of cane on de groun." The loaders sat around their carts or loaded very slowly, frequently stopping to rest when a cart was only half finished. As Furguson went from spell to spell, the men made remarks like "Lawd busher, de spirit na tek me fe wuk today," or "Me nah feel fe wuk so, busher." Meanwhile the cutters and transport team, though sympathetic to the loaders' situation, were pressuring the busher to get their cane to the weigh station during premium time.

Finally, Furguson called to Will Kennedy, a Dover cutter who was also a small time ganja dealer and asked if he had "weed fe sell." Kennedy, however, had sold most of his supply on Saturday and had only a small amount left. The only two men in Dover who had a sufficient supply were Faircough, a fisherman and vendor, and Peace-and-Love, the very man Furguson had suspended.

Kennedy went to Faircough's yard, as requested by Mr. Furguson, but Mrs. Faircough told him that her husband had not yet returned from the fishing beach. On his way to the beach, Kennedy stopped to see Peace-and-Love, who had returned late the night before from another parish with a crocus bag of kali. Peace-and-Love carefully packaged a pound-weight of weed, putting it in his lunch case with his thermos. When the two men returned to Dover, "busher nah know fe laf or vex." However, every man got a "good cigar fe smoke and nah raise up till done," and "all three hundred fifty ton of cane loaded by noon and three hundred more by three o'clock."

Whatever the real or perceived effects on individual productivity, the lateral cooperation in work efforts, enhanced by ganja smoking, is itself a boon to production. Ganja provides the impetus to accomplish work on both the individual and group level. It has traditionally been advantageous for cane workers to smoke ganja, and remains so for hand-loading gangs; farmer-laborers in Leyburn and fishing crews in Buckland also derive distinct economic benefits through the social use of ganja. Generally speaking, the relationships established in ganja-smoking circles are beneficial in helping individuals of all three communities deal with the limitations of the socioeconomic milieu in which they work and live. In some situations, such as the loading spells of Chelsea and co-working groups in Leyburn, a fairly rigid system of mutual obligations revolves around ganja use. Workers are compelled to give ganja, accept ganja, and repay ganja, and failure to do so may result in withdrawal of co-operation and support from co-workers. Despite the class-linked stigmas attached to heavy ganja use, users tend to associate initiation to smoking with the entrance to a responsible life. Caleb Lucas, for instance, a typical young farmer-laborer and heavy ganja user in Leyburn, claimed that when he began to smoke regularly in his early twenties, ganja "mek I check out my life and see the life I was living until then wasn't good. It mek I take better care of money, for me have business to look about, . . . and me decide fe rest woman awhile." It was during this introspective period of his life that Caleb established the union with this present mate and began farming on a piece of leased land. He now has two children and, while still renting the rooms in which he lives, has applied for a government subsidy to build his own home on a plot of land which he recently purchased. Caleb combines farming with wage labor for the tobacco company and two of the larger farmers in the district. To accomplish all this, he worked in a partner relationship with two of his peers. All three men are heavy ganja users and smoke regularly together in work and leisure contexts.

Until Caleb started smoking routinely with co-workers, he had been regarded as one of the local "rude boys"—working irregularly, wasting what little money he earned in the rum shop, and "sporting women."[12] Though he had the coveted opportunity to go to Canada for farm work, Caleb behaved so poorly on the first trip that he was never invited back. For Caleb, ganja symbolizes the transition from a careless to a conscientious life.

In contrast, George Cunningham, a slightly older farmer from the same community, recently gave up smoking because it "makes men lose their ambition, . . . their plans in life. The police know every man in the district who smokes weed, so you must take a chance every day." (It is of interest that George made this comment in the same week that he planted twenty-five ganja roots for domestic use). While George has successfully combined farming with off-farm labor for several years, he recently inherited more land room and found himself in a position to do full-time farming with the assistance of his two teenage sons. Work partnerships, established when still relying on wage-labor opportunities, were suddenly less useful and George began to minimize his participation in them, including the smoking of ganja. In addition, George had become legally married within the year, and his wife complained often about his consuming ganja and setting a poor example for the children.

Though these men hold opposing views on the motivational value of ganja, each is correct, for their positions reflect different life stages with different options and different goals. For Caleb, heavy ganja use is an integral part of the cooperative work efforts that accompany the early years of his role as an accountable farmer, husband, and father, For George, who has already accumulated resources and is in the process of assuming a middle-class life style, the ganja relationships and obligations that once had been necessary now have become liabilities that hinder his social and economic advancement.

NOTES

1. Reports from farm managers and headmen indicate that the strongest producers are generally faster workers. The reverse, however, is not always the case.

2. The actual size of the Wilmington property is 1,863 acres, but a large proportion is waste land or tide land which is unusable for planting cane.

3. The total acreage for Ipswich, the estate's largest farm, is 2,078

4. The annual bonus payment is one of the major incentives in estate work. It represents a form of enforced savings. A few workers claim they would prefer to have higher pay and forget the bonus, but more typical comments include "Me love it to god. . . . Me can buy a pig or shegoat." The bonus payment is also timed to occur in late November, immediately prior to holiday season, which enhances its attractiveness among workers.

5. This attitude was clearly illustrated when, after I received approval to conduct field work on the estate, upper management scheduled Wilmington and Ipswich as the first farms to be studied because their gangs were "better mannered" and "more cooperative."

6. "Bad cane" refers to any special condition of the cane which makes it more difficult or time consuming to reap, such as the presence of vines or cow itch or its location in steep gullies. According to an agreement between management and the unions, cutters working in any of these conditions are supposed to be awarded additional compensation in the range of ten to twenty cents per ton.

7. Theoretically, all seven gangs on the estate are interchangeable and are supposed to work whenever they are needed. Thus acreage would be distributed evenly among all workers on the estate. However, cutters become extremely upset when they have to travel long distances to work, or work under a busher whom they are unused to. They become equally annoyed when another gang is brought in to work their home farm. For example, approximately mid-crop the Ipswich gang was brought in to help cut a piece of Northfield wet-land cane in order to hasten reaping before the rains. Because the work was allocated on a first come, first served basis, some of the Ipswich men were assigned rows of cane while Northfield men were sent away. That evening an "accidental" cane fire burned several acres of cane on Ipswich, forcing management to recall Ipswich workers to their home farm for several days. While the bushers of both farms were certain that the fire had been started by Northfield men, they didn't bother to pursue the matter; they also disrelish the problems which accompany the transfer of gangs from one farm to another.

8. According to workers and union organizers, bonus payments are awarded to farm managers who reduce costs or maintain them at the same level.

9. According to management, forty is the age at which workers begin to decline in productivity. Unfortunately, however, men below the age of thirty or thirty-five are generally regarded as notoriously difficult workers. Though they are fast and powerful, they are said to be unreliable, inconsistent in their performance, and difficult to supervise. Thus, by the time a laborer has settled down to what is regarded as a good, responsible worker, he is almost past his most productive years.

10. Occasionally, the labor situation is so bad that the contractor is hired by the estate to finish the reaping season.

11. If the cart cannot be spotted within a certain range of the pile of cut cane, the loaders are supposed to receive additional monetary compensation for cane carried on their heads to the cart.

12. During this time he also contracted gonorrhea, which he claims to have cured by using a preparation of ganja tonic.

REFERENCES

Davidson, R. B. 1973. "The labour force in the Jamaican sugar industry." In *Work and family life: West Indian perspectives*, ed. Lambros Comitas and David Lowenthal. Garden City, NY: Anchor Books.
Rubin, Vera, and Lambros Comitas. 1975. *Ganja in Jamaica*. The Hague: Mouton.

Chapter 6

Conclusion

In this final chapter we will draw the implications of the research we have discussed, all of which deals with the question of how the independent variable, marijuana use, is related to the dependent variable, job performance. In attempting to assess the effects of marijuana on job performance, it is desirable that multiple methods be used because this makes methodological triangulation possible. Each research method has its own strengths and weaknesses, as we have attempted to show throughout this volume. By examining multiple studies, conducted using multiple approaches, readers can critically evaluate competing conclusions. Given the methodological limitations of each approach and the inconsistent results, the research does not support the claim that the independent variable has any consistent effect on the dependent variable. This does not mean that marijuana has been *proven* to have no effect on job performance; nor does it mean that we have no information about the relationship between these variables.

In our introductory chapter, we discussed the politically polarized character of public discourse about marijuana in the U.S. today. We described two dichotomous factions which we called the Responsible Living position and the Individual Liberty position. We argued that partisans committed to each side see their perspective as reasonable, moral, and their cause as serving the best interest of the society as a whole. It seems probable that the statement above—that the available, scientifically sound evidence does not show that marijuana has any consistent effect on job performance—will mean entirely different things to advocates of each of these drug policy perspectives. Furthermore, despite the desirability of more research on this topic, those who set human resources policies for companies and those responsible for making public policy must decide whether to commit the resources necessary to reduce or eliminate marijuana use on the job.

Policy decisions are currently being made on the basis of the evidence presently available.

The conclusions we present here will not include recommendations to decision-makers in the public or private sectors about the proper way to regulate workplace marijuana. They will, however, summarize the research discussed in the book, identify hypotheses to be tested in future research and attempt to clarify the choices faced by organizations and communities with respect to cannabis. Recommendations will be made about ways to improve the process used in making decisions in politically contentious policy areas and about how to evaluate relevant information in such settings. We first turn to the scholarly implications of past research on marijuana and job performance

SUMMARY OF CURRENT EVIDENCE AND DIRECTIONS FOR FUTURE RESEARCH

Findings from past research do not support the claim that there is a direct, causal relationship between marijuana and job performance. As the controlled experiments show, individuals given marijuana in experimental settings perform less effectively on tasks measuring attention, learning, memory, and psychomotor skills related to performance at many jobs. However, the results of the Kagel et al. experimental micoreconomy show that these performance decrements do not necessarily reduce job productivity. Further, acute marijuana intoxication reduces performance in driving simulations, but its effects are not consistent in actual driving situations. This suggests that the results of the controlled experiments may not generalize to actual work settings. The field research using survey methods showed a *significant positive relationship* between some measures of self-reported marijuana use and wages among young adult men in the mid and late 1980s. However, there was a significant *negative* relationship between some measures of self-reported marijuana use and labor force participation (hours worked) among young adult men in the mid and late 1980s. Relationships are different for young women. Individuals who test positive for marijuana in pre-employment drug screens are more likely to experience turnover, accidents, and absenteeism that should reduce their overall productivity. The Normand et al. study included in Chapter 3 concluded that pre-employment testing was cost-effective for the U.S. Postal Service because positive test results were a statistically significant predictor of turnover and absenteeism; however, this study did not confirm the finding of other researchers that on-the-job accidents and injuries are more frequent among employees who failed such tests. Though objective measures show no consistent relationship between marijuana use and motivation to work, the *perceptions* of its effects on motivation vary widely across cultures.

Those who argue that marijuana use reduces job performance make the implicit assumption that the substance produces changes in users which directly cause decreased effectiveness at the job. It is difficult to reconcile the facts with this assumption. It seems unlikely that marijuana would simultaneously increase wages and decrease hours worked. If marijuana did have a direct, causal effect on performance, it seems unlikely that those who work under the influence of marijuana in different cultures would have diametrically opposed views of its effects. It also seems unlikely that marijuana would produce different effects in men and women. Finally, the fact that effects seem more consistent in experiments and simulations than in real world settings is not easily explained under the assumption of a straightforward, causal link between cannabis use and behavioral changes in users.

In contrast, it seems more likely that marijuana has subjective effects that may distract users, but that these effects can often be dismissed at dosages associated with recreational use, so that for some individuals marijuana has no impact on job productivity at all. In this case, we would not expect research to reveal a consistent relationship between marijuana use and workplace behavior. Apparent effects reported in some studies would be spurious correlations produced by methodological limitations of different types of research. In the discussion which follows, we will not be attempting to prove that marijuana has no effects on job performance, which would amount to attempting to prove the null hypothesis. We will simply argue that the spurious correlation model of the observed effects of marijuana is more consistent with the facts listed above than is the direct cause model.

The results of the experimental research seem to agree with the commonly reported subjective effects of acute marijuana intoxication such as "experiencing vivid colors, sounds, and tastes" and "being easily distracted" (Stafford, 1992: 201–203). This suggests that marijuana makes sensory input more interesting and therefore more difficult to ignore. Thus, an intoxicated person would be more easily distracted when performing tasks requiring attention, learning, memory, and psychomotor skills in an experimental setting and would perform less effectively at them. If, however, the effects are weak, a person motivated to attend to work might be able to "dismiss" the drug's effects and work as effectively as they would without it. This may be particularly true for relatively repetitive and difficult tasks like agricultural labor. If workers have the ability to dismiss the effects of the drug while they are actually working or driving, this would explain the fact that marijuana has more consistent negative effects in driving simulations than in actual driving situations and the fact that marijuana use did not reduce the productivity of agricultural laborers in the anthropological field studies.

If marijuana has no direct, causal effect on performance, the positive relationship between marijuana use and wages among young men and the negative relationship between marijuana use and hours worked could be due to the fact that those who have higher wages and work fewer hours smoke more marijuana. In other words, these results are produced not by the effects of marijuana on wages and hours worked but the effects of greater amounts of money and free time on marijuana use among young men.

Spurious correlation may also account for the pre-employment drug testing results. These studies show that positive tests on pre-employment marijuana screens are positively related to job-related problems that should translate into lower productivity, though the effect sizes are small. If, however, marijuana use has no overall effect on job performance, the relationships between pre-employment drug tests and subsequent job problems may be due to some third-variable cause such as selection bias (i.e., pre-employment drug screens tend to identify careless and thoughtless marijuana users rather than *all* marijuana users).

In the anthropological field research, use of marijuana was *positively* associated with some measures of performance and local folklore portrayed marijuana as a drug that could be used to increase productivity. If marijuana has *no* overall effect on performance, the popular association between use and performance may have to do with the cultural context in which it is used. In the Costa Rican and Jamaican studies, those who *want* to work are more likely to use marijuana, so the high levels of productivity and use may both be caused by motivation to work hard.

This explanation also accounts for the difference in the relationship between reported marijuana use and wages between men and women. If the common folklore in our culture suggests that marijuana smoking is more acceptable for young men than for young women (as was once believed about cigarette smoking), then young women who choose to use it may have personal characteristics that would account for the apparent differences in "effects" of marijuana on men and women.

White (1991) argued for the spurious correlation explanation (and against the direct cause model) in understanding marijuana and delinquency. His data show that some of the relationships between marijuana use and delinquency can be explained by other variables. The same appears to be true for the relationship between marijuana use and job performance. If so, policies aimed at limiting use cannot be justified on the grounds that they will have predictable effects on job productivity. If, as this review suggests, there is no consistent causal relationship between marijuana use and job performance, it is not certain that any policy dealing with employee marijuana use will have appreciable economic benefits.

Though a variety of research methods have been used to examine the relationship between marijuana use and productivity, the vast majority of research has been conducted using quantitative as opposed to qualitative methods. Quantitative methods involve the development of numerical measures and the use of statistical analysis, while qualitative methods usually focus on detailed observation and description of phenomena. The controlled experiments, survey research, and pre-employment drug testing studies have all used quantitative data and statistical analyses to test hypotheses regarding the relationship between various measures of use and various measures of performance. This research has produced divergent results. It may be that qualitative methods will help us understand how marijuana fits into the work lives of its users. Though the ethnographic field research conducted by anthropologists represents a good beginning, it can be extended in a number of ways.

The ethnographic studies conducted so far have been conducted outside the

United States and have focused on small groups of workers in a relatively narrow range of jobs. Future research might focus on American workers in jobs that involve less manual labor and more managerial and professional responsibilities. Ethnographic studies in large bureaucratic organizations such as the Postal Service would be useful in supplementing the quantitative data currently available on the relationship between marijuana use and performance in these organizations.

Other qualitative methods that do not demand researchers to live among those being studied might be useful for studying larger populations. Users who have not experienced problems at work because of their marijuana use might be asked to provide written description of their patterns of use and their own views on how the drug relates to their work life. Analysis of these written records provided by users might give insights into the patterns of use and the reasons for use that are not detrimental to job performance.

Another recommendation for future research is that researchers continue to use multiple research methods to address this issue. The use of multiple research methods as described above will allow for "triangulation" on the question of the relationship between marijuana use and job performance. Denzin (1978) and Jick (1979) define triangulation as the combination of multiple methodologies in the study of the same phenomenon in an attempt to achieve convergence in results that provide the basis for a more complete understanding of the phenomenon. The concept of triangulation is based on Campbell and Fiske's "multiple operationism" (1959), which involves the use of multiple methods to compensate for the limitations and weaknesses of each individual method. The first author, among others, has argued for the use of triangulation in research on a number of topics related to performance in the workplace (Schwenk, 1982).

Some models of the research process suggest that research proceeds in phases and that certain types of methodology should predominate at each phase. For example, Heishman and Henningfield argue that research should progress from laboratory research for addressing basic research questions to workplace assessment for verifying laboratory results (Heishman & Henningfield, 1990: 173). Early in the process of investigating a phenomenon, according to McGrath, field studies should predominate as researchers attempt to understand the phenomenon (McGrath, 1964). Later, more quantitative methods including survey research should build on what has been learned in field studies. Laboratory experiments and computer simulations should follow as researchers manipulate variables they have identified and determine the casual relationship between them. Finally, researchers should return to the field to conduct confirmatory studies to verify relationships between variables that have been observed in laboratory experiments.

Our own view differs slightly from that of McGrath. We have observed that the research process rarely proceeds in an orderly fashion with certain types of research predominating at any particular phase. Instead, research begins with an initial conception of the area of investigation. Conceptual work involves guesses about the important research questions in the area as well as the most important variables and how they may be related to each other. This work is based not on field research but on personal observation, reading, and discussion of the topic and it results in an initial conceptual framework that guides even exploratory field research. This point is illustrated in the ethnographic research discussed earlier.

Based on this initial work, both quantitative and qualitative research should be conducted concurrently. It is essential that those conducting both types of research communicate extensively with each other and that the results of early research influence the sorts of research questions dealt with in later studies and the design of these studies.

This communication is especially important if the results of different types of research conflict with each other, as they do on the topic of marijuana use and job performance. Such conflict might result from problems in the operationalization of variables in the laboratory settings, from the effects of confounding variables in the field settings, or from the biases of individual researchers in interpreting the findings. Because field researchers are familiar with the properties of variables in their natural settings, they can assist laboratory researchers in identifying potential errors in operationalizing these variables in controlled settings. On the other hand, laboratory researchers can assist field researchers in identifying potential confounding variables present in field settings. In developing laboratory experiments to represent the essential features of a phenomenon that occurs in the field, laboratory researchers must make judgments about which features must be included and which represent irrelevant or confounding variables. These judgments should be communicated to field researchers.

Once potential problems in operationalization and potential confounding variables have been identified, their effects can be examined through both laboratory and field research. Laboratory researchers can change the structure of important variables according to the suggestions of field researchers and attempt to replicate previous laboratory experiments with the newly defined variables. They can also attempt to operationalize the confounding variables and introduce these into laboratory experiments to assess their effects in interaction with the variables of primary interest. The field researchers, following the suggestions of laboratory researchers about potential confounding variables, can conduct field studies in new sites where some of these confounding variables will not be present.

There are at least three possible future studies that would help to determine whether the results of past research are due to spurious correlation. The first focuses on the results of past experimental research on performance at various tasks dealing with job-related skills and abilities. If marijuana has effects that cannot be dismissed, then users' level of motivation to dismiss the effects should be irrelevant. It is also possible, that the effects of marijuana would disappear if users were motivated to dismiss them. This suggests the following hypothesis:

H1: The task performance of subjects motivated to perform well will be less affected by marijuana intoxication than the performance of subjects not motivated to perform well.

This hypothesis could be readily tested by comparing the performance of intoxicated subjects who are *rewarded* for performing well at a set of tasks similar to those used in past controlled experiments with intoxicated subjects who are paid the same amount regardless of their performance. Since the experimental research has generally been conducted by individuals with training in medicine rather than management, *motivation* to perform well at tasks has not been incorporated into previous experiments. If, however, the effects of marijuana intoxication can be dismissed, an experiment in which subjects were motivated to dismiss the effects should provide evidence of this ability. It would, however, be difficult to design incentives in laboratory experiments that would have the same effects as those used on the job. An alternative approach using survey research might involve asking respondents about their level of commitment to their jobs and their motivation to perform well. Negative relationships between marijuana use and job performance may be stronger for those who have low levels of commitment to their jobs.

The second study has to do with the relationship between attitudes and expectations about marijuana, marijuana use, and performance. These attitudes may be important in explaining the relationship between marijuana and productivity. Collecting data on these attitudes in future survey research would help to address the question of whether beliefs about the effects of the drug account for any of the observed relationships between use and performance.

H2: Individuals' beliefs about the effects of marijuana and the beliefs of their co-workers will moderate the relationship between marijuana use and performance.

This hypothesis could be addressed in future field research by collecting information on respondents' attitudes and the attitudes of co-workers toward marijuana use as well as data on actual use. The relative importance of beliefs about use versus actual use could then be assessed.

The final study would attempt to address questions of causality in past survey research using the NLSY database. The positive relationship between marijuana use and wages may be due to a positive effect of marijuana on job productivity or the positive relationship may have another cause, possibly the fact that those who earn more money are likely to use more marijuana. This suggests the following hypothesis:

H3: Job performance (wages) predicts future marijuana use better than marijuana use predicts future job performance.

Data on marijuana use and wages would be collected from the 1988 and 1990 data in the NLSY, and the relationships between these variables at these two times would be assessed. If we find a stronger relationship between 1988 wages and 1990 marijuana use than between 1988 marijuana use and 1990 wages, this would argue that differences in job performance (wages) lead to differences in marijuana use, rather than the reverse.

Needless to say, these three hypotheses do not exhaust the possibilities for future research on marijuana and work performance. A short list of topics would include the effects of recreational use versus acute intoxication on the job, possible "hangover effects" on work performance, the effects of marijuana on different types of jobs requiring different physical and mental capabilities, and the differential effects of marijuana on employees of different cultural backgrounds and genders. Readers are encouraged to identify other topics that may have escaped our notice. The relationship between job performance and marijuana use is much more complex and interesting than the discussions of the topic in popular news media would suggest.

PUBLIC CHOICE, DECISION RULES, AND STANDARDS OF PROOF

The findings of the body of research discussed here do not support the proposition that marijuana has a consistent, causal effect on job performance. As we stated above, this inference is not equivalent to the conclusion that cannabis has no effect on workers. Intellectual honesty and scientific integrity allow researchers to state only that currently available knowledge is inconclusive with regard to the causal impact of marijuana on job performance. The scientific method does not allow the researcher to prove that a variable such as drug use has no effect on the outcome of interest. Tests of statistical significance provide information on the probability that an observed effect is simply a random occurrence. These tests are designed to minimize the chance that inquirers will mistakenly conclude that two factors are related to each other when, in fact, they are not. They are very good at detecting and measuring effects, but they provide no measure of noneffects; that is, they can't tell us precisely when to decide that something has no impact on something else.

If science cannot automatically provide a final answer to the question of whether marijuana effects job performance, policy-makers must choose a decision rule to be applied to the problem; they must adopt or create a structure for the decision process and develop some way to resolve competing claims. Decision rules are the explicit or implicit choices made about the method that will be used to reach a final conclusion. We are all aware that different institutions and different choice situations require different decision rules. For example, in judicial proceedings, the plaintiff (the party who initiates a legal action) bears the burden of proof. In a criminal case, the state (the plaintiff) must prove the defendant guilty beyond a reasonable doubt; the defendant is presumed innocent until proven guilty. In civil matters, the plaintiff must prove his or her case by a preponderance of the evidence. While the civil plaintiff must meet a weaker standard of proof than the one applied in criminal matters, it is still the responsibility of the party initiating the case to show evidence of injury or loss. Another way to characterize the problem of burden of proof is to ask what the default option is in any given decision problem; that is, what option will go into effect if no action is taken? Obviously, in legal proceedings, if a case is not proven by the plaintiff or not initiated at all, the existing status quo will continue. The criminal defendant will go free; the civil plaintiff will receive no reparations.

Food and drug regulation by the U.S. government also uses a number of different decision rules in dealing with the wide variety of substances under its control. The Food and Drug Regulation Act of 1938 created the Federal Food and Drug Administration. The original legislation defined the class of medications consumers could purchase only with a doctor's prescription, and it placed the burden of proof on the manufacturers of prescription drugs to provide evidence that their products were safe. The standard for new drug approval was expanded in 1963, requiring the makers to prove new drugs' effectiveness as well as their safety. At the same time as substances making therapeutic claims were placed under these regulations, political and economic realities limited the scope and nature of the FDA's authority. Many widely used over-the-counter drugs, vitamins, herbal remedies, and other products were designated as "Generally Recognized as Safe" (or GRAS). These products were allowed to remain on the market pending review by the FDA, placing the burden of proof on the agency to show that they were unsafe.

Questions of where the burden of proof should fall and what standard of proof should be applied in a particular choice situation are the decision rules to be followed in that context, the rules that give structure to the decision process. When business and government policy-makers must take action regarding marijuana use by workers, decision rules often become confusing. Students of public and private policy-making have pointed out that in some respects such confusion is inevitable or even functional (Lindblom, 1959; Simon, 1976; Steinbruner, 1974) in that it results from limitations on human information processing capacity and facilitates compromise and incremental decision-making. Nevertheless, clarifying the decision rules to be used in relation to marijuana regulation could make policies in this area more rational and more transparent, improving shareholders', stakeholders' and constituents' ability to hold corporate and government agents accountable. It would also constitute a first step toward more productive discussion of a contentious political issue and toward stronger democracy (Barber, 1984).

In Chapter 1 we discussed the highly conflictual character of public debate on issues related to drug use in general and with regard to marijuana in the workplace in particular. Mythical numbers, poorly documented and biased data often come to dominate discourse on this subject (Singer, 1971; Reuter, 1984). Evidence presented on each side of the conflict is frequently chosen because it supports the position advocated by its purveyors and the self-interest of those responsible for producing it. Similarly, advocates seldom wish to specify the decision rules they are assuming should be used in a given situation. They implicitly apply standards that justify their positions. Such ambiguity can lead to the misuse of otherwise sound data, turning useful information into mythical numbers. This process appears to have occurred in relation to the NIDA/NIAAA report, *Economic Costs of Drug and Alcohol Abuse, 1992* (Harwood et al., 1998). The report's title and its conclusion that substance abuse cost the nation $246 billion in 1992 were widely publicized by committed supporters of drug-free workplace policies, who saw them as providing strong evidence that tougher measures to eliminate employee drug and alcohol abuse are needed (Institute for a Drug-Free Workplace, 1998, 1999). Citing estimates of economic effects to justify workplace drug policies implies that such policies should be adopted because of the economic benefits they will produce. However, closer examination of the report's findings, discussed in Chapter 1, shows that it provides little or no evidence that preventing substance abuse by workers would be cost-effective for employers.

Drug-free workplace policies may be justified on many grounds. Partisans committed to what we referred to in our introductory chapter as the "Responsible Living" position on this issue feel strongly that the country has a moral obligation to prevent use of intoxicating substances. They argue that there are compelling ethical reasons that the federal government should do everything possible to eliminate drug abuse. These justifications do not depend on the economic benefits that might or might not result from decreasing use of illicit substances. For Responsible Living advocates, it is not necessary to prove that marijuana has a negative causal impact on job performance in order to justify efforts to make workplaces drug-free, in part because the purely financial consequences of drug use are not as important as the moral and ethical effects. Partisans of this perspective also feel that the burden of proof regarding marijuana regulation should fall upon those favoring more permissive policies. Consequently, they demand that employers do everything possible to deter drug use unless and until their opponents offer conclusive evidence that such policies do not increase sobriety.

On the other hand, for those committed to what we have called the "Individual Liberty" position on drug policy, the lack of proof that marijuana and other intoxicants cause diminished worker safety and productivity has dramatically different implications. Opposing any unnecessary limits on personal lifestyle choices, partisans in this camp would prefer to place the burden of proof regarding the value of the drug-free workplace on its advocates. This side feels that policy-makers should be required to show that existing laws are not already too intrusive. Strong economic evidence that pre-employment drug testing and other workplace anti-drug measures are cost effective would be necessary to convince committed Individual Liberty partisans that pre-employment drug testing and other such practices are justified. These advocates would further argue that those favoring interference with private, informed decisions by adults should be required to prove that the policies they support are the least constraining alternatives available.

It seems likely that rational policy-making in relation to the legal status and modes of regulation of marijuana will require multiple decision rules. It would be helpful if this fact could be made explicit and appropriate rules specified. For example, therapeutic claims made for medical marijuana suggest that it should be held to the "proven safe and effective" standard applied to new prescription medicines. Federal drug czar Barry McCaferty and other opponents of medical marijuana have suggested that this is the standard that should be met. However, due to its widespread use currently and historically, it will not be possible to patent smoked marijuana. Consequently, pharmaceutical manufacturers cannot afford to expend the millions of dollars required to perform the extensive testing required by the FDA new drug approval process. In this respect, marijuana is similar to many products classified as GRAS under food and drug law. Obviously, decisions regarding the overall legal status of marijuana will have to resolve the question of where the burden of proof should fall and what standard of proof the substance must meet in order to change the status quo of complete prohibition.

On its face, the issue of marijuana in the workplace appears to be an economic problem that may be decided primarily on the basis of economic efficiency. Many supporters of drug-free workplace policies have given implicit support to this premise by calling attention to the 1998 report, *Economic Costs of Drug and Alcohol Abuse, 1992* and arguing that it shows that expanded efforts to eliminate employee drug use are needed because of the of costs it describes. This argument is misleading, however, both because of the content of the report and because of its implications for the criteria that should be used in making decisions about employee drug policies. From the perspective of economic efficiency, the causal effect of marijuana on job performance, the probability that any effect exists and the size of possible causal impacts, should be central to decision-making regarding the drug-free workplace. The evidence currently available, including the NIDA/NIAAA *Economic Costs* report, strongly suggests that marijuana has no direct, negative effect on workers' productivity. Thus, efforts to create a marijuana-free workplace may not be economically justified.

For strong supporters of the Responsible Living point of view on drug policy, the low probability of direct economic benefits from drug-free workplace policies does not prove that such policies should not be adopted. Committed advocates of this perspective feel all reasonable efforts should be made to deter drug use, regardless of the immediate economic consequences of those efforts. From their viewpoint, marijuana prohibition is what economists refer to as a public good. Public goods, as opposed to private goods, are societal benefits that will be under-provided by market mechanisms alone.

The literature on public choice (see Ostrom, 1990 for a brief review) has shown that certain categories of goods, notably those that cannot be divided into discrete increments and those from which those who do not pay cannot be excluded, will not be produced in economically efficient amounts by actors in the private marketplace. National defense is considered the classic example of such a pure public good: Once it is provided effectively for any segment of the population, the whole country benefits. If national defense were privatized and some people refused to buy any of this private good, they would be able to "free ride" on the contributions of their neighbors toward the country's security. They could not be excluded from the benefits for which others had paid. Consequently, we give the state the power to collect taxes to purchase national defense and require that all citizens contribute to the provision of this good.

The United States Congress has determined that the use of certain drugs is so injurious to the public health and welfare that their prohibition constitutes a public good, a good which private individual and corporate action will not produce without government intervention. The drug-free workplace appears to be part of this public good, so even though companies may not see an improvement in their bottom lines from reducing employee substance abuse, the federal government must require or induce them to take steps toward this goal. The Drug-Free Workplace Act of 1988 requires employers doing business with the federal government to use pre-employment drug testing, and its 1998 extension allocates funds for voluntary programs to encourage smaller employers to develop anti-drug policies. It is very unlikely that the benefits of a drug-free workplace can be captured by individual employers. If this is the case, the costs of implementing this policy in effect constitute a tax on employers, a tax which must ultimately be paid by consumers through increased prices. This policy may be entirely consistent with citizen preferences; however, businesses, their owners, employees, and customers should hold policy-makers accountable by requiring them to make the decision rules and evidence justifying their choices explicit.

SOCIAL SCIENTIFIC INQUIRY AND STRONG DEMOCRACY

Strong, effective popular participation demands that ordinary citizens be able to recognize and critique mythical numbers and ambiguous decision rules. It may seem difficult for the nonexpert to sort through the many studies, reports, and highly publicized, often biased, evidence presented by advocates on different sides of contentious policy debates like the one surrounding workplace marijuana. Our intent is to help readers critically evaluate complex social scientific evidence and the uses to which it's put. We would like to close the book with some basic guidelines for evaluating economic, political, and social research dealing with controversial public policy issues.

Even though many public policy choices do involve technical complexities, such complexities should not be allowed to obfuscate the values at stake in the decision. We feel that citizens can and should be skeptical consumers of the evidence and arguments presented by the committed advocates who tend to dominate political debate. In the absence of broadly based, critical attention from the population potentially affected, public policy dialog seems often to become highly polarized. As we have argued above, such polarization leads to the proliferation of mythical numbers and unclear decision rules, symptoms of "thin" democracy (Barber, 1984).

Research on individuals' development of social identities (Aho, 1994; Berger & Luckman, 1967) shows that once one has become committed to a group identity, the goals and values of the group become integral to one's world view. Committed partisans tend to interpret policy-relevant information in biased ways (Vallone, Ross, & Lepper, 1985). Advocates will feel justified in attempting to control the way outsiders view issues of concern to them. Individuals who identify strongly with a particular policy perspective will have difficulty listening to proponents of alternative options; they may even feel obligated to discourage objective evaluation of the evidence for and against their position.

Strong democracy requires citizens to resist efforts by partisans to limit the terms of debate in the public policy arena. Substantial grassroots attention to and involvement in community policy-making will improve citizens' ability to hold members of the governing elite accountable. It will also help prevent the dysfunctional biases held by advocacy groups from dominating policy choices. In the interest, then, of improving readers' ability to critically evaluate policy-relevant social scientific research, thereby strengthening democracy, we offer some basic guidelines for the examination of information coming from fields like economics, sociology, anthropology, and political science.

The skeptical research consumer should ask who (a) conducted, (b) funded, and (c) published the findings in question. The interests and credentials of all three should be clearly disclosed. As voters and shoppers, American consumers are, for the most part, well aware of the need for skepticism about the messages they receive and the importance of recognizing the persuasive intent of much of the public communication surrounding them. Science cannot and should not ask its audience to suspend that skepticism. In fact, skepticism is the hallmark of true scientific inquiry and one of the primary characteristics that the reader should expect to find in high quality social and economic research. Findings should be stated in a manner that makes their limitations clear and does not overgeneralize their relevance. Questions that remain unanswered should be discussed; aspects of the research topic requiring further study should be outlined.

Skepticism regarding social science research is necessary; however, skepticism should not lead to complete rejection of this body of knowledge in toto. As with other modes of investigation, social science methods can be used well or they can be used poorly. Social science frequently addresses highly controversial issues, such as the effects of marijuana on work. Because it enters into policy territory where dialogue is emotionally charged, it may appear that social inquiry is inevitably biased.

This book's main goal is to refute this proposition. We offer this review of multiple studies applying multiple, diverse methods to a controversial question as an example of useful social inquiry. Combining findings from different perspectives makes the sort of triangulation discussed above possible. The strengths of one method may make up for the weaknesses of another; questions one approach is incapable of answering can be addressed by a different one.

The skeptical consumer of psychological, political, economic, and other types of social scientific research should also ask how many studies have examined the hypotheses being examined. Does the study under consideration review previous work on the topic? Does it clearly explain prior results and discuss the ways in which it confirms or contradicts them? Unique, path-breaking research addressing a new issue or overturning the received wisdom of the day may be very exciting and get a great deal of publicity, but a single experiment, field study, survey, or other set of findings can only suggest directions for further exploration in the future. Multiple studies by multiple authors are necessary before any result can be considered well supported.

What about assessing the quality of individual pieces of research? Here are some specific guidelines for judging social scientific studies:

1. Generally, work published in peer-reviewed journals has met technical standards widely accepted among professionals knowledgeable about its subject matter. As mentioned in the introduction to this volume, some caution is appropriate regarding reliance on this criterion; it is not foolproof. At the same time, it is an appropriate screen to use in identifying high quality research.

2. Statistical significance of quantitative research results is also an initial screen to use in evaluating a study's importance. It provides a measure of the probability that an association between two factors is due to chance. Keep in mind that this probability varies inversely with (a) the *number* of subjects included in the study, and (b) the *strength* of the connection between the variables. Therefore, a study that detects a significant association may have discovered a strong connection between the factors it examined, or it may have found a weak connection between factors in a large number of subjects, or both the strength of the results and the sample size may be great. The practical importance of statistically significant findings can vary immensely depending on which of these possibilities exist. Do not confuse statistical robustness with effect size.

3. Remember that correlation does not prove causation. During the eighteenth century, hot, humid air was believed to be the cause of malaria because the disease could readily be observed to occur with alarming frequency in such environments (the relationship between these two variables was highly significant, statistically!). Later generations discovered the third variable, the mosquito, which actually *caused* the deadly disease. The need to gather additional evidence beyond mere association in order to establish a casual linkage between factors being examined is clear. Here, we come back to our recommendation that multiple methods be used to triangulate on the true relationship connecting variables of interest. Controlled experiments, though creating unrealistically simple test situations, do enable researchers to demonstrate causality. Other methodological approaches can tell us more about the complex web of interconnecting conditions we see in the real world.

By combining quantitative measures of association (obtained through analysis of surveys, archival records, and other statistical sources), experimental findings, and rich qualitative data from studies like the anthropological field research on the use of ganja reported here, we can sort out true causal relationships.

No scientific discipline can claim to make public or private policy decisions. Virtually all collective decisions involve many choices about how to structure the problem at hand. In addition to questions about *who* will make the decision (obviously a potentially contentious issue), at some point policy-makers must, explicitly or implicitly, answer crucial questions about the decision rules they will follow. Who bears the burden of proof in the current situation? What is the default option if no action is taken? What standards of proof must be met before a decision is reached and what will count as evidence in meeting that standard?

Advocates involved in controversial policy areas, such as employment of marijuana users, seldom wish to "waste time" clarifying the structure of a decision problem. However, when decisions are delegated to corporate managers, elected government officials, or other agents in the public or private sector, the accountability of those agents will be greatly increased if they are required to specify how they are approaching the problem to make the decision's structure explicit. In this context, then, arguments and evidence relevant to the decision can be evaluated much more effectively than if the structure remains ambiguous.

References

Abel, E., 1970. "Marijuana and memory." *Nature*, 227: 1151–1152.

Abel, E., 1971. "Marijuana and memory: Acquisition or retrieval?" *Science*, 173: 1038–1040.

Agarwal, A., B. Sethi, S. Gupta, 1975. "Physical and cognitive effects of chronic bhang (cannabis) intake." *Indian Journal of Psychiatry*, 17: 1–17.

Aho, J., 1994. *This Thing of Darkness: A Sociology of the Enemy*. Seattle: University of Washington Press.

Aldrich, M., 1977. "Tantric cannabis use in India." *Journal of Psychedelic Drugs*, 9: 227–233.

Azorlosa, J., S. Heishman, M. Stitzer, and J. Mahaffey, 1992. "Marijuana smoking: Effect of varying delta-9 tetrahydrocannabinol content and number of puffs." *Journal of Pharmacology and Experimental Therapeutics*, 26: 114–122.

Barber, B., 1984. *Strong Democracy*. Berkeley: University of California Press.

Barite, E., W. Beaver, R. White, P. Blacken, and P. Adams, 1972. "The effects of chronic use of marijuana on sleep and perceptual-motor performance in humans." In M. Lewis (Ed.) *Current Research in Marijuana*. New York: Academic Press.

Barnett, G., V. Lick, and T. Thompson, 1985. "Behavioral pharmacokinetics of marijuana." *Psychopharmacology*, 85: 51–56.

Bech, P., L. Rafaelsen, and O. Rafaelson, 1973. "Cannabis and alcohol: Effects on estimation of time and distance." *Psychopharmacologia*, 32: 373–381.

Blank, D., and J. Fenton, 1989. "Early employment testing for marijuana: Demographic and employee retention patterns." In S. Gust and M. Walsh (Eds.) *Drugs in the workplace: Research and evaluation data*. Rockville, MD: National Institute on Drug Abuse: 139–150.

Block, R., R. Farinpour, and K. Braverman, 1992. "Acute effects of marijuana on cognition: Relationships to chronic effects of smoking techniques." *Pharmacology, Biochemistry, and Behavior*, 43: 907–917.

Block, R., S. Farnham, K. Braverman, R. Noyes, and M. Ghoneim, 1990. "Long-term marijuana use and subsequent effects on learning and cognitive functions related to school achievement: A preliminary study." *NIDA Research Monograph Series*, 101: 96–111.

Block, R., and M. Ghoneim, 1993. "Effects of chronic marijuana use on human cognition." *Psychopharmacology*, 110: 219–228.

Bompey, S., 1988. "Drugs in the workplace: From the batter's box to the boardroom." In S. Bompey (Ed.) *Alcohol and Drug Abuse in the Workplace: The Complete Resource Guide*. Washington, DC: Bureau of National Affairs.

Bowman, M., and R. Pihl, 1973. "Cannabis: Psychological effects of chronic heavy use." *Psychopharmacologia*, 29: 159–170.

Braff, D., L. Silverton, D. Saccuzzo, and D. Janowsky, 1981. "Impaired speed of visual information processing in marijuana intoxication." *American Journal of Psychiatry*, 138: 613–617.

Brannen, J., 1992. *Mixing Methods: Qualitative and Quantitative Research*. Aldershot, England: Avebury.

Brill, N., and R. Christie, 1974. "Marijuana use and psychosocial adaptation." *Archives of General Psychiatry*, 31: 713–719.

Broad, K., and B. Feinberg, 1995. "Perceptions of ganja and cocaine in urban Jamaica." *Journal of Psychoactive Drugs*, 27: 261–276.

Brookoff, D., C. Cook, C. Williams, and C. Mann, 1994. "Testing reckless drivers for cocaine and marijuana." *New England Journal of Medicine*, 331: 518–522.

Burroughs, W., 1957. "Letter from a master addict to dangerous drugs." *British Journal of Addiction*, 53: 119–131.

Campbell, D., and D. Fiske, 1959. "Convergent validation by the multitrait-multimethod matrix." *Psychological Bulletin*, 56: 81–105.

Carlin, A., and E. Trupin, 1977. "The effect of long-term chronic marijuana use on neuropsychological functioning." *International Journal of Addictions*, 12: 617–624.

Carter, W., 1980. *Cannabis in Costa Rica*. Philadelphia: ISHI Press.

Casswell, S., and D. Marks, 1973a. "Cannabis and temporal disintegration in experienced and naive subjects." *Science*, 179: 803–805.

Casswell, S., and D. Marks, 1973b. "Cannabis-induced impairment of performance on a divided attention task." *Nature*, 241: 60–61.

Castillo, R., 1990. "Depersonalization and meditation." *Psychiatry*, 53: 158–168.

Chait, L., 1990. "Subjective and behavioral effects of marijuana the morning after smoking." *Psychopharmacology*, 100: 328–333.

Chait, L., M. Fischman, and C. Schuster, 1985. " 'Hangover' effects the morning after marijuana smoking." *Drug and Alcohol Dependence*, 15: 229–238.

Chait, L., and J. Perry, 1994. "Acute and residual effects of alcohol and marijuana, alone and in combination, on mood and performance." *Psychopharmacology*, 115: 340–349.

Clark, L., R. Hughes, and E. Nakashima, 1970. "Behavioral effects of marijuana." *Archives of General Psychiatry*, 23: 193–198.

Cohen, S., 1976. "The 94-day cannabis study." *Annals of the New York Academy of Sciences*, 282: 211–220.

Crancer, A., J. Dille, J. Delay, J. Wallace, and M. Haykin, 1969. "Comparison of the effects of marijuana and alcohol on simulated driving performance." *Science*, 164: 851–854.

Crouch, D., D. Webb, L. Peterson, P. Buller, and D. Rollins, 1989. "A critical evaluation of the Utah Power and Light Company's substance abuse management program: Absenteeism, accidents, and costs." In S. Gust and M. Walsh (Eds.) *Drugs in the workplace: Research and evaluation data*. Rockville, MD: National Institute on Drug Abuse.

Crow, S., and S. Hartman, 1992. "Drugs in the workplace: Overstating the problems and the cures." *Journal of Drug Issues*, 22: 923–937.

Culver, C., and F. King, 1974. "Neuropsychological assessment of undergraduate marijuana and LSD users." *Archives of General Psychiatry*, 31: 707–711.

Darley, C., and J. Tinklenberg, 1974. "Marijuana and memory." In L. Miller (Ed.) *Marijuana: Effects on Human Behavior*. New York: Academic Press

Darley, C., J. Tinklenberg, W. Roth, S. Vernon, and B. Kopell, 1977. "Marijuana effects on long-term memory assessment and retrieval." *Psychopharmacology*, 52: 239–241.

Denzin, N., 1978. *The Research Act (second edition)*. New York: McGraw-Hill.

Dittrich, A., K. Battig, and I. von Zepplin, 1973. "Effects of delta-9-transtetrahydro-cannabinol on memory, attention, and subjective state." *Psycho-pharmacologia*, 33: 369–376.

Dixon, J., 1963. "The depersonalization phenomenon in a sample population of college students." *British Journal of Psychiatry*, 109: 371–375.

Doblin, R., and M. Kleiman, 1995. "The medical use of marijuana: The case for clinical trials." *Journal of Addictive Diseases*, 14: 5–14.

Donovan, J., 1996. "Problem-behavior theory and the explanation of adolescent marijuana use." *Journal of Drug Issues*, 26: 379–404.

Dornbush, R., G. Clare, A. Zaks, P. Crown, J. Volavka, and M. Fink, 1972. "Twenty-one day administration of marijuana in male volunteers." In M. Lewis (Ed.) *Current Research in Marijuana*. New York: Academic Press.

Dreher, M., 1982. *Working Men and Ganja: Marijuana Use in Rural Jamaica*. Philadelphia: ISHI Press.

Entin, E., and P. Goldzung, 1973. "Residual effects of marijuana on learning and memory." *Psychological Review*, 23: 169–178.

Evans, M., R. Martz, D. Brown, B. Rodda, G. Kiplinger, L. Lemberger, and R. Forney, 1973. "Impairment of performance with low doses of marijuana." *Clinical Pharmacology and Therapeutics*, 14: 936–940.

Foltin, R., M. Fischman, J. Brady, D. Bernstein, R. Capriotti, M. Nellis, and T. Kelly, 1990. "Motivational effects of smoked marijuana: Behavioral contingencies and low-probability activities." *Journal of the Experimental Analysis of Behavior*, 53: 5–19.

Gianutsos, R., and A. Litwack, 1976. "Chronic marijuana smokers show reduced coding into long-term storage." *Bulletin of the Psychonomic Society*, 7: 277–279.

Gieringer, D., 1988. "Marijuana, driving, and accident safety." *Journal of Psychoactive Drugs*, 20, 93–101.

Grant, I., J. Rochford, T. Fleming, and A. Stunkard, 1973. "A neuropsychological assessment of the effects of moderate marijuana use." *Journal of Nervous and Mental Disorders*, 156: 278–280.

Grinspoon, L., and J. Bakalar, 1993. *Marijuana: Forbidden Medicine*. New Haven, CT: Yale University Press.

Grinspoon, L., and J. Bakalar, 1995. "Marijuana as medicine: A plea for reconsideration." *Journal of the American Medical Association*, 274: 1838.

Halikas, J., R. Weller, C. Morse, and R. Hoffman, 1983. "Regular marijuana use and its effect on psychosocial variables: A longitudinal study." *Comprehensive Psychiatry*, 24: 229–235.

Hansteen, R., R. Miller, L. Lonero, L. Reid, and B. Jones, 1976. "Effects of cannabis and alcohol on automobile driving and psychomotor tracking." *Annals of the New York Academy of Sciences*, 282: 240–256.

Harris, M., 1993. "Drugs in the workplace: Setting the record straight." *Journal of Drug Issues*, 23: 727–732.

Harris, M., and L. Heft, 1992. "Alcohol and drug use in the workplace: Issues, controversies, and directions for future research." *Journal of Management*, 18: 239–266.

Harrison, L., 1995. "The validity of self-reported data on drug-use." *Journal of Drug Issues*, 25: 91–111.

Hartman, S., and S. Crow, 1993. "Drugs in the workplace: Setting Harris straight." *Journal of Drug Issues*, 23: 733–738.

Harwood, H., D. Fountain and G. Livermore, 1998. *Economic Costs of Drug and Alcohol Abuse, 1992.* Washington, DC: U.S. Government Printing Office.

Heishman, S., and J. Henningfield, 1990. "Application of human laboratory data for the assessment of performance in workplace settings: Practical and theoretical considerations." In S. Gust, J. Walsh, L. Thomas, and D. Crouch (Eds.) *Drugs in the Workplace: Research and Evaluation Data* (Volume II) Rockville, MD: National Institute on Drug Abuse.

Heishman, S., M. Stitzer, and S. Yingling, 1990. "Effects of THC content on smoking behavior, subjective reports, and performance." *Pharmacology, Biochemistry, and Behavior*, 34: 173–179.

Hendin, H., A. Pollinger, and R. Ulman, 1981. "The function of marijuana abuse for adolescents." *American Journal of Drug and Alcohol Abuse*, 8: 441–456.

Hollister, L., 1986. "Health aspects of cannabis." *Pharmacological Reviews*, 38: 1–18.

Husain, S., and I. Kahn, 1985. "An update on cannabis research." *Bulletin of Narcotics*, 37: 3–15.

Institute for a Drug-Free Workplace, 1998. *Gallup Survey.* Institute for a Drug-Free Workplace, http://www.drugfreeworkplace.org.

Institute for a Drug-Free Workplace, 1999. Institute for a Drug-Free Workplace, http://www.drugfreeworkplace.org.

Jick, T., 1979. "Mixing qualitative and quantitative methods: Triangulation in action." *Administrative Science Quarterly*, 24: 602–611.

Johnston, L., P. O'Malley, and J. Bachman, 1994. *National Survey Results on Drug Use from the Monitoring the Future Study* (Volumes 1 and 2). Rockville, MD: National Institute on Drug Abuse. Publication # 94–3810.

Jones, R., and N. Benowitz, 1976. "The 30-day trip—Clinical studies of cannabis tolerance and dependence." In M. Braude and S. Szara (Eds.) *The Pharmacology of Marijuana.* New York: Raven Press.

Jones, R., and G. Stone, 1970. "Psychological studies of marijuana and alcohol in man." *Psychopharmacologia*, 18: 108–117.

Kaestner, R., 1994a. "New estimates of the effect of marijuana and cocaine on wages." *Industrial and Labor Relations Review*, 47: 454–470.

Kaestner, R., 1994b. "The effect of illicit drug use on the labor supply of young adults." *Journal of Human Resources*, 24: 126–155.

Kagel, J., R. Battalio, and C. Miles, 1980. "Marijuana and work performance: Results from an experiment." *Journal of Human Resources*, 15: 373–395.

Kelly, T., R. Foltin, C. Emurian, and M. Fischman, "Multidimensional behavioral effects of marijuana." *Progress in Neuropsychopharmacology and Biological Psychiatry*, 14: 885–902.

Kerlinger, F., 1973. *Foundations of Behavioral Research*. New York: Holt, Rinehart, and Winston.

Kleiman, M., 1989. *Marijuana: Cost of Abuse, Costs of Control*. Westport, CT: Greenwood Press.

Klonoff, H., 1974. "Marijuana and driving in real-life situations." *Science*, 186: 317–324.

Klonoff, H., and M. Low, 1974. "Psychological and neuropsychological effects of marijuana in man: An interaction model." In L. Miller (Ed.) *Marijuana: Effects on Human Behavior*. New York: Academic Press.

Kupfer, D., 1973. "A comment on the 'amotivational syndrome' in marijuana smokers." *American Journal of Psychiatry*, 130: 1319–1322.

Kvalseth, T., 1977. "Effects of marijuana on human reaction time and motor control." *Perceptual and Motor Skills*, 45: 935–939.

Lindblom, C., 1959. "The science of muddling through." *Public Administration Review*: 79–88.

MacAvoy, M., and D. Marks, 1975. "Divided attention performance of cannabis users and nonusers following cannabis and alcohol." *Psychopharmacologia*, 44: 147–152.

MacDonald, S., 1995. "The role of drugs in workplace injuries: Is drug testing appropriate?" *Journal of Drug Issues*, 25: 723–734.

McGrath, J., 1964. "Toward a theory of method for research on organizations." In W. Cooper (Ed.) *New Perspectives in Organizational Research*. Somerset, NJ: Wiley.

Manno, J., G. Kiplinger, S. Haine, I. Bennett, and R. Forney, 1970. "Comparative effects of smoking marijuana or placebo on human motor and mental performance." *Clinical Pharmacology and Therapeutics*, 11, 808–815.

Manno, J., G. Kiplinger, N. Scholz, R. Forney, and S. Haine, 1971. "The influence of alcohol and marijuana on motor and mental performance." *Clinical Pharmacology and Therapeutics*, 12: 202–212.

Margolis, R., and N. Popkin, 1980. "Marijuana: A review of the medical research with implications for adolescents." *Personnel and Guidance Journal*, 59: 7–14.

Mathew, R., W. Wilson, D. Humphreys, J. Lowe, and K. Weith, 1993. "Marijuana use and cognitive functioning." *Biological Psychiatry*, 33: 431–441.

McBay, A., and S. Owens, 1981. "Marijuana and driving." In L. Harris (Ed.) *Problems of Drug Dependence*. Washington, DC: U.S. Government Printing Office.

McDaniel, M., 1988. "Does pre-employment drug use predict on-the-job suitability?" *Personnel Psychology*, 41: 717–729.

McGlothlin, W., and L. West, 1968. "The marijuana problem: An overview." *American Journal of Psychiatry*, 125: 370–378.

Melges, F., 1976. "Tracking difficulties and paranoid ideation during hashish and alcohol intoxication." *American Journal of Psychiatry*, 133: 1024–1028.

Melges, F., J. Tinklenberg, L. Hollister, and H. Gillespie, 1970a. "Marijuana and temporal disintegration." *Science*, 168: 1118–1120.

Melges, F., J. Tinklenberg, L. Hollister, and H. Gillespie, 1970b. "Temporal disintegration and depersonalization during marijuana intoxication." *Archives of General Psychiatry*, 23: 204–210.

Mellinger, G., 1978. "Drug use, academic performance, and career indecision." In D.

Candel (Ed.) *Longitudinal Research on Drug Use: Empirical Findings and Methodological Issues*. Washington, DC: Hemisphere Press.

Mellinger, G., R. Somers, S. Davidson, and D. Manheimer, 1976. "The amotivational syndrome and the college student." *Annals of the New York Academy of Sciences*, 282: 37–55.

Mendelson, J., T. Babour, J. Kuehnle, A. Rossi, J. Bernstein, N. Mello, and I. Greenberg, 1976a. "The effects of marijuana use on human operant behavior: Individual data." In M. Braude and S. Szara (Eds.) *Pharmacology of Marijuana*, New York: Raven Press.

Mendelson, J., T. Babour, J. Kuehnle, A. Rossi, J. Bernstein, N. Mello, and I. Greenberg, 1976b. "Behavioral and biological aspects of marijuana use." *Annals of the New York Academy of Sciences*, 282: 186–210.

Mendhiratta, S., V. Varma, R. Dang, A. Malhotra, K. Das, and R. Nehra, 1988. "Cannabis and cognitive functions: A re-evaluation study." *British Journal of Addictions*, 83: 749–753.

Mendhiratta, S., N. Wig, and S. Varma, 1978. "Some psychological correlates of long-term heavy cannabis users." *British Journal of Psychiatry*, 132: 482–486.

Meyer, R., R. Pillard, L. Shapiro, and S. Mirin, 1971. "Administration of marijuana to heavy and casual marijuana users." *American Journal of Psychiatry*, 128, 198–203.

Miller, L., W. Drew, and G. Kiplinger, 1972. "Effects of marijuana on recall of narrative material and Stroop Color-Word performance." *Nature*, 237: 172–173.

Millsaps, C., R. Azrin, and W. Mittenberg, 1994. "Neuropsychological effects of chronic cannabis use on the memory and intelligence of adolescents." *Journal of Child and Adolescent Substance Abuse*, 3: 47–55.

Miranne, A., 1979. "Marijuana use and achievement orientation of college students." *Journal of Health and Social Behavior*, 20, 194–199.

Morningstar, P., 1985. "Thandai and Chilam: Traditional Hindu beliefs about proper uses of cannabis." *Journal of Psychoactive Drugs*, 17: 141–165.

Moskowitz, H., R. Shea, and M. Burns, 1974. "Effects of marijuana on the psychological refractory period." *Perceptual and Motor Skills*, 38: 959–962.

Moskowitz, H., K. Zeidman, and S. Sharma, 1976. "Visual search behavior while viewing driving scenes under the influence of alcohol and marijuana." *Human Factors*, 18: 417–432.

Murray, J., 1986. "Marijuana's effects on human cognitive functions, psychomotor functions, and personality." *Journal of General Psychology*, 113: 13–55.

Nahas, G., 1985. "Critique of a study on ganja in Jamaica." *Bulletin on Narcotics*, 37: 15–30.

National Institute on Drug Abuse, 1998. *Economic Costs of Drug and Alcohol Abuse, 1992*. Washington DC: U.S. Printing Office.

Normand, J., S. Salyards, and J. Mahoney, 1990. "An evaluation of preemployment drug testing." *Journal of Applied Psychology*, 75: 629–639.

Ostrom, E., 1990. *Governing the Commons*. Cambridge, England: Cambridge University Press.

Page, J., 1983. "The amotivational syndrome hypothesis and the Costa Rica study: Relationships between methods and results." *Journal of Psychoactive Drugs*, 15: 261–267.

Page, J., W. Fletcher, and W. True, 1988. "Psychosociocultural perspectives on chronic cannabis use: The Costa Rican follow-up." *Journal of Psychoactive Drugs*, 20: 57–65.

Pandina, R., E. Labouvie, V. Johnson, and H. White, 1990. "The relationship between alcohol and marijuana use and competence in adolescence." *Journal of Health and Social Policy*, 1: 89–108.

Parker, E., I. Birnbaum, H. Weingartner, J. Hartley, R. Stillman, and R. Wyatt, 1980. "Retrograde enhancement of human memory with alcohol." *Psychopharmacology*, 69: 219–222.

Parish, D., 1989. "Relation of pre-employment drug testing result to employment status: A one-year follow-up." *Journal of General Internal Medicine*, 4: 44–47.

Pickworth, W., M. Rohrer, and R. Fant, 1997. "Effects of abused drugs on psychomotor performance." *Experimental and Clinical Psychopharmacology*, 5: 235–241.

Pope, H., and D. Yurgelun-Todd, 1996. "The residual cognitive effects of heavy marijuana use in college students." *Journal of the American Medical Association*, 275: 521–527.

Pope, H., A. Gruber, and D. Yurgelun-Todd, 1995. "The residual neuropsychological effects of cannabis: The current status of research." *Drug and Alcohol Dependence*, 38: 25–34.

Rafaelsen, O., P. Bech, H. Christiansen, H. Christrup, J. Nyobe, and L. Rafaelsen, 1973. "Cannabis and alcohol: Effects on simulated car driving." *Science*, 179: 920–923.

Reed, H., 1974. "Cognitive effects of marijuana." In J. Mendelson, A. Rossi, and R. Meyer (Eds.) *The Use of Marijuana: A Physiological and Psychological Inquiry*. New York: Plenum Press.

Reuter, P., 1984. "The (continued) vitality of mythical numbers." *Public Interest*, 75: 135–147.

Rickles, W., M. Cohen, C. Whitaker, and K. McIntyre, 1973. "Marijuana-induced state-dependent verbal learning." *Psychopharmacologia*, 30: 349–354.

Robbe, H., and J. O'Hanlon, 1993. *Marijuana and Actual Driving Performance*. Washington, DC: Department of Transportation.

Rochford, J., I. Grant, and G. LaVigne, 1977. "Medical students and drugs: Further neuropsychological and use pattern considerations." *International Journal of Addictions*, 12: 1057–1065.

Roth, W., J. Tinklenberg, C. Whitaker, C. Darley, B. Koppell, and L. Hollister, 1973. "The effect of marijuana on tracking task performance." *Psychopharmacologia*, 33: 259–265.

Rubin, V., and L. Comitas, 1975. "Psychological assessment." In V. Rubin and L. Comitas (Eds.) *Ganga in Jamaica: A Medical Anthropological Study of Chronic Cannabis Use*. Mouton, France: The Hague.

Satz, P., J. Fletcher, and L. Sutker, 1976. "Neuro-psychological, intellectual, and personality correlates of marijuana use in native Costa Ricans." *Annals of the New York Academy of Sciences*, 282: 266–306.

Schwartz, R., 1991. "Heavy marijuana use and recent memory impairment." *Psychiatric Annals*, 21: 80–82.

Schwartz, R., P. Gruenwald, M. Klitzner, and P. Fedio, 1989. "Short-term memory impairment in cannabis-dependent adolescents." *American Journal of Disadvantaged Children*, 143: 1214–1219.

Schwenk, C., 1982. "Why sacrifice rigor for relevance? A proposal for combining laboratory and field research in strategic management." *Strategic Management Journal*, 3: 213–225.

Schwenk, C., 1985. "The use of participant recollection in the modeling of organizational decision processes." *Academy of Management Review*, 10: 496–503.

Segal, J., 1990. "Developing return-to-work agreements." *HR Magazine*, 39: 86–89.

Sethi, B., J. Trivedi, and H. Singh, 1981. "Long-term effects of cannabis." *Indian Journal of Psychiatry*, 23: 224–229.

Siegel, S., 1956. *Nonparametric Statistics for the Behavioral Sciences*. New York: McGraw-Hill.

Simon, H., 1976. *Administrative Behavior (third edition)*. New York: Free Press.

Singer, M., 1971. "The vitality of mythical numbers." *The Public Interest*, 23: 135–147.

Solowij, N., P. Michie, and A. Fox, 1991. "Effects of long-term cannabis use on selective attention: An event-related potential study." *Pharmacology, Biochemistry, and Behavior*, 40: 683–688.

Stafford, P., 1992. *Psychedelics Encyclopedia*. (3rd Edition). Los Angeles: Tarcher.

Stefanis, C., J. Boulougouris, and A. Liakos, 1976. "Clinical and psychophysiological effects of cannabis in long-term users." In M. Braude and S. Szara (Eds.) *The Pharmacology of Marijuana*. New York: Raven Press.

Steinbruner, J., 1974. *The Cybernetic Theory of Decision*. Princeton, NJ: Princeton University Press.

Sussman, S., C. Dent, and A. Stacy, 1996. "The relationship of pro-drug use myths with self-reported drug use among youth at continuation high schools." *Journal of Applied Psychology*, 26: 2014–2037.

Sussman, S., A. Stacy, C. Dent, T. Simon, and C. Johnson, 1996. "Marijuana use: Current issues and new research directions." *Journal of Drug Issues*, 26: 695–734.

Swan, N., 1995. "Marijuana, other drug use among teens continues to rise." *NIDA Notes: National Institute on Drug Abuse*, 10: 8–9.

Tart, C., 1971. *On Being Stoned: A Psychological Study of Marijuana Intoxication*. Palo Alto, CA: Science and Behavior Books.

Teherune, K., 1994. *The Incidence and Role of Drugs in Fatally Injured Drivers*. Washington, DC: Department of Transportation.

Trice, H., and P. Steele, 1995. "Impairment testing: Issues and convergence with employee assistance programs." *Journal of Drug Issues*, 25: 471–503.

Ungerleider, J., and T. Andrysiak, 1985. "Therapeutic issues of marijuana and THC (Tetrahydrocannabinol)." *International Journal of Addictions*, 20: 691–699.

Vachon, L., A. Sulkowski, and E. Rich, 1974. "Marihuana effects on learning, attention, and time estimation." *Psychopharmacologia*, 39: 1–11.

Vallone, R., L. Ross, and M. Lepper, 1985. "The hostile media phenomenon." *Journal of Personality and Social Psychology*, 49: 577–585.

Varma, V., A. Malhotra, R. Dang, K. Das, and R. Nehra, 1988. "Cannabis and cognitive functions: A prospective study." *Drug and Alcohol Dependence*, 21: 147–152.

Weckowicz, T., G. Collier, and L. Spreng, 1977. "Field dependence, cognitive functions, personality traits, and social values in heavy cannabis users and non-user controls." *Psychological Reports*, 41: 291–302.

White, H., 1991. "Marijuana use and delinquency: A test of the 'independent cause' hypothesis." *Journal of Drug Issues*, 21: 231–256.

Wig, N., and V. Varma, 1977. "Patterns of long-term heavy cannabis use in North India and its effects on cognitive functions: A preliminary report." *Drug and Alcohol Dependence*, 2: 211–219.

Wilson, W., E. Ellinwood, R. Mathew, and K. Johnson, 1994. "Effects of marijuana on performance of computerized cognitive-neuromotor test battery." *Psychiatry Research*, 51: 115–125.

Wish, E., 1990. "Preemployment drug screening." *Journal of the American Medical Association*, 264: 2676–2677.

Woodward, J., 1962. *Industrial Organization: Theory and Practice*. London: Oxford University Press.

Zimmer, L., and J. Morgan, 1995. "Exposing marijuana myths: A review of the scientific evidence." The Lindesmith Center. http://www.norml.org/myths/Lindesmith/index.shtm.

Zwerling, C., J. Ryan, and E. Orav, 1990. "The efficacy of preemployment drug screening for marijuana and cocaine in predicting employment outcomes." *Journal of the American Medical Association*, 264: 2639–2643.

Index

About the Editors

CHARLES R. SCHWENK recently retired from his position as Professor of Management at the Kelly School of Business, Indiana University. His research specialties are strategic management and business policy, and he has published on these topics in such journals as *Academy of Management Review*, *Decision Sciences*, and *Strategic Management Journal*, where he currently serves on the editorial board. He is also author of another book, *The Essence of Strategic Decision Making*.

SUSAN L. RHODES currently disabled, is a former Assistant Professor of Political Science at the University of Kentucky. Her research interests include public policy making, criminal justice policy, and public choice, and her articles have appeared in such periodicals as *American Politics Quarterly*, *Law and Society Review*, and *Criminal Justice Policy Review*.

ISBN 1-56720-291-8

HARDCOVER BAR CODE